Hiking Olympic National Park

A Guide to the Park's Greatest Hiking Adventures

Second Edition

Erik Molvar

FALCONGUIDES®

GUILFORD, CONNECTICUT
HELENA, MONTANA
AN IMPRINT OF THE GLOBE PEQUOT PRESS

FALCONGUIDES®

Copyright © 1997, 2008 Morris Book Publishing, LLC.

Falcon and FalconGuides are registered trademarks of Morris Book Publishing, LLC.
Text design by Nancy Freeborn
Maps created by Daniel Lloyd © Morris Book Publishing, LLC.
Interior photos by Erik Molvar.

Library of Congress Cataloging-in-Publication Data
Molvar, Erik.
  Hiking Olympic National Park : a guide to the national park's greatest
hiking adventures / Erik Molvar. – 2nd ed.
      p. cm.
  Includes index.
  ISBN-13: 978-0-7627-4119-9
  1. Hiking–Washington (State)–Olympic National
Park–Guidebooks. 2.
Trails–Washington (State)–Olympic National
Park–Guidebooks. 3.
Olympic National Park (Wash.)–Guidebooks. I. Title.
  GV199.42.W220496 2008
  796.5'10979798–dc22
                                        2007049925

Printed in the United States of America
10 9 8 7 6 5 4 3 2 1

To buy books in quantity for corporate use
or incentives, call **(800) 962–0973**
or e-mail **premiums@GlobePequot.com.**

Contents

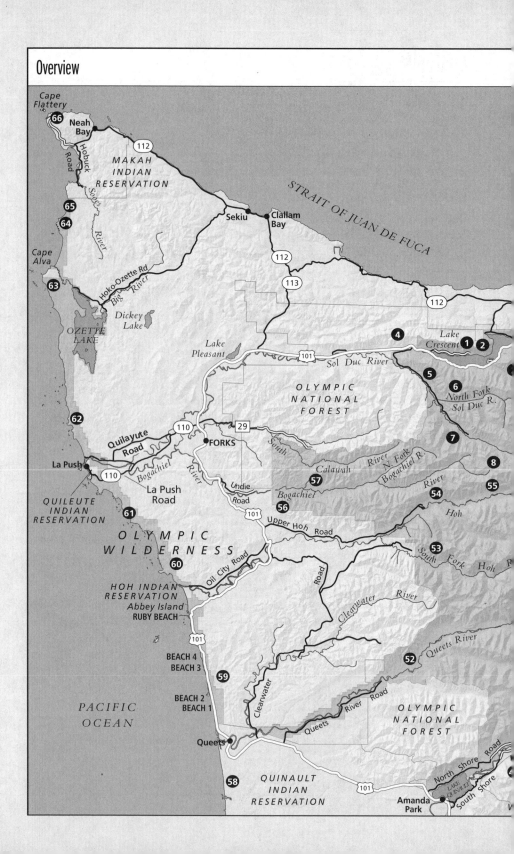

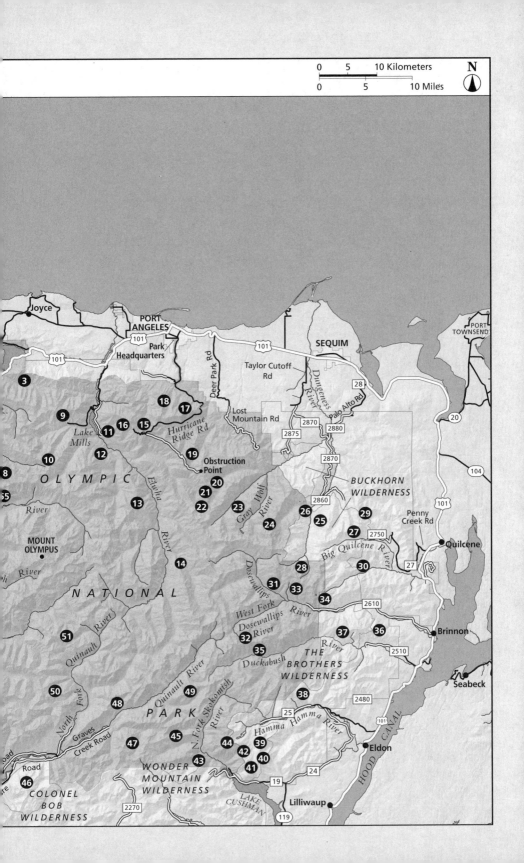

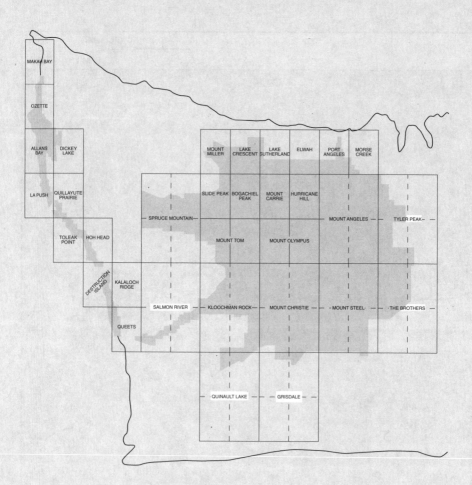

Map labels: MAKAH BAY, OZETTE, ALLANS BAY, DICKEY LAKE, LA PUSH, QUILLAYUTE PRAIRIE, TOLEAK POINT, HOH HEAD, DESTRUCTION ISLAND, KALALOCH RIDGE, QUEETS, SALMON RIVER, KLOOCHMAN ROCK, SPRUCE MOUNTAIN, SLIDE PEAK, BOGACHIEL PEAK, MOUNT CARRIE, HURRICANE HILL, MOUNT MILLER, LAKE CRESCENT, LAKE SUTHERLAND, ELWAH, PORT ANGELES, MORSE CREEK, MOUNT TOM, MOUNT OLYMPUS, MOUNT ANGELES, TYLER PEAK, MOUNT CHRISTIE, MOUNT STEEL, THE BROTHERS, QUINAULT LAKE, GRISDALE

Acknowledgments

During the course of writing this book, I have received valuable assistance from a variety of agency personnel and local residents, only a few of whom are mentioned here. Ruth Scott served as a primary liaison throughout the project and has been a wellspring of information. Bill Baccus was a wizard at procuring and reviving walking wheels. Tom Shindler of Custom Correct Maps provided additional distance data and valuable information on the "Additional Trails." Nelsa Buckingham shared with me her veritable treasure trove of botanical information. Geological information presented here relies heavily on the works of R. W. Tabor and W. M. Cady. Bruce Moorhead, Susan Schultz, Chuck McDonnell, Dave Conca, Kirstie Ray, Bryan Bell, Jerry Freilich, Hank Warren, Jim Halvorson, Molly Erickson, Susan Graham, and the entire revegetation crew provided supplementary information and advice. A special thanks to Pat Pratt at the Camera Corner for the excellent darkroom work and for keeping my camera and soul together during my research.

Introduction

Olympic National Park encompasses the glacier-clad spires that crown the peninsula as well as the wild and windswept beaches of the Pacific coast. It shelters a rare temperate rain forest ecosystem found only in a few pockets elsewhere in the world. The Olympic Mountains have been isolated from other ranges for millennia, and this isolation has led to the development of a unique alpine community of plants and animals. Some of these are found nowhere else on Earth. This bountiful ecosystem provides a refuge where weary city dwellers can seek inspiration in the midst of nature's majesty.

The uniqueness of this area was recognized in the late 1800s, when the region was set aside as a forest reserve. President Theodore Roosevelt created a national monument within the reserve in 1909, in part to protect the forest subspecies of elk that now bears his family name. National park status came in 1937, and the additional protection of wilderness status for the remote parts of the park was conferred in 1984. At the same time, five adjoining blocks of national forest land were declared wilderness, protecting 91,000 additional acres of this diverse and beautiful ecosystem. The park and its surroundings have been internationally recognized as a biosphere reserve and a world heritage site.

An extensive network of trails provides access into the most remote corners of the mountains, and a well-planned series of wilderness routes allows hikers to take in most of the Olympic coastline. There are 581 miles of maintained trails within the national park, and hundreds more on the adjoining national forest lands. This book covers all of the maintained trails and designated routes within the park and the adjacent wilderness areas. These trails provide a full spectrum of recreation opportunities, from short strolls to extended journeys that penetrate to the heart of the mountains.

The Making of the Mountains

The Olympic Peninsula appears to be attached to the northwest corner of the continent as an afterthought. In geological terms, this impression is absolutely correct. The peninsula is actually the eastern end of the Juan de Fuca Plate, a small terrane that collided with the much larger continental plate millions of years ago. The resulting folding and faulting of the earth's crust produced the mountains we see today.

These mountains had their genesis on the bottom of the ocean. Cracks in the sea floor allowed molten magma to well up into the water, forming a deep-sea range of volcanoes. These seamounts were already quite old when the Juan de Fuca Plate approached the rim of North America. As the plates collided, enormous pressures

◀ *Hiking up Mount Townsend*

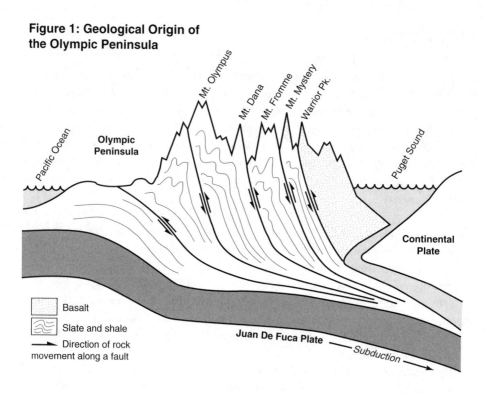

Figure 1: Geological Origin of the Olympic Peninsula

Mt. Olympus
Mt. Dana
Mt. Fromme
Mt. Mystery
Warrior Pk.

Pacific Ocean

Olympic Peninsula

Puget Sound

Continental Plate

Basalt
Slate and shale
Direction of rock movement along a fault

Juan De Fuca Plate — Subduction

pushed the seamounts upward. The Juan de Fuca Plate began to dive underneath the margin of the continent, but the seamounts were wedged against the continental plate, and movement ground to a halt. Beds of sedimentary and metamorphic rock piled up behind the seamounts like boxcars behind a derailed steam engine, with deep faults between them (see Figure 1). The ancient undersea lava beds now form a horseshoe of crags that stretches from Lake Crescent through Mount Constance and The Brothers and extends southwest as far as Lake Quinault. This "pillow basalt" is resistant to erosion, and as a result many of the highest peaks in the range occur within this narrow belt. The interior ranges are a mix of sandstone, shale, and slate. The border between these two formations is a zone of heavy faulting where hot springs well up through the earth's crust.

The newly created mound of high country was soon dissected by streams, which carved a system of shallow valleys in a radial pattern. With the coming of the ice ages, these valleys filled with glaciers, which deepened them into the U-shaped clefts that we see today. At the same time, an enormous Cordilleran ice sheet filled the Puget Sound basin and lapped against the base of the Olympics like a great frozen sea. It dammed up the waterways, forming huge glacial lakes that extended far into the mountains. Lake Crescent and Lake Cushman are remnants of these glacial lakes, and granite erratics brought in by the ice sheet can be found in certain parts of the peninsula.

The glacial ice receded in recent times, leaving remnants of the great valley glaciers stranded high on the flanks of the tallest peaks. These glaciers still gouge away at the rock, surging and retreating with annual changes in snowfall and temperature. Flowing water is now the dominant sculptor of the landscape, fueled by the heavy rains and snows for which the area is known. Raging rivers have carved deep canyons in the valley floors once planed flat by glaciers. The result is a series of elevated, well-drained terraces that rise high above the courses of most major rivers.

Biogeography of an Island Range

Because the Olympic Mountains have long been isolated from other alpine areas by a sea of lowland forest, their flora and fauna have many characteristics of an island assemblage. During the ice ages, the entire peninsula was sheathed in ice, with the exception of three refuge areas. One was a strip along the coastline, while the other two were nunataks, high mountaintops surrounded by ice. These two mountaintop refugia were located above the Gray Wolf–Dungeness basin in the northeast and in the Moonlight Dome area near the southern end of the mountains. All three refugia must have had an environment similar to Arctic tundra, surrounded as they were by vast fields of ice.

The plants and animals that could live in such an extreme environment survived, while other species went extinct. Some have been able to repopulate the Olympics from the distant Cascade Range, but species that cannot disperse across lowland basins were never able to return to suitable habitats on the peninsula. Notably absent in historical times were the mountain goat, grizzly bear, pika, red fox, and golden-mantled ground squirrel. Many of the alpine plants were able to survive here as Miocene and Pliocene relicts in pocket populations; their nearest relatives now exist in the eastern Rocky Mountains, where glaciation did not wipe the slate clean.

These millennia of isolation have resulted in genetic drift, and new species have arisen here that are unique to the Olympic Peninsula. The Olympic aster, Flett's violet, and Piper's bellflower are among the best-known endemic wildflowers; it is instructive to note that each is an inhabitant of alpine tundra. Among mammals, the Olympic marmot, Olympic snow mole, and Olympic yellow-pine chipmunk have evolved coloration patterns and behaviors that mark them as distinct from their closest relatives. There are also the Beardslee and Crescenti trout, a number of beetles and butterflies, a salamander, and even several species of slugs that are found only on the Olympic Peninsula.

The interference of modern man has also left its mark upon the ecosystem. Roosevelt elk were driven to the brink of extinction by overhunting in the late 1800s, and predator control efforts led to the eradication of the timber wolf by the mid-1920s. The loss of wolves and the resulting expansion of coyotes into the Olympic

Figure 2: Forest Life Zones
of the Olympic Peninsula

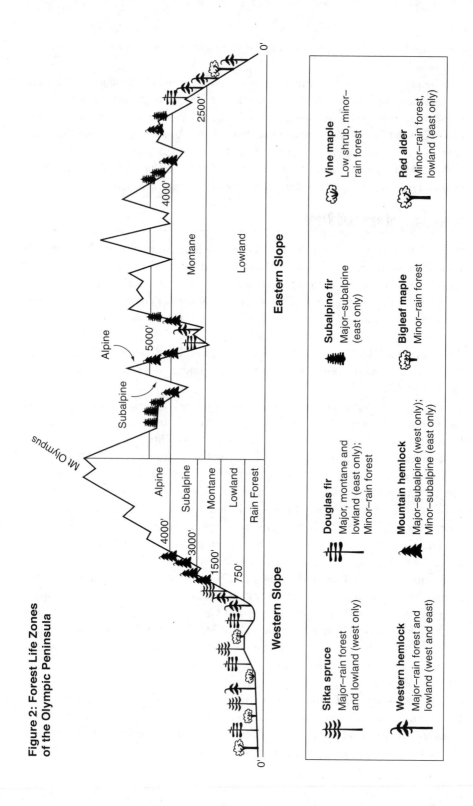

peninsula may be the reason that the Olympic marmot is currently declining toward possible extinction. Mountain goats were introduced to these mountains at about the same time, and had in recent years begun to overpopulate their range. In the interest of preserving native plant species, the National Park Service embarked on a program to relocate the goats to the Cascades. Many of them were successfully removed before the program was terminated, although several hundred still remain.

Original Inhabitants

The Olympic peninsula has been a site of human habitation since Pleistocene times. The earliest record comes from the vicinity of Sequim, where mammoth remains showing evidence of butchering were dated at 12,000 years before the present. During the intervening centuries, a rich and complex coastal Indian culture emerged on the lowlands surrounding the mountains. The economy revolved around hunting and gathering, with salmon and marine mammals forming the staples of the coastal villages. The tribes made forays deep into the mountains during summer, a fact attested to by numerous finds of stone points in the high valleys.

Coastal Indian culture revolved around permanent winter villages made up of cedar longhouses. Summer excursions were made to hunt elk or gather shellfish. Native carvers constructed masks that are now considered high art. These masks are still used in religious ceremonies that reaffirm the ties between the tribe and the natural world. Prominent families added to their prestige by holding lavish potlatches, during which they gave away most of their possessions as gifts. In many respects, the Indians of the Northwest Coast were quite similar culturally to the Europeans who explored the area much later.

The Indians of the Olympic Peninsula are organized into a number of distinct bands that persist to this day. On the eastern side of the peninsula, the Twana people are divided into the Quilcene (meaning "saltwater people") and the Skokomish (meaning "fresh-water people"). To the north, the S'Klallam tribe includes the coastal element found near Sequim as well as the more inland-oriented Elwha band. The Makah of the Cape Flattery area were perhaps the most ocean-oriented of the tribes, and relied heavily on marine mammals for their subsistence. The Quileute, Queets, and Quinault people to the south also hunted marine mammals but based their economies most heavily on bountiful runs of steelhead and salmon.

The Olympic Forests

One of the hallmark features of Olympic National Park are its vast expanses of unbroken forest. Some of the stands have not been greatly disturbed in more than 1,000 years, and the result is an old-growth community of outstanding diversity. Some of the largest specimens of coniferous trees in the world are found here, with boles that approach 20 feet in diameter and crowns that soar more than 200 feet into the sky. Beyond the borders of the park, state and private timberlands are an ecological wasteland dedicated solely to the production of timber products. In this area, the widespread clear-cutting and resulting forest fragmentation are destroying the habitat of the endangered spotted owl, and as a result the barred owl is moving in, further displacing the spotted owls from their natural habitat. It is only through the foresight of early conservationists that some of the primeval Olympic forest has survived.

The lowland valleys of the west are covered in a rain forest of enormous ecological value. This area receives an average of more than 12 feet of rain annually, most of which falls during winter months. Morning fogs roll in from the ocean, sustaining the mighty Sitka spruce, which grows only within 20 miles of the ocean. These fogs are critical to this species of tree because it cannot control the amount of water that it loses to transpiration. Bigleaf and vine maple are prominent hardwoods, and western hemlock, Douglas fir, and red cedar round out the important overstory species.

A lush growth of *epiphytes,* or plants that grow on tree surfaces, suffuses the understory of the rain forest with a greenish glow. Club mosses, lichens, and licorice ferns all make their home on living and dead trees. Saplings and shrubs grow from the mat of mosses that covers fallen tree trunks, which are thus known as nurse logs. The abundance of dead wood and complex structure of the forest canopy creates a large number of ecological niches for mammals and birds. Roosevelt elk maintain the openness of the rain forest by browsing out brush and young hemlock saplings, which in turn encourages the growth of herbaceous ground cover such as oxalis and violets.

Moving up in elevation, a lowland forest dominates the lower slopes of the foothills (see Figure 2). Western hemlock is dominant here, although Douglas fir may be prevalent in areas with a history of fire. This forest type also occupies all of the low country on the eastern side of the peninsula. It grades into a montane forest on the middle slopes. This forest type has little understory growth and occupies well-drained soils. Silver firs show up as the montane forest becomes subalpine in character. Near timberline, lingering snows determine the distribution of trees, and the conical mountain hemlock and subalpine fir predominate. These spire-shaped trees shed winter snows easily by virtue of their tall and slender growth form.

Above timberline, plant communities are strongly determined by minute differences in microclimate. The few conifers that grow here are sculpted into low-growing *krummholz* forms by windblown ice and snow. Lingering snowfields may promote the growth of such plants as avalanche lilies or bistort, and in extreme cases may prevent any plants from taking root at all. In contrast, well-drained sites may be as desiccated as a desert, and only water misers like shrubby cinquefoil can survive in such places. Other plants, such as phlox and penstemon, specialize in colonizing cracks in the rock itself, where little or no soil is present. In general, timberline habitats are dominated by lush swards dotted with wildflowers, although a kind of alpine desert can be found in places in the northeast corner of the mountains.

How to Use This Guide

The primary intent of this guide is to provide information that will help hikers choose day hikes and backpacking trips according to their desires and abilities, as well as to provide a detailed description of the trail system for interpretation of the natural features found along the trails. This guide is intended to be used in conjunction with topographic maps, which can be purchased at ranger stations, local gift and sporting goods stores, or through the U.S. Geological Survey. The most accurate topographic maps for the Olympic Peninsula belong to the Custom Correct® series, and they include mileages that have been proofed with a walking wheel. Addresses for map distributors can be found in appendix D. The appropriate quadrangle maps (several are usually required) are listed for each featured hike in this guidebook, and the corresponding Custom Correct map appears in italics.

Each trail description begins with a statistical section describing the physical characteristics of the trail for quick and easy reference. Overall distance is listed in miles, and an overview describes the hike type: day hike, backpack, extended trip, or wilderness route. Extended trips cannot be reached by road, while wilderness routes represent abandoned trails and cross-country routes, where the only indication of a trail might be an occasional cairn. This description is followed by a difficulty rating. The difficulty rating can be interpreted as follows: *Easy* trails can be completed without difficulty by hikers of all abilities, hikes rated *Moderate* will challenge novices, *Moderately Strenuous* hikes will tax even experienced travelers, and *Strenuous* trails will push the physical limits of the most Herculean hiker.

The "Trail type" section is an index to the maintenance level and modes of transport allowed on the trail. Note that mountain bikes are banned from all wilderness and most national park trails. Primary trails are maintained early in the summer, and these trails are easy to find and have no obstructions to passage. Secondary trails have lower maintenance priority; hikers might expect to find downed timber on such a trail, and stock parties may have to duck under a few tree limbs. Both Foot and Primitive trails are open exclusively to hikers. The former are well maintained, while the latter are often faint and difficult to follow.

"Best season" provides an index of when the trail will generally be passable without special aids like crampons, ice axes, or skis. It does not necessarily reflect a schedule of trail maintenance, which varies unpredictably from year to year. This is a relative measure, and late snowstorms may delay the opening of a trail beyond the time published here. Indeed, during years of heavy snowfall, some of the later-opening trails may never become passable without ice axe and crampons. If there are higher-elevation sections of a "year-round" trail that will generally not be open until mid-June, that will be noted in this section. Use this guidebook to get a general feel for the dates when the trail is usually open, and check with local authorities before your trip to get the latest trail conditions.

After "Best season" comes information about elevation gain and loss, maximum elevation (altitude), the appropriate maps for the hike (see above), and driving directions to the trailhead.

The driving directions are followed by "The Hike," a detailed interpretive description of the trail, including geologic and ecological features, fishing opportunities, campsites, and other important information. Photographs have been included to give the reader a visual preview of some of the prominent features seen along the trail. An elevation profile accompanies each trail description and provides a schematic look at the major elevation gains and losses incurred during the course of the trip.

Following the hike description are the "Key Points," a mile-by-mile list of landmarks, trail junctions, and gradient changes. Distances were recently developed using a walking wheel, primarily by the author himself. These mileages are more reliable than the distances posted on current trail signs and maps, and these new measurements have been adopted as the official mileages of the national park and will appear on the new maps and trail signs as they are replaced over time.

Planning Your Trip

It is important to gather as much current information as possible before starting out on a wilderness expedition. Permits are required for overnight expeditions into Olympic National Park, and a few areas that receive heavy use have quotas that limit the number of visitors. In most cases, however, the permits are filled out at trailhead self-registration stations. For further information, a list of addresses and phone numbers for these ranger stations is provided in appendix D. Campers are encouraged to use established campsites and to practice minimum impact camping techniques where these are unavailable. In the wilderness, each of us is a passing visitor, and we should leave no trace of our travels or camping to mar the wilderness experience of other travelers.

The key to a quality hiking experience is good planning. Hikers who underestimate the distance or time required to complete a trip may find themselves hiking in the dark, a dangerous proposition at best. An experienced hiker traveling at a fast clip without rest stops can generally make 3 miles per hour on any terrain, and perhaps more if the distance is all downhill. Hikers in less than peak physical condition or who are new to the sport have a maximum speed of 2.5 miles per hour. Note that these rates do not include stops for rest and refreshment, which add tremendously to the hiker's enjoyment and appreciation of the surroundings. Eight miles a day is a good goal for travelers new to backpacking, while old hands can generally cover at least 12 miles comfortably. We recommend traveling below top speed, focusing more attention on the surrounding natural beauty and less on the exercise of hiking itself.

A Few Words of Caution

Weather patterns in the Olympic Mountains can change frequently and without warning. Cold temperatures can occur even during the height of summer, and nighttime temperatures routinely dip into the 40s and even 30s on clear nights. Thunderstorms may suddenly change cloudless days into drenching misery, so carry appropriate rain gear at all times. Ponchos are generally sufficient for day hikes, but backpackers should carry full rain suits: water from drenched vegetation will quickly soak travelers who rely solely on ponchos for protection. Snowfall is always a distinct possibility in the high country, and hikers on overnight expeditions should carry clothing and gear with this possibility in mind. Detailed short-range forecasts are available at ranger stations and are usually reliable.

In general, snows linger in the high country into mid-June. This month traditionally receives the heaviest rainfall of the summer, with drier weather coming in late July and August. The first snowstorms visit the high country in mid-October, and by the end of this month a deep blanket of snow may cover the passes. Hikers who head for the high country in early summer should check with local rangers for current trail conditions. In many cases, ice axes and crampons will be required, especially on high passes with northern exposures. October marks the beginning of the rainy season in the park, and the drizzle does not let up until late April.

Drinking water from the pristine streams and lakes of the Olympic Peninsula is quite refreshing, but all such sources may contain a microorganism called *Giardia lamblia*. Giardia is readily spread to surface water supplies through the feces of mammals and infected humans, causing severe diarrhea and dehydration when ingested by humans. Water can be rendered safe for drinking by boiling it for at least five minutes or by passing it through a filter system with a mesh no larger than 2 microns. Iodine tablets and other purification additives are not considered effective against giardia. No natural water source is safe, and a single sip of untreated water can transmit the illness. Symptoms (gas, cramps, nausea, and diarrhea) usually appear within three weeks and demand medical attention.

Many of the wild animals in Olympic National Park may seem almost tame. In the absence of hunting, these creatures have lost their natural fear of humans. However, they remain wild, finely attuned to their environment and sensitive to human disturbance. Feeding wildlife human food may cause the animal digestive problems and may erase the wild instincts that keep the animal alive during times of scarcity. Black bears are particularly troublesome in their quest for human food. Campers must hang their food in a tree or from a cache wire, at least 10 feet above the ground and 6 feet away from the tree trunk. In some areas, special bear-resistant food canisters must be used. These bears are able climbers and will raid food containers that are hung too close to the trunk. Other animals are more of a nuisance than a danger. Deer and mountain goats often hang around campsites and try to steal sweat-soaked clothing and saddle tack. At higher elevations, rodents dwelling in rockslides may chew their way into a pack in search of food or salt. Along the Olympic coastline, raccoons have become crafty camp raiders in their opportunistic quest for food.

The Olympic Peninsula has one of the highest mountain lion populations in the nation. Because of their reclusive habits, they are rarely seen by hikers. However, they can present a real threat if encountered at close range. The current wisdom is that hikers encountering a cougar should behave aggressively in order to scare it off. Remain standing and never turn your back on a cougar or attempt to run away. Such behavior may incite an attack. Report all sightings at the nearest ranger station.

Fording Streams and Rivers

There are only a few places in Olympic National Park where trails cross major rivers without the benefit of a bridge. Bear in mind, however, that footlogs and bridges can be washed out during floods. Unbridged stream crossings are labeled as fords on the maps provided in this book. Streams are typically highest in early summer, when snowmelt swells the watercourses with silty discharge. Water levels also rise following rainstorms. Glacial rivers on the western side of the peninsula rise on warm afternoons as the meltwater from the glaciers surges downstream. Stream crossings should always be approached with caution; even a shallow stream can harbor slippery stones that can cause a sprained ankle or worse. However, wilderness travelers can almost always make safe crossings by exercising good judgment and employing a few simple techniques.

When you get to the water's edge, the first thing you'll probably think is, "This is going to be really cold!" It will be even colder if you try to cross barefooted. Since most folks don't like to hike around in wet boots all day, we recommend bringing a pair of lightweight canvas sneakers or river sandals specifically for the purpose of fording streams. Wearing something on your feet will prevent heat from being conducted from your feet to the stream cobbles and will give you superior traction for a safer crossing. Walking staffs add additional stability when wading streams. Some manufacturers make special staffs for wading with metal tips, and some even telescope down to manageable proportions. If you use one of these, remember not to lean too hard on it; your legs should always bear most of the burden.

Before entering the stream, unclip your hip belt and other restrictive straps; having the straps undone could save you from drowning. Water up to knee-depth can usually be forded without much difficulty; midthigh is the greatest safe depth for crossing unless the water is barely moving. Once you get in up to your crotch, your body starts giving the current a broad profile to push against, and you can bet that it won't be long before you are swimming.

When wading, discipline yourself to take tiny steps. The water will be cold, and your first impulse will be to rush across and get warm again, but this kind of carelessness frequently results in a dunking. While inching your way across, your feet should seek the lowest possible footing, so that it is impossible to slip downward any farther. Use boulders sticking out of the streambed as braces for your feet; these boulders will have tiny underwater eddies on their upstream and downstream sides, and thus the force of the current against you will be reduced by a fraction. When emerging from the water, towel off as quickly as possible with an absorbent piece of clothing. If you let the water evaporate from your body, it will take with it additional heat that you could have used to warm up.

Some streams will be narrow, with boulders sticking up from the water beckoning you to hopscotch across without getting your feet wet. Be careful, because you are in prime ankle-spraining country. Rocks that are damp at all may have a film of slippery algae on them, and even dry rocks might be unstable and roll out from underfoot. To avoid calamity, step only on boulders that are completely dry, and do not jump onto an untested boulder, since it may give way. The best policy is to keep one foot on the rocks at all times, so that you have firm footing to fall back on in case a foothold proves to be unstable.

How to Follow a Faint Trail

Some of the trails that appear on maps of the Olympic Peninsula are quite faint and difficult to follow. Visitors should have a few elementary trail-finding skills in their bag of tricks, in case a trail peters out or a snowfall covers the pathway. A topographic map and compass—and the ability to use them—are essential insurance against disaster when a trail takes a wrong turn or disappears completely. There are also a few tricks that may aid a traveler in such a time of need.

Maintained trails on the Olympic Peninsula are marked in a variety of ways. Signs bearing the name of the trail are present at most trail junctions. The trail signs are usually fashioned of plain wood, with the script carved into them. They sometimes blend in well with the surrounding forest and may go unnoticed at junctions where a major trail meets a lightly traveled one. These signs sometimes contain mileage information, but this information is often inaccurate.

Along the trail, several kinds of markers indicate the location of maintained trails. In forested areas, old blazes cut into the bark of trees may mark the path. In spots where a trail crosses a gravel streambed or rock outcrop, piles of rocks called cairns may mark the route. Cairns are also used in windswept alpine areas. These cairns are typically constructed of three or more stones placed one on top of the other, a formation that almost never occurs naturally.

In the case of an extremely overgrown trail, markings of any kind may be impossible to find. On such a trail, the techniques used to build the trail serve as clues to its location. Well-constructed trails have rather wide, flat beds. Let your feet seek level spots when traveling through tall brush, and you will almost always find yourself on

The North Fork of the Sol Duc River ▶

Mountain goat at Appleton Pass

the trail. Old sawed logs from previous trail maintenance can be used to navigate in spots where the trail bed is obscured; if you find a sawed log, then you must be on a trail that was maintained at some point in time. Switchbacks are also a sure sign of an official trail; wild animals travel in straight lines and rarely zigzag across hillsides.

Trail specifications often call for the clearing of all trees and branches for several feet on each side of a trail. In a forest situation, this results in a distinct "hall of trees" effect, where a corridor of cleared vegetation extends continuously through the woods. Trees grow randomly in a natural situation, so a long, thin clearing bordered by tree trunks usually indicates an old trail bed. On more open ground, look for trees that have lost all of their lower branches on only one side. Such trees often indicate a spot where the old trail once passed close to a lone tree.

When attempting to find a trail that has disappeared, ask yourself where the most logical place would be to build a trail given its source and destination. Trail builders tend to seek level ground where it is available, and often follow the natural contours of streamcourses and ridgelines. Bear in mind that most trails avoid up-and-down motion in favor of long, sustained grades culminating in major passes or hilltops. Old trail beds can sometimes be spotted from a distance as they cut across hillsides at a constant angle.

Zero-Impact Hiking and Camping

One of the aims of this book is to encourage people to heft a knapsack or backpack and stride out on any of the wonderful trails in Olympic National Park and the surrounding national forests. But many of these same trails already receive moderate to heavy use, and they're showing signs of wear. Erosion is a problem where an army of boots has shortcut switchbacks; litter seems to beget more litter, especially near trailheads and at backcountry campsites; and unofficial trails have proliferated across some high alpine meadows, marring the otherwise wild scene.

Fortunately, all of these problems are avoidable—as are most impacts caused by backcountry visitors—if a few simple guidelines are heeded. Remember: The goal is to leave no trace of your passing.

Advanced Planning to Minimize Impacts

Much of the wear and tear that occurs in Olympic National Park could be reduced by careful planning before the trip. Visitors should contact local authorities (see appendix D) to find out about areas that are particularly sensitive to disturbance or receive heavy use. Since the goal of most wilderness travelers is to visit pristine and untrammeled areas, the avoidance of the most popular sites can only enhance one's wilderness experience.

We encourage travelers to plan their routes using established trails whenever possible, as these travel corridors are least susceptible to damage. Alpine habitats above the timberline are particularly fragile, and travelers who lack thorough training in minimum impact techniques should cross them only on designated trails. Backcountry visitors can also travel more lightly by moving about in small groups. Small groups stress the landscape to a much smaller degree, especially around campsites, and they also lend themselves to greater flexibility in route choice and on-the-spot problem solving. Groups of two to six are optimal, while groups larger than ten hikers have a much greater potential for environmental damage and should be split up into smaller components.

The proper equipment can also help visitors reduce their visual presence and trampling effects in the wilderness. Dark-hued or muted clothing, tents, and packs help make you less conspicuous to other travelers. One bright-yellow or orange shirt can be carried to attract attention in an emergency. Hiking shoes with a shallow tread design are gentler on plants and soils and also won't clog with mud. Backpackers can also carry a pair of smooth-soled camp shoes—sport sandals, boat shoes, or moccasins. These feel terrific after a day on the trail, and they greatly reduce wear and tear on plants and soils around camp.

On the Trail

Please stay on established trails. Cutting switchbacks or crossing previously untracked ground leaves behind footprints and trampled plants—signs that may invite the next person to follow in your footsteps. Eventually enough footsteps lead to damaged plants and soils, erosion, and unwanted "social" trails.

Try to avoid travel when trails are saturated with rain or snowmelt. When muddy conditions are unavoidable (as is often the case in the Olympic rain forests), resist the temptation to skirt around puddles or boggy spots in the trail. This only widens the tread, and your feet will likely get soaked from brushing against ground plants anyway.

If you must travel off trail, look for trample-resistant surfaces: sand, gravel, snow (if it's not too steep), glacial till, or a streambed below the high water mark. Parties traveling cross-country should spread out in a line abreast rather than travel single file. This reduces the potential for creating new and unwanted trails and erosion in pristine areas. Leave your route unmarked—no blazes, cairns, flagging, or arrows scratched in the dirt.

As you hike along, always be conscious to reduce short- and long-term disturbances in the environment. Making loud noises can be helpful in avoiding encounters with bears and mountain lions where visibility is limited, but it also disturbs the less dangerous wildlife as well as other travelers. If you do spot wildlife along the trail, be careful to stay outside the animal's comfort zone. If an animal changes behavior as a result of your presence, you are too close. You may also chance upon sites of historical or archaeological significance as you travel on the Olympic Peninsula. These sites are an irreplaceable treasure of national importance and are protected by federal law. Enjoy them without rendering any changes to the site. Be especially respectful of local cultures, and ask permission before entering tribal lands.

Be courteous and considerate to people you meet on the trail. Downhill hikers should yield to those going up. Motorbikers yield to all other trail users, mountain bikers yield to pack stock and hikers, and hikers yield to pack stock. Take the opportunity to say hello and exchange news of the trail. Remember—we are each in our own way pursuing the same goal of having fun in the backcountry.

Selecting a Campsite

Plan your route so that you can camp in established campsites that are officially listed in this guide. Pitch your tent in the center of the bare ground so as not to trample vegetation. Snow and river gravel bars, as far as possible from the water, are good choices, as are dry meadows of sedge and grass. Shorelines of lakes and stream banks are particularly sensitive to disturbance. Keep all campsites at least 200 feet from the nearest lake or stream. Alpine meadows are also very fragile and should be avoided by campers, especially heather and huckleberry communities. And camp well away from travel corridors—this will increase your own seclusion and help other parties preserve their wilderness experience.

On the coast, camp on the beach above the high tide line rather than in the forest. Sand and cobbles are probably the most impact-resistant surface found anywhere, and storm tides eventually erase nearly all trace of human activity. If you have a campfire, it should be built well away from driftwood piles and below the high tide mark. This way, all traces of your campfire will be erased by the next incoming tide.

When leaving any campsite, be sure that the area is returned to its natural state. Make an extra check around the area to be sure that you don't leave any belongings or litter. Leaves, duff, and twigs should be scattered about to camouflage your tent site and any high foot-traffic areas.

Campfires

Even where campfires are allowed, consider doing without one. The torrential rains found in this part of the country often make dry firewood a scarce commodity. A lightweight stove is a far superior alternative for cooking, and light can be supplied by a flashlight or candle lantern. If you build a fire, do so only where downed, dead wood is abundant. Use sticks small enough to be broken by hand, and gather only as much as you need. Keep the fire small and brief. The fire should be built in an existing fire ring or a fire pan (a metal tray or scrap of flame-resistant canvas under a 6-inch mound of dirt). Do not build new rock fire rings, and dismantle those that you find outside of designated campsites.

A fire should never be left unattended, and once it's out make sure the ashes are cold. The cold ashes should be scattered; leave the fire ring clean and pack out any unburned trash.

Human Waste Disposal

Many people are surprised to learn that human waste, even when properly buried in a "cat hole" under ideal conditions, requires a year or more to decompose naturally. Any fecal bacteria present will remain viable (that is, ready to infect) for that length of time. The decomposition process is slowed even more when waste is concentrated (as in a group latrine) or deposited in excessively dry, wet, or cold conditions.

Once the traveler understands these facts, it is easy to see that natural composting can't always keep pace with the amount of human waste that is deposited, particularly at heavily used backcountry campsites. The problem is compounded when the site is near a lake or stream (as are many popular campsites) because runoff or groundwater can easily carry fecal material and disease to the surface water. Wildlife—and other campers—then rely on the same source for drinking water. This can result in disastrous consequences.

The Olympic marmot, a rodent endemic to the Olympic Mountains

Many of the camping areas in Olympic National Park are provided with old-fashioned outhouses. Use these rustic facilities whenever nature calls, and practice minimum impact disposal techniques where they are unavailable. Increasingly, land managers are asking (and in some places requiring) people to pack out human waste. Boaters on many western rivers have been doing this for years, and mountain climbers, including those on Mount Olympus, are now handed plastic bags for this purpose in several national parks. Thanks to the staff at Yosemite National Park, all backcountry visitors now have a clean, easy, and secure way to join the ranks and pack out waste. It's called the "poop tube."

You can make your own poop tube from a piece of 4-inch-diameter PVC plastic pipe, the kind used for plumbing. Cut the pipe to length as needed for the number of days you'll be in the backcountry; a 2-foot section is enough for five to seven days for most folks. Then glue a cap on one end and a threaded adapter for a screw-on plug on the other end. Some travelers duct tape a piece of nylon webbing onto the side of the tube so that it can be strapped onto the outside of a pack.

To use the tube, defecate into a paper lunch bag. Then sprinkle in a handful of kitty litter to absorb moisture and reduce odors. Shake the bag to distribute the kitty litter, then roll it up and slide it into the tube. Used toilet paper can go in the tube as well. Screw in the plug and you're done. At the end of the trip, empty the contents into a non-flush vault or "pit" toilet (ask land managers beforehand to recommend a specific outhouse). The paper bags will quickly decay (use only unwaxed bags to ensure that they do) and won't clog the pump used to clean out the vault. Never put human waste into trash cans or Dumpsters—it creates a health hazard and is illegal.

If you decide instead to use the cat hole method and bury your waste in the backcountry, follow a few simple guidelines:

- Look for an out-of-the-way site in stable soil at least 200 feet (about 70 paces) from surface water. Avoid places that show signs of flooding, carrying runoff, or groundwater seepage.

- Make sure the site is at least 200 feet from campsites, trails, and other centers of human activity.

- Look for a site with a healthy layer of topsoil at least 6 inches deep. The ground should be moist (but not saturated) and easy to dig in.

- With a small hand trowel, dig a cat hole 6 to 8 inches deep. Keep the sod lid intact. Set it aside and pile all the dirt next to the hole.

- Squat and aim for the hole. Deposit used toilet paper in the hole (burning it is unnecessary and risky if conditions are dry or windy).

- When covering the waste, use a stick to stir in the first handful or two of soil. This hastens the decomposition process. Add the remaining soil and replace the sod lid. Scrape leaves and duff around the site to camouflage your efforts. Remember to clean your hands well before handling food or cooking utensils.

- Unless local regulations state otherwise, it's usually best to dig individual cat holes rather than a group latrine. And always use the outhouse if one is provided.

Washing

The key to cleaning up in the backcountry is to keep soap, oils, and all other pollutants out of the water. Mountain lakes and streams have a delicate balance of nutrient inputs and outputs. Soaps and dishwater dumped into alpine waterways encourage the growth of microbes that can deplete dissolved oxygen in the water, making it uninhabitable to many species of fish. In addition, aquatic plants and fish are extremely sensitive to soap (even the biodegradable kind) and can die from contact with it.

To wash cooking and eating utensils, carry water in a clean bowl or pot at least 200 feet from water sources. Use little or no soap—water warmed on the stove will unstick most food and grease. Use a plastic scrubbie and a little muscle for stubborn residues. Scatter wash water over the ground in an out-of-the-way spot at least 200 feet from surface water and 100 yards from any likely campsite. In bear country, pick out food scraps before scattering the water and pack them out with other garbage.

For personal bathing, a good dousing and scrubbing with a soapless washcloth will suffice for all but extended trips. Again, carry the water at least 200 feet from surface water. There are also rinse-free soaps and shampoos on the market that are designed specifically for backpackers.

Regulations and Guidelines Specific to Olympic National Park

- Backcountry campers must obtain a permit, which is available for $5 at ranger stations in Port Angeles, Forks, and on the south shore of Lake Quinault and at many trailheads.
- Campfires are not permitted above 3,500 feet. Where fires are allowed, they must be built in existing fire rings.
- Pets are prohibited in the backcountry and in some frontcountry areas.
- Nearly all trails in the park are closed to mountain bikes; some trails are off-limits to horses.
- Weapons are prohibited throughout the park.
- The group size limit for overnight trips is twelve people and/or eight head of stock.
- Limits for overnight use are in effect for several backcountry areas of the park, including the Ozette Loop, Lake Constance, Flapjack Lakes, Grand Valley, and the Seven Lake Basin.

Regulations Specific to National Forest Wilderness Areas

- Mechanized vehicles and motorized equipment are strictly prohibited.
- Campfires are not permitted above 3,500 feet elevation.
- Group size is limited to twelve people and/or eight head of stock.
- Livestock may not be tethered to trees or shrubs for longer than thirty minutes.
- Transportation of unprocessed vegetative matter such as hay or grain is prohibited.

For more information about zero-impact techniques, pick up a copy of *Wild Country Companion,* available from The Globe Pequot Press at www.globepequot.com or by phone at (800) 243-0495. And contact the National Leave No Trace Skills and Ethics Education Program at 288 Main Street, Lander, WY 82520, or phone (800) 332-4100.

Legend

▨▨▨▨	Wilderness/National Boundary
═══	Paved Road
≡≡≡	Interstate Highway
■ ■ ■ ■	Jeep Road
▬▬▬	Dirt/Gravel Road
────	Creek
▧▧▧▧	National Forest Boundary
────	River
▬▬▬	Described Trail
– – – –	Other Trail
··········	Cross-country Route
⬭	Glacier
▪	Country above 3500' Elevation
⬬	Lake
x^{7524}	Mountain Peak
⋀	Campsite
⚑	Ranger Station
⌣ʳ	Pass/Saddle
▪	Building
▭178	Forest Road
🄸44➤	Trailhead
④	State Road
②	US Highway
⚇	Spring
⊙	Point of Interest
⊕	Coastal Beach Marker
//	Falls

Mount Jupiter and Constance Peak, as seen on the Jupiter Ridge hike

Sol Duc–
Lake Crescent

This northern fringe of the Olympic Mountains is dominated by heavily forested peaks. The low basins were originally carved by glaciers and now bear the drainages of the Lyre and Sol Duc Rivers. Sol Duc means "sparkling waters," and this great stream is born in an area of tremendous geothermal activity. Waters heated by molten magma rise through faults in the Juan de Fuca Plate, leaking to the surface at Sol Duc Hot Springs. These waters have been harnessed in swimming pool form at a full-scale resort within the park.

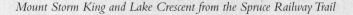

Mount Storm King and Lake Crescent from the Spruce Railway Trail

Lake Crescent is one of the primary attractions of the area. This large body of water is clear and cold, surrounded by imposing peaks. This lake attained its current size when a landslide blocked its eastern outlet, and the water level rose until it poured over the northern lip of the basin to form the Lyre River. This new outlet stream was too turbulent to admit the passage of sea-run rainbow and cutthroat trout that inhabited the lake, and these isolated stocks evolved into the Beardslee and Crescenti trout, respectively.

There are ranger stations near Sol Duc Hot Springs (which is open only three to four days per week) and on Barnes Point on the south shore of Lake Crescent (which does not offer backcountry permits). The Sol Duc Hot Springs Resort, Lake Crescent Lodge, and Log Cabin Resort provide lodgings within the national park, and there are campgrounds near the hot springs and at the western end of Lake Crescent. An entrance fee is charged at the Sol Duc Hot Springs Road. The Fairholm general store at the western end of Lake Crescent is the only nearby source of supplies.

1 Pyramid Peak Trail

A 3.5-mile day hike to the summit of Pyramid Mountain.

Difficulty: Moderately strenuous.
Trail type: Secondary.
Best season: Late May to mid-October.
Elevation gain: 2,400 feet.

Maximum elevation: 3,050 feet.
Topo maps: Lake Crescent; Custom Correct *Lake Crescent–Happy Lake Ridge.*

Finding the trailhead: Take U.S. Highway 101 west from Lake Crescent to reach a junction with Camp David Jr. Road at mile 220.9. Follow this improved gravel road for 1.6 miles to the North Shore picnic area. The trail begins at a signpost on the main road.

The Hike

This trail makes a steady ascent of a minor peak on the northern boundary of the park, with views of both Lake Crescent and the Strait of Juan de Fuca. Cougars are

Mount Storm King and Happy Lake Ridge

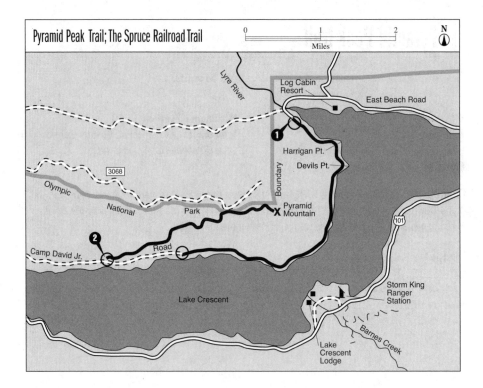

Pyramid Peak Trail; The Spruce Railroad Trail

0   1   2   N

Miles

Lyre River

Log Cabin
Resort

East Beach Road

Harrigan Pt.

Devils Pt.

Boundary

3068

Olympic

National   Park

X Pyramid
Mountain

101

Camp David Jr.   Road

Storm King
Ranger
Station

Lake Crescent

Barnes Creek

Lake
Crescent
Lodge

occasionally sighted on the dry slopes of the mountain. The trek begins by ascending gradually out of the cedar-dominated valley bottom and onto the drier slopes above. Here a mixed forest of Douglas fir and bigleaf maple is underlain by Oregon grape and salal. Early openings in the trees offer views of Lake Crescent and Aurora Ridge beyond it. After 1.5 miles the trail crosses two intermittent streams and begins to climb more briskly across the fluted face of the ridge.

After another 0.5 mile the path zigzags up to a saddle in the ridge, where a poorly placed clear-cut interrupts the forest. Vancouver Island can be seen, as well as the patchwork scars of clear-cuts covering the slopes to the north. As the trail climbs along the north slope of the ridge, it enters a dark forest of hemlock and red cedar. This forest type thrives in the moist soils that occur on slopes shaded by the bulk of the ridge.

After mounting a series of false summits, the trail arrives at a second saddle that offers views to the south. Just beyond it lies the summit of Pyramid Mountain. Here an old lookout shack harks back to World War II, when observers were stationed at this spot to watch for Japanese aircraft that might attack the naval bases of Puget Sound. Views from the summit are sweeping, fea-

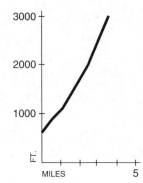

turing the cobalt waters of Lake Crescent and the rugged summits of Mount Storm King and Happy Lake Ridge rising beyond it. Far beyond the Strait of Juan de Fuca, the snow-clad cone of Mount Baker rises above lesser peaks of the Cascades.

Key Points

0.0   Trailhead.

3.5   Summit of Pyramid Mountain.

2 The Spruce Railroad Trail

A 4-mile point-to-point day hike along the north shore of Lake Crescent. (See map on page 26.)

Difficulty: Easy.
Trail type: Primary (mountain bikes allowed).
Best season: All year.
Elevation gain: 260 feet.

Elevation loss: 260 feet.
Maximum elevation: 700 feet (Devils Point).
Topo maps: Lake Crescent; Custom Correct *Lake Crescent–Happy Lake Ridge.*

Finding the trailhead: Take U.S. Highway 101 to a junction with East Beach Road, at mile 232 just east of Lake Crescent. Follow this winding, paved road 3.2 miles, passing the Log Cabin Resort and turning left onto another paved road bearing a sign for the Spruce Railroad Trail. This road crosses the Lyre River and reaches a parking area near some private residences. The trail begins from a sign on the west side of the road.

The Hike

This trail offers a gentle stroll along the north shore of Lake Crescent, making a point-to-point hike that is discussed here from east to west. It follows an old rail bed that was built during World War I to transport Sitka spruce from the then-inaccessible western part of the peninsula to the aircraft factories. Sitka spruce has a superior ratio of strength to weight, and was therefore coveted for the making of biplane airframes. The railroad was completed in a remarkable time of only six weeks, but the war was over before the first logs rolled eastward on the rails. The railway was active through the 1950s, when it was abandoned and subsequently turned into a trail. It is one of the only trails in Olympic National Park where mountain bikes are permitted.

The trail begins by running inland from North Shore Road, climbing gently to reach the old railroad grade. As the rail bed runs southward, it passes through a mixed forest of red alder and Douglas fir, skirting inland to avoid private residences along the lakeshore. It then descends to the shoreline, although dense trees screen out views of the water. A rough spur path to Harrigan Point brings the traveler to a grassy spit that offers the first unobstructed vistas of the hike.

A short distance farther, the main trail climbs a bit to round the rocky headland of Devils Point. An old tunnel was blasted through the bedrock of the point to accommodate the railway, but it has since been sealed off with rocky debris. The point itself offers fine views of the north arm of the lake and Mount Storm King

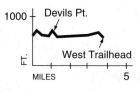

rising above the waters to the south. Pacific madrones thrive in the thin soils of this sunny locale. A bridge soon arches above the waters of a narrow and rocky cove, and its turquoise depths have a gemlike clarity. The imposing rock faces that rise all around this inlet are the exposed foundation of Pyramid Peak.

Just beyond the bridge are fine views of the western arm of the lake, with the towering green wall of Aurora Ridge dominating its south shore. The next stretch of shoreline is frequently punctuated by openings where the trail skirts the base of sheer cliffs. Lake Crescent Lodge occupies the alluvial delta of Barnes Creek on the far side of the lake. A second tunnel is soon reached, and the eastern entrance of this one has not been blocked. The tunnel is choked with rubble and rotting timber, however, and exploring it would be an unsafe proposition. Old sections of rail are reminiscent of earlier times as the path makes its way through sun-dappled groves of red alder to reach the western trailhead. Just before arriving at the trailhead outhouse, the path departs from the rail bed and drops to meet the end of Camp David Jr. Road.

Key Points

0.0 East trailhead.

0.8 Harrigan Point.

1.1 Devils Point

2.9 Second tunnel.

4.0 West trailhead.

3 Mount Storm King

A 1.9-mile day hike from Storm King Ranger Station partway up Mount Storm King.

Difficulty: Strenuous.
Trail type: Foot.
Best season: Late May to mid-October.
Elevation gain: 2,100 feet.

Maximum elevation: 2,650 feet.
Topo maps: Lake Crescent; Custom Correct *Lake Crescent–Happy Lake Ridge.*

Finding the trailhead: Take U.S. Highway 101 to mile 228 on the south shore of Lake Crescent, then take a short side road north to the Storm King Ranger Station. The trail begins from this point and crosses underneath the highway.

The Hike

This trail offers a steep ascent that ends at a viewpoint high on the flanks of Mount Storm King. The trip starts out on the paved nature trail that crosses underneath the highway and into the bottomland forest beyond. The rich alluvial delta of Barnes

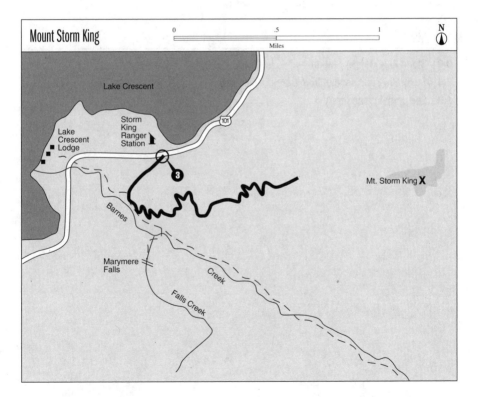

Creek supports an old-growth stand of grand fir and red cedar where towering progenitors rise above a mix of younger trees. Just before the walkway reaches a footlog over Barnes Creek, the Storm King Trail breaks away to the left.

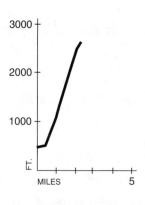

This narrow path climbs steeply out of the bottomland and onto drier slopes pocked with sunny openings where bigleaf maples thrive. The trail soon crosses a broad terrace with poorly drained soils that support a lush growth of forest similar to that found in the creek bottoms. The trail then resumes its calf-burning climb through young Douglas firs and a scattering of smooth-barked madrones. Several openings allow fine views of the forested convolutions of Aurora Ridge. About two-thirds of the way up, the path crests the first of two knobs that overlook Lake Crescent. The second knob, 0.5 mile farther up, affords the most spectacular views of the route. The deep azure of the lake provides a stunning foreground for vistas of Vancouver Island and the Strait of Juan de Fuca. After an additional climb of 0.2 mile, the trail reaches its official terminus at a high overlook above the Barnes Creek valley. The rocky crest of Happy Lake Ridge can be seen above the head of the drainage. A primitive path leads from this point to the summit; it is steep and exposed, and should only be attempted by skilled climbers.

Key Points

0.0 Storm King Ranger Station.

0.5 Storm King Trail departs from Barnes Creek Trail.

1.9 End of maintained trail.

4 Mount Muller

A 12.9-mile (round-trip) day hike or backpack loop over Mount Muller.

Difficulty: Moderately strenuous.
Trail type: Primary.
Best season: Early May to mid-October.
Elevation gain: 3,150 feet.
Elevation loss: 3,150 feet.

Maximum elevation: 3,748 feet (Mount Muller summit).
Topo maps: Snider Peak, Mount Muller; Custom Correct *Lake Crescent–Happy Lake Ridge.*

Finding the trailhead: From Lake Crescent, drive west on U.S. Highway 101 to mile 151. A dirt road across from Forest Road 2918 runs north past an electrical substation to the well-marked trailhead.

The Hike

This newly created trail forms a 13-mile loop, visiting a long stretch of subalpine meadows atop Mount Muller. The mountain's relatively low elevation (3,748 feet) and proximity to the Strait of Juan de Fuca combine to melt winter snows early. As a result, this trail offers excursions into the high country at a time when trails in the interior of the Olympics are still snowbound. Outstanding wildflower displays and splendid views of Mount Olympus and the Sol Duc Valley make this trail a fine complement to the existing trail system. Hikers desiring a shorter trip can make a one-way 2.9-mile jaunt to the summit from an alternate trailhead on Forest Road 3040.

The trail begins beside Littleton Creek and immediately offers a choice of directions for hiking the loop. This book will cover the trail in a clockwise motion, following the narrow path that runs north beside the stream. It soon climbs onto drier slopes, ascending steadily through a forest of young Douglas fir. The trail then appropriates an old jeep track that once gave access to manganese prospects on the steep mountainside. After a few switchbacks the path leaves the jeep trail behind and embarks on a more gradual ascent along the west face of a finger ridge. Gaps in the trees allow early views of Olympus and the Sol Duc Valley, and an isolated spring provides a dependable (though muddy) water source.

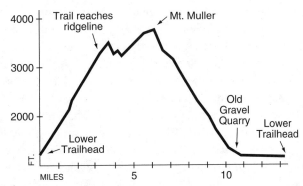

View from Mount Muller of Lake Crescent and Mount Storm King

The grade becomes quite moderate as the path approaches the main ridgetop. Here it enters a meadow of tall grass interrupted by ragged conifers. Grouse find an ideal mix of cover and food here, and often explode from the underbrush beside the trail. The origin of the meadow is told by the charred stumps that are scattered about, a silent reminder of a fire that razed the forest in the 1920s. The lower slopes were soon covered with Douglas fir saplings, but the drier ridgetops favored grasses, salal, and kinnikinnick. The trail crests the ridgetop and is joined by a 0.5-mile spur that rises from FR 3040. An unfinished spur trail rides the ridgeline west to Kloshe Nanitch; renovations on this historic and striking fire lookout were recently completed.

The main trail swings east along the ridgetop, crossing grassy meadows filled with the blossoms of lupine, Olympic daisy, and paintbrush. After a gentle climb the path crosses a bald knob and then begins descending toward the next saddle. Look through a window in the hills to glimpse Mount Baker beyond the watery expanse of Puget Sound. As the trail loses elevation, it enters a forest of young silver fir and mountain hemlock; the trees have interlocking crowns that block out the sun. The forest is periodically broken by grassy openings and fine views of the Olympic Mountains. Mounts Olympus and Tom cradle the icy swath of the White Glacier between them, while the solitary peak of Mount Appleton rises above the verdant hills farther west.

The trail reaches a low point dubbed Thomas Gap, then begins to climb steadily toward the summit of Mount Muller. Open meadows allow sweeping vistas along the way, and wildflowers carpet these lush openings. A few isolated monoliths of basalt

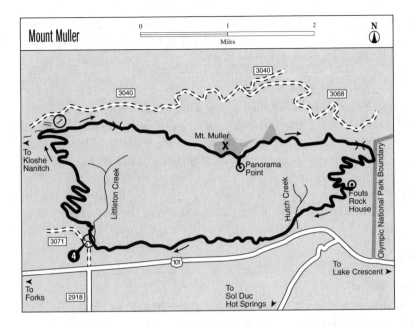

rise from the rounded hilltop like the menhirs of a lost race of primitives. Near the top of the peak, a spur path takes off to the left, climbing the remaining 0.1 mile to the tree-cloaked summit. A better view can be had from a knob known as Panorama Point just a few hundred yards to the east along the main trail. This bare outcrop rises sheer above the valley of the Sol Duc, offering vistas down its entire length and an outstanding view of Lake Crescent. The lake's deep blue waters lie cupped in the forest of the foothills like a giant sapphire nestled amid folds of green velvet. Mount Storm King guards the foot of the lake, while Mount Baker rises on the eastern horizon.

The ground cover soon changes to a sward of beargrass, a lily that sends up bulbous clumps of flowers every three to five years. Subalpine firs become common in the overstory as the terrain gets rougher. The trail jogs to the north to avoid several jagged outcrops of basalt before beginning the long and often steep descent into a pass called Mosley Gap. The last of the distant views are found here; a montane forest of Douglas fir closes around the path as it drops onto the south slope of the ridge and makes its way down a gently sloping toe of the mountain.

The trail soon leaves this shallow ridgetop to descend westward across steeper slopes. It soon enters a forest rockscape of mossy boulders and outcrops, and a faint spur trail runs east to a boulder formation known as Fouts Rock House. Ferns have begun to invade the understory, and the forest takes on a decidedly lowland aspect as the shallow benches slope away to the valley floor. Hutch Creek marks the bottom of the grade, and the noisy passage of cars can be heard on nearby US 101.

Beyond this stream is a well-tended grove where vine maples and red alders grow in regular clumps, with wide alleyways between them that allow passage of the trail. The conifers return just before the path reaches an old gravel quarry. The path across the quarry is indistinct, but the trail is marked by signs at both ends. Soon after passing this opening, the trail crosses a boggy creek where a forest wetland forms critical breeding habitat for frogs and salamanders.

Beyond it lies a series of shelterwood cuts, and the trek follows a maze of old logging roads through the thinned timber. One brief island amid the logging activity holds a fine stand of red alder, their stately white trunks rising from a carpet of wood sorrel. This hardwood is worthless as lumber but plays an important ecological role: Its roots harbor bacteria that return nitrogen to the forest soil. The cuts soon return, and the path finds its way onto an active trunk road. It follows the road for 0.4 mile before leaving it and gradually becoming a path again. It passes among Douglas fir infested with witches' broom, a parasite that causes the foliage of a tree to form a dense ball. Slender alders rise above the trail as it goes the final distance to return to the trailhead.

Key Points

0.0   Trailhead.

3.0   Ridgetop junction with trails to Kloshe Nanitch and FR 3040. Turn right.

5.5   Junction with spur trail to summit of Mount Muller.

10.1   Old gravel quarry.

12.9   Trail returns to original trailhead.

5 Aurora Ridge

A 22.7-mile backpack over Aurora Ridge from the Sol Duc Hot Springs Road to the Storm King Ranger Station.

Difficulty: Moderately strenuous.
Trail type: Primitive between Aurora Springs and Barnes Creek; otherwise secondary.
Best season: Mid-June to mid-October.
Elevation gain: 4,680 feet.

Elevation loss: 5,390 feet.
Maximum elevation: 4,800 feet.
Topo maps: Mount Muller, Lake Crescent, Lake Sutherland; Custom Correct *Lake Crescent-Happy Lake Ridge.*

Finding the trailhead: Take U.S. Highway 101 west from Lake Crescent to mile 219. Then follow Sol Duc Hot Springs Road south for 2.5 miles to the well-marked trailhead.

The Hike

This trail is well-defined from Sol Duc Hot Springs Road to Aurora Springs, but then it disappears in the open meadows behind Aurora Peak. It becomes distinct again as it approaches the Barnes Creek drainage. The grade into the Barnes Creek valley is

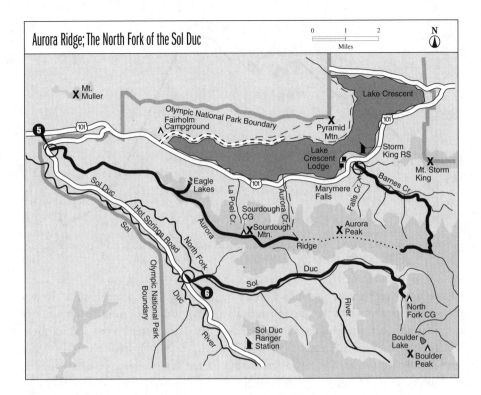

long and steep, and hikers who attempt the hike should approach from the west to avoid having to climb it.

After the initial plunge into the forest, the trail swings south, following an old roadbed shaded by red alder. It begins to climb rather vigorously after 0.5 mile, leaving the road and alders behind in favor of the hemlock-clad slopes above. The brief but stiff ascent leads to ridgetop benchlands bearing the enormous boles of old-growth trees. After reaching the ridgeline the trail wanders among tiny hillocks. The shaded understory bears only a thin growth of mosses here. The general trend of the country is upward, but there are numerous level sections and even a few substantial descents. As the trail gains altitude, huckleberry bushes invade the understory, and early season travelers will note the nodding white blossoms of the wood nymph.

Upon crossing a broad depression between hillocks, the trail reaches a spur path that leads northward to the Eagle Lakes.

The Aurora Ridge Trail continues to gain elevation, and the forest floor comes alive with avalanche lilies following the melting of winter snows. Just before reaching Sourdough Peak, the trail crosses a wide opening studded with low-growing junipers. Lupines, paintbrushes, and bistorts poke up through the shrubs to provide a colorful accompaniment to a stunning view of the Olympus massif. Shortly thereafter a faint track climbs away to the north, running a short distance to Sourdough Camp and its

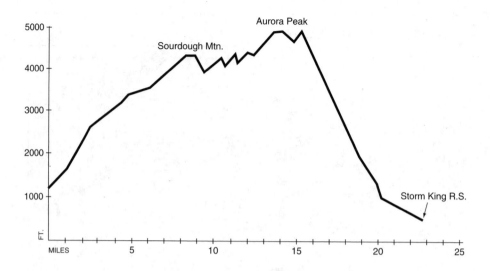

collapsed shelter. This site occupies a rather soggy meadow amid subalpine and silver firs; a ravine just north of this site provides a supply of water. For most of the summer season, water on this trail is extremely scarce. Carry extra water bottles and fill them whenever possible. Other sources include Eagle Lakes, which have plenty of water year-round, and Aurora Springs, a fluctuating source that may not provide water in late August. Beyond Aurora Springs, hikers will find no water until descending into the Barnes Creek drainage, 4 miles away.

After the main trail descends into the next saddle, it drops onto the northern side of the ridge and passes a number of small glades. It returns to the ridgeline before meeting the Aurora Creek Trail, which drops away swiftly toward the shores of Lake Crescent. Stay right as the Aurora Ridge Trail returns to the southern slope of the ridge to pass behind Aurora Peak. The trail descends to Aurora Springs, then becomes difficult to pick out in the tangle of grasses and game trails. To the southeast Boulder Peak and Mount Appleton rise above the unbroken forest of the North Fork Sol Duc Valley. The path descends for a time, then climbs again to enter the forest. After cruising through the timber for several miles, the trail reaches a much larger complex of meadows. It is virtually impossible to follow here; stay uphill and head for the ridgeline as the meadows end to regain the trail.

Sawed logs mark the trail as it drops to the south of one more summit on its way to a major trail junction. The Aurora Divide cutoff (discussed at the end of this section) runs southeast from this point to join the Happy Lake Ridge Trail. To complete this hike, turn left onto a trail that descends into the Barnes Creek drainage. This trail drops down through mountain hemlocks, passing a collection of tiny snowmelt ponds surrounded by heather and twisted saplings. This is a favorable spot to pitch a tent. Snow lingers late in this area but is more of a nuisance than a hazard.

The trail then begins a foot-pounding descent that lasts for 4.5 miles. After a short distance the trees give way to an open brushfield that offers good views of the ridges behind Mount Storm King, as well as an excellent opportunity to be mauled by devil's club. After reaching the bottom of the brushfield, the trail continues to plummet through a mixed stand of Douglas fir and hemlock, with occasional views of the tumbling watercourse that runs down the wooded vale.

At the main Barnes Creek valley, the route reaches a junction with the Barnes Creek Trail. Turn left and keep descending past a small stream with its attendant campsite. The descent continues as the trail wanders in and out of the bottomlands, crossing two substantial tributaries on footlogs. Just beyond the second stream is a log across Barnes Creek itself. As the descent slows, note the incursion of western red cedar into the forest overstory. The trail emerges at the much wider Marymere Falls Trail; bear right for the brief and flat jaunt through the forest and under the highway to reach the Storm King Ranger Station.

Aurora Divide Option: This trail follows a ridgetop for 1.8 miles to connect the Aurora Ridge hike with Happy Lake Ridge. From the Aurora Ridge junction, the trail climbs through the forest to reach the western slopes of Lizard Head Peak. After passing a spring that occupies a steep ravine, the path runs southward onto the crest of a sinuous ridge. Mount Appleton can be seen from openings in the trees, along with the rocky knob of Boulder Peak. The trail then climbs steadily to meet the Happy Lake Ridge Trail.

Key Points

0.0	Sol Duc Hot Springs Road.
5.5	Junction with Eagle Lakes spur trail. Stay right.
8.3	Sourdough camping area.
10.4	Junction with Aurora Creek cutoff trail. Stay right.
11.3	Aurora Springs. Trail maintenance ends.
15.1	Junction with Aurora Divide cutoff trail. Turn left to begin descent.
18.7	Junction with old Upper Barnes Creek Trail. Bear left.
22.0	Junction with Marymere Falls Trail. Turn right.
22.3	Junction with Lake Crescent Lodge cutoff trail. Stay right.
22.7	Storm King Ranger Station.

6 The North Fork of the Sol Duc

A 9-mile backpack up the North Fork of the Sol Duc River to the end of the trail. (See map on page 35.)

Difficulty: Moderate.
Trail type: Secondary.
Best season: All year.
Elevation gain: 1,890 feet.

Elevation loss: 440 feet.
Maximum elevation: 2,900 feet (shelter).
Topo maps: Mount Muller, Lake Crescent; Custom Correct *Lake Crescent–Happy Lake Ridge.*

Finding the trailhead: Take U.S. Highway 101 west from Lake Crescent to mile 219. Then follow Sol Duc Hot Springs Road south for 8.2 miles. The parking area is marked by a sign on the west side of the road; the trail leaves from the east side.

The Hike

This trail follows the valley of the North Fork of the Sol Duc River, which has remained undisturbed by fire and human activities for centuries. The wild and remote character of this drainage is surprising given its easy access. The trail offers pleasant hiking as far as the second ford, after which it is no longer maintained. Numerous wades across the stream are required to reach the North Fork Shelter, but beyond this point it is no great feat to bushwhack upward through the open forests of a spur ridge to connect with the Happy Lake Ridge Trail.

The trail begins by climbing over the low ridge that separates the two forks of the Sol Duc. Upon reaching the banks of the North Fork, a knee-deep ford leads the hiker among the glassy green pools and chattering riffles. Once on the far bank, the trail follows the river upstream, rising gently as it traverses a bottomland stand of moss-hung bigleaf maples. This plant community is more typical of the rain forest bottoms of the peninsula's western rivers; it is found along the North Fork because the unique configuration of the mountains produces a pocket of moist climate here.

The trail soon finds its way to the water's edge, which it follows as the river swirls lazily across flutes and whorls of soft bedrock. After a time the path moves inland again to enter a true rain forest of mighty conifers. (Though this area might not meet the rainfall criterion of a true rain forest, it is ecologically identical to forests on the western part of the peninsula that do.) Sitka spruce and hemlock rise from skirtlike bases that formed as the saplings put down roots around a nurse log or rotting stump. The pattern is repeated in the newest generation of trees: Hemlock seedlings carpet the deadfalls and stumps that litter the forest floor. Sword ferns and vine maples dot the understory, rounding out this ancient plant community.

A campsite occupies a grassy glade at mile 3.1, after which the path climbs onto the slopes above the valley floor. It maintains a constant height of about 100 feet above the water as it continues eastward. These well-drained hillsides, crisscrossed by mossy brooks, support a lowland forest of Douglas fir and western hemlock more typical of the eastern slope of the peninsula. The valley ultimately widens out, and tall, evenly spaced Douglas firs rise from the level benches. This even-aged stand of shade-intolerant trees indicates that a forest fire probably swept the area about 250 years ago.

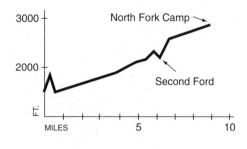

After passing a small camp on the wooded terraces, the trail begins to climb steadily and turns northeast to enter a major side valley. At mile 6.3 the path descends into a moss-lined canyon, where a tiny campsite marks the end of the maintained trail. The old trail bed fords the stream just above this spot and climbs over a hillside before dropping back to the stream. It makes innumerable fords of the creek, and it almost makes sense to hike straight up the streamcourse. The primitive trail peters out at the North Fork Shelter, which is set amid silver firs at the base of Happy Lake Ridge.

Key Points

0.0   Trailhead.

1.0   Knee-deep ford of North Fork of the Sol Duc River.

6.3   Second ford and end of maintained trail.

9.0   North Fork Shelter.

7 Mink Lake–Little Divide

A day hike or backpack 2.5 miles to Mink Lake, or 7.6 miles to Deer Lake.

Difficulty: Moderately strenuous.
Trail type: Primary to Mink Lake; foot beyond.
Best season: Late June to mid-October.
Elevation gain: 2,940 feet.

Elevation loss: 1,060 feet.
Maximum elevation: 4,140 feet.
Topo maps: Bogachiel Peak; Custom Correct *Seven Lakes Basin-Hoh.*

Finding the trailhead: From U.S. Highway 101, take Sol Duc Hot Springs Road 11 miles to Sol Duc Hot Springs Resort. The trail leaves from a sign at the northwest corner of the parking lot.

The Hike

This trail provides an alternate route to the High Divide and also accesses the end of the Bogachiel River Trail. It begins at Sol Duc Hot Springs Resort. The trail soon splits away from the more heavily trodden Lover's Lane route. Rocky traveling leads across a bottomland forest filled with a lush growth of sword ferns. As the trail begins

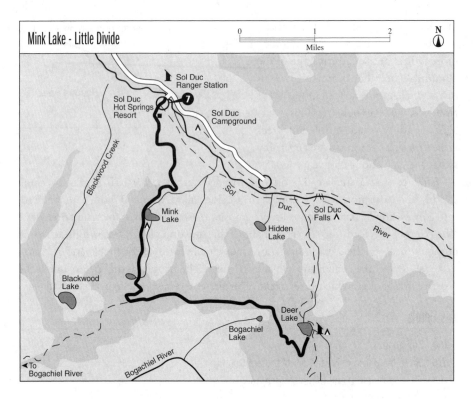

a gradual climb of the valley wall, a more xeric plant community of Douglas fir and highbush blueberry replaces the lowland forest. On its way up, the trail flirts with Mink Creek, its chuckling waters splashing just out of sight in the forest. After 2.5 miles a spur path leads down to the weedy shore of Mink Lake. This shallow pond is set among the folds of forested hills and has a camping area and shelter near its head.

The main trail runs past the western shore of the lake and crosses a number of small rivulets as the forest thins out. It soon reaches the head of the valley, a delightful bowl where miniature trees and shrubs grow amid a rockscape reminiscent of a Japanese garden. The climb steepens as the path heads for the ridgetop, crossing heather-filled swales and fir-clad hummocks along the way. On the ridgeline is an intersection with the Bogachiel River Trail; turn left to continue the trek along the crest of the Little Divide.

This hogback is heavily clad in silver firs that allow only fleeting glimpses of Mount Tom through the branches. After 0.9 mile the ridgetop broadens and cups several stagnant pools within its folds. The going is

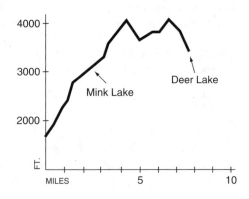

easy here, but the path soon drops onto the wooded south slope of a hillock and begins a series of vigorous ups and downs. Miniscule Bogachiel Lake appears to be quite close to the trail on most maps, but in reality it lies a long distance below the trail and can scarcely be seen through the trees. After climbing onto a saddle in the ridge, the path wanders through subalpine parkland on the north-facing slope before beginning a long descent through the trees. The trail reaches its terminus on the south shore of Deer Lake, where it meets the High Divide Loop.

Key Points

0.0 Sol Duc Hot Springs trailhead.

0.1 Junction with Lover's Lane Trail. Turn right.

2.5 Mink Lake.

4.3 Junction with Bogachiel River Trail. Turn left.

7.6 Junction with High Divide Loop, south shore of Deer Lake.

8 The High Divide Loop

A 17.6-mile (round-trip) backpack that climbs to the spine of the High Divide.

Difficulty: Moderately strenuous.
Trail type: Primary.
Best season: Mid-July to mid-October.
Elevation gain: 4,020 feet.

Elevation loss: 4,020 feet.
Maximum elevation: 5,370 feet.
Topo maps: Bogachiel Peak, Mount Carrie; Custom Correct *Seven Lakes Basin–Hoh*.

Finding the trailhead: From U.S. Highway 101, drive about 13 miles on the Sol Duc Hot Springs Road to a large parking lot at its end. The trail departs from the south end of this lot.

The Hike

This trail offers an outstanding ridge walk along the alpine divide of the Hoh River, featuring magnificent views of Mount Olympus and passing several beautiful lake basins along the way. Sunrises and sunsets are particularly spectacular here, with sublime displays of alpenglow on the snow-clad peaks. Because of the popularity of the area, a reservation system has been put in place for the trail to ensure visitors of a wilderness experience. Permits are available at the Sol Duc Ranger Station and must be obtained in person.

From the trailhead a broad path winds eastward through the towering bottomland forest. The trail forks at the Sol Duc Falls shelter; travelers can approach the loop from either direction, but it will be discussed here as a counterclockwise trek. Follow the right fork down to the river, where a pack bridge and viewing area allow close inspection of this unusual cataract. As the river wore a channel through the stone of

Lunch Lake

the valley floor, it encountered a hard, resistant stratum of stone that is tilted vertically and cuts diagonally across the river channel. Immediately south of this hard layer was a layer of weak, easily eroded rock through which the waters soon wore a deep path. The result is Sol Duc Falls, where the river spills in an angled curtain across the sill of resistant rock and lands 20 feet below in a deep cleft.

The High Divide Trail runs south from the falls, passing a junction with the Lover's Lane Trail before climbing up the sloping wall of the valley. The damp woods of the bottomland soon give way to a montane forest underlain by spindly blueberry bushes. Jungles of devil's club occupy some of the damp swales. A pack bridge spans the mossy channel of Canyon Creek, which flows from Deer Lake. One last pitch of climbing remains before the trail crosses a level basin to reach the lake itself. Deer Lake is a popular camping area surrounded by ponds and sluggish streams that form a breeding ground for frogs and mosquitoes. Wet meadows of sedges and cottongrass are interspersed with rocky knolls that support a sparse growth of subalpine fir. A sign identifies the location of designated campsites.

After rounding the eastern shore of Deer Lake, the trail ascends gradually through a subalpine forest underlain by blueberry bushes. The path soon climbs over the low divide to the east, and the forest opens up into a delightful meadowland dotted with snowmelt ponds and decorated with pink and white heather blossoms. Here the route begins to climb more vigorously on its way to the crest of the High Divide. After achieving the ridgetop, the trail drops onto the south face, running level for

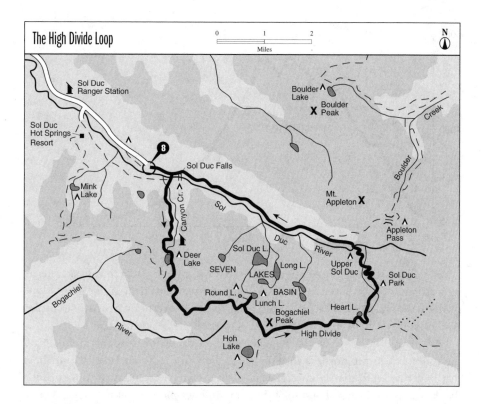

The High Divide Loop

0   1   2
Miles

N

Sol Duc
Ranger Station

Sol Duc
Hot Springs
Resort

Mink
Lake

Sol Duc Falls

Canyon Cr.

Sol

Boulder
Lake
Boulder
X Peak

Boulder Creek

Mt.
Appleton X

Appleton
Pass

Deer
Lake

Sol Duc L.

SEVEN

LAKES

Round L.

Lunch L.

BASIN

Long L.

Duc

River

Upper
Sol Duc

Sol Duc
Park

Heart L.

Bogachiel

River

Bogachiel
Peak
X

High Divide

Hoh
Lake

some distance as it circumnavigates a wooded point. The forest soon gives way to a
spectacular alpine bowl, guarded to the south by a jagged spur of Bogachiel Peak. The
next saddle is a jumble of boulders, and amid the tilted rock is a junction with the
Seven Lakes Basin Trail.

A brief side trip to the west offers the traveler a chance to explore the meadowy
basins and sparkling tarns of the Seven Lakes Basin. Turn north at the junction as the
path slips through a rocky pass and makes a long descent down a stone staircase to
reach the valley floor. Due to the basin's north-facing aspect, glaciers lingered here
until fairly recently to carve a series of cirque lakes that have not yet been filled with
sediment. The trail splits after 0.5 mile, offering spurs to Round and Lunch Lakes.
Looming above the lakes are the oddly twisted summits of the High Divide, rising
like miniature ranges above the flats of the basin. Adventurous hikers can explore
some of the more remote lakes of the basin, but stick to maintained trails to prevent
further impact, and camp only at designated campsites.

Meanwhile the High Divide Trail continues to climb as it makes its way up the
slopes of Bogachiel Peak. It makes a brief sojourn onto the ridge crest well below the
summit, where snow lingers late into the summer and an ice axe may be required. It
then wanders back onto the south slope, bypassing the summit to arrive at a high col
and an intersection with the Hoh Lake Trail. Views of the Olympus massif expand
to fill the entire southern horizon as the path crosses the slopes high above the Hoh

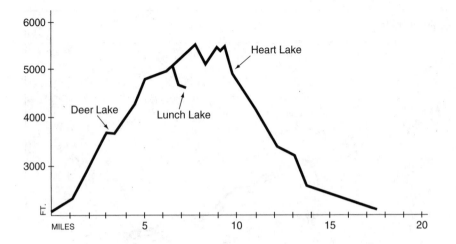

River valley. A short spur path soon climbs to the summit of Bogachiel Peak, offering an aerial view of the Seven Lakes Basin. Watch for marmots high on the grassy slopes of the peak and golden eagles cruising the thermals overhead. Speedwell, heather, lupines, and avalanche lilies brighten the verdant slopes beside the trail.

As the trail drops down the ridgeline to the east, firs obscure the mountains to the south, but to the north is an unimpeded view of the Seven Lakes Basin. Snows that linger late into the summer prevent plant growth here and maintain a primordial landscape of bare soil and rock. The trail follows the crest of the ridge, dipping and rising with the changing contours until it reaches a junction above aptly named Heart Lake. Straight ahead lies the Cat Peak Trail, discussed at the end of this section, while the loop trail descends to the north. This track passes the emerald waters of Heart Lake, then follows its babbling outlet stream downhill. The entire basin is filled with heather-blueberry meadows. There are several colonies of marmots in residence here, and Roosevelt elk are frequent visitors during morning and evening.

The meadows persist as far as Sol Duc Park, where a camping area is nestled in a grove of large hemlocks and silver firs. Beyond this point the trail descends briskly as it drops from the hanging valley of the Bridge Creek basin into the deeper defile of the Sol Duc Valley. The path soon enters a forest of tall conifers, then crosses a footlog over the rushing flow of the Sol Duc. Good camping sites are scattered along the river at regular intervals for the next 3 miles.

After passing a junction with the Appleton Pass Trail, the loop trail skirts the edge of a deep cleft that the river has carved into the bedrock of the valley floor. After a time the valley widens and the forest understory disappears to reveal evenly spaced ranks of old-growth Douglas fir and western hemlock. In many cases the mighty boles rise more than 100 feet before the first branches emerge. After 1.5 miles of traveling among these venerable pillars, the trail reaches the shelter at Sol Duc Falls and completes the loop. The remaining 0.7 mile is covered on the wide path that runs west along the river to reach the trailhead.

Cat Peak primitive trail: Despite its designation, this trail is well built and easy to follow, although hikers may have to negotiate an occasional deadfall. It begins at a junction with the High Divide Loop on the ridge above Heart Lake and runs eastward, following the ridgeline. After passing behind a nameless mountain, the trail drops through open parkland covered in avalanche lilies and dwarf blueberries. The ice-robed bulk of Mount Olympus looms across the Hoh Valley, almost near enough to touch. To the east, Cat Peak marks the beginning of the Bailey Range.

After a steady descent the trail meets an unmarked spur in the low saddle at the head of Cat Creek. The smaller trail descends northward into the Cat Basin, while the main trail continues eastward. The forest soon closes around it, opening briefly to give views of Cat Peak and later Mount Olympus. After 2.9 miles the maintained trail ends at a signpost. Rolling meadows allow excellent vistas of Olympus and its retinue of lesser peaks. Skilled mountaineers can proceed eastward into the Bailey Range from this access point.

Key Points

0.0 Trailhead.

0.1 Junction with spur from Sol Duc Campground. Go straight.

0.7 Loop trail splits at Sol Duc Falls shelter. Turn right.

0.9 Junction with Lover's Lane Trail. Bear left.

3.3 Foot of Deer Lake.

3.5 Junction with Mink Lake–Little Divide Trail at head of Deer Lake. Bear left.

5.2 Trail crests High Divide.

6.7 Junction with Seven Lakes Basin spur trail. Bear right.

7.6 Junction with Hoh Lake Trail. Stay left.

7.7 Junction with Bogachiel Peak spur trail. Stay right.

9.6 Junction with Cat Peak Trail. Turn left and start descending.

10.0 Heart Lake.

10.8 Trail crosses Bridge Creek. Sol Duc Park Camp.

12.3 Footlog over Sol Duc River. Upper Sol Duc Camp.

12.9 Junction with Appleton Pass Trail. Go straight.

17.6 Trail returns to parking area.

Additional Trails

The **Marymere Falls Trail** is an easy stroll from the Storm King Ranger Station to a 90-foot waterfall. The first part of the trail is barrier-free as it passes through a grove of old-growth Douglas fir on the Barnes Creek delta.

The **Upper Barnes Creek Trail** is no longer maintained. The old tread runs up to the divide, then ends abruptly in the face of sheer rocks.

The **Fairholm Campground Trail** makes a 0.8-mile loop through the forest west of Lake Crescent.

The **Aurora Creek Trail** is an extremely steep path that climbs from the shore of Lake Crescent to intercept the Aurora Ridge Trail.

The **Ancient Groves Trail** is a self-guided nature walk in the bottomland forest of the Sol Duc Valley.

The **Lover's Lane Trail** follows the west bank of the Sol Duc River from the hot springs to Sol Duc Falls. It can be combined with the first mile of the High Divide Loop and the Sol Duc Campground Trail for a 4-mile loop trip.

The **Sol Duc Campground Trail** connects the hot springs resort with the High Divide trailhead via both loops of the automobile campground.

Elwha River– Hurricane Ridge

The high alpine meadows of Hurricane Ridge are easily reached from Port Angeles via a paved road and are extremely popular with day hikers. The entire length of Hurricane Ridge from Obstruction Point to Hurricane Hill escaped glaciation during the ice ages, and so served as a refuge for alpine plants and animals. The result is an outstanding diversity of wildflowers, featuring several species that are found nowhere else in the world. There are excellent opportunities to view alpine wildlife, particularly black-tailed deer and Olympic marmots.

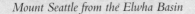

Mount Seattle from the Elwha Basin

Visitors who desire a more remote wilderness experience should consider the valley of the Elwha River, which penetrates to the geographic center of the park. The Elwha band of S'Klallams once had a village that has since been flooded by the dam at Lake Mills, and these people ranged far up the valley in pursuit of elk. Later, members of the Press Expedition chose this corridor in their crossing of the range. In the late 1800s, homesteading activity occurred in the Geyser Valley part of the drainage, and several sturdy cabins remain to this day. Olympic Hot Springs, once a developed resort, has been returned to a more natural state and offers a wild alternative to the Sol Duc facility. In addition, the Elwha Dam, which has long blocked migrations of salmon, is slated for demolition in 2009, which will help to restore the ecological integrity of this beautiful river.

Both Hurricane Ridge and Olympic Hot Springs Roads have fee entrance stations on them. There are full-fledged visitor centers in Port Angeles and at Hurricane Ridge, and a ranger station in the Elwha Valley. This latter station also offers interpretive ranger walks free of charge on a set schedule. There is camping at Heart o' the Hills at the bottom of Hurricane Ridge Road and also at the Elwha and Altaire campgrounds in the Elwha Valley. Port Angeles offers all services required by the traveler.

9 The Happy Lake Ridge Loop

A 15.2-mile (round-trip) backpack that climbs to the crest of Happy Lake Ridge.

Difficulty: Moderately strenuous.
Trail type: Primary.
Best season: Late June to mid-October.
Elevation gain: 4,070 feet.
Elevation loss: 4,150 feet.

Maximum elevation: 5,300 feet.
Topo maps: Mount Carrie, Lake Sutherland; Custom Correct *Lake Crescent-Happy Lake Ridge.*

Finding the trailhead: From U.S. Highway 101 west of Port Angeles, follow Olympic Hot Springs Road, which ascends the Elwha Valley into the park. Stay on the main road, bearing right at Elwha, go past the Altaire campground, and continue to the parking area and trailhead at the end of the road.

The Hike

This trail provides access to the pools of Olympic Hot Springs, then climbs up to an alpine ridgetop for sweeping views of the peaks to the south. The path is heavily traveled as far as the Boulder Creek campground, but the ridge walk itself receives only light traffic. For the first 2.2 miles, the trek follows an old paved road along the forested banks of Boulder Creek. This road ends at a junction below the Boulder Creek campground. The spur path to Olympic Hot Springs continues along the creek, then crosses it and turns east to reach the hot pools. There was once a developed resort here, but it has long since been torn down. The pools have been returned to a more natural state and are scattered across the hillside above the stream.

Travelers bound for the ridge should turn right at the intersection as the roadbed climbs into the sprawling Boulder Creek camping complex. The trail exits the western end of the campground as a dirt track that rises and falls through a creekside forest of Douglas fir and hemlock. An intersection with the Appleton Pass Trail is located 0.6 mile beyond the camping area. Turn right and begin the ascent as the trail winds its way into the valley of Boulder Creek's North Fork. A few gaps in the forest canopy allow views of the sawtooth ridges that form the western wall of the valley. The forest changes markedly as the trail approaches Boulder Lake. First is an extensive stand of Alaska cedar, followed by a mixture of subalpine firs and open glades. The lake itself is on a spur trail 150 yards west of the main route; it offers camping and fishing opportunities. Its clear waters are bordered to the east by open meadows and on the west by the steep, wooded slopes of Boulder Peak. This is the last source of surface water until Happy Lake.

The Happy Lake Ridge Trail bears northeast from the Boulder Lake junction, climbing steeply up a spur ridge that allows occasional views of the lake. Upon reaching the crest of the main ridge, the trail turns east and levels out considerably. Tiny

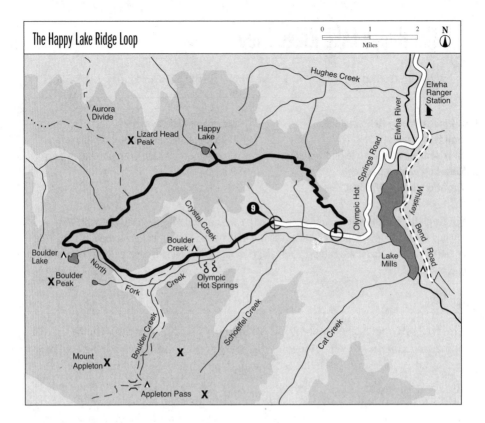

ridgetop meadows of pink heather are hemmed in by dense stands of subalpine fir. After a shallow descent into a broad saddle, the trail surmounts the next knob. Here forest fires have thinned the trees, creating outstanding vistas of Boulder and Everett Peaks as well as the craggy summits surrounding Appleton Pass. The path soon drops onto the northern slope of the ridge as it climbs toward a junction with the Aurora Divide cutoff trail (discussed under the Aurora Ridge hike).

At this junction the cutoff trail lies straight ahead, while the Happy Lake Ridge Trail jackknifes sharply to the southwest. Take a look to the south as this trail descends into the next saddle. The pinnacles and glaciers of Mount Olympus are framed by Appleton Pass, and the northern Baileys rear majestically skyward farther east. The path soon dives into the forest, tracking the vigorous ups and downs of the ridgetop. It emerges into meadows just west of the Happy Lake spur trail, allowing views of a rugged basalt outlier of the main ridge. Happy Lake is 0.5 mile distant, in a shallow basin filled with meadows and firs.

The main trail runs through level country for a time before dropping through a series of dips. Upon departing the ridgeline for wooded southern slopes, the route passes several openings that allow a last vista of the Bailey Range. The trail then begins a long slog downward through heavy timber. After 1 mile the trail rounds a spur and

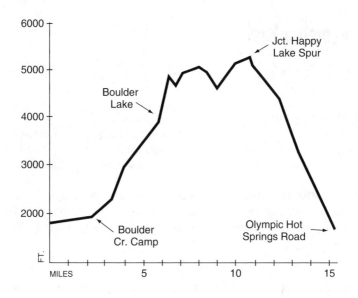

enters an old burn site. In some places the fire burned in the understory, leaving the mature trees intact. In other spots the flames carried into the canopy, completely razing the forest. Pole-size second-growth trees occupy these heavily burned sites. The trail emerges on Olympic Hot Springs Road, about 2.5 miles east of the trailhead.

Key Points

0.0   Appleton Pass trailhead.

2.2   Junction with Olympic Hot Springs spur trail. Bear right.

2.3   Boulder Creek campground.

3.1   Junction with Appleton Pass Trail. Turn right and begin ascent.

5.8   Spur trail to Boulder Lake. Through hikers bear right.

8.3   Junction with Aurora Divide cutoff trail. Turn right.

10.8   Junction with spur trail to Happy Lake. Bear right to complete the loop.

15.2   Trail returns to Olympic Hot Springs Road.

10 Appleton Pass

A 10.1-mile backpack from Olympic Hot Springs Road to the Sol Duc River.

Difficulty: Moderately strenuous.
Trail type: Primary.
Best season: Late June to mid-October.
Elevation gain: 3,310 feet.

Elevation loss: 2,060 feet.
Maximum elevation: 5,120 feet.
Topo maps: Mount Carrie; Custom Correct
Lake Crescent–Happy Lake Ridge.

Finding the trailhead: From U.S. Highway 101 west of Port Angeles, follow Olympic Hot Springs Road, which ascends the Elwha Valley into the park. Stay on the main road, bearing right at Elwha, go past the Altaire campground, and continue to the parking area and trailhead at the end of the road.

The Hike

This trail runs from Boulder Creek over a beautiful alpine saddle to reach the Sol Duc River. It begins on the old paved road to Olympic Hot Springs, which it follows for the first 2.2 miles of the trek. The road ends at the Boulder Creek campground, where a spur path crosses the creek to reach the hot pools. Follow the main trail through the campground and out its western side. A brief jaunt through rolling forest leads to a junction with the Happy Lake Ridge Trail, where the traveler will bear left.

The trail soon descends from wooded slopes into the damp creek bottoms and then crosses a footlog over the North Fork of Boulder Creek. The path bears southeast for a short period before climbing along the banks of the South Fork. This stream features two spectacular waterfalls that can be reached on short spur trails. The lower falls is 25 feet high and drops into a clear pool surrounded by mossy bedrock. Below the cataract the creek winds in tight S-curves through a deep channel in the stone. The graceful limbs of cedar and hemlock lean out over the rushing waters. The upper falls is the taller of the two, but because its spur path runs to the lip of the cascade, it is difficult to gain a viewpoint that reveals its full glory.

The main trail crosses the South Fork just above the upper falls and begins a steady climb. It flattens out a bit upon reaching a loosely wooded

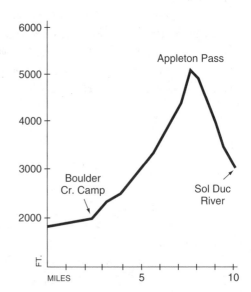

Mountain goats at Appleton Pass

vale, and avalanche fields lead down to the water's edge from the slopes to the west. Near the head of the valley, the forest opens out into an open bowl densely vegetated with cow parsnip and tall grasses. The blossoms of tiger lilies and bluebells add color to the scene, and a braided cascade drops into the basin from the flanks of Mount Appleton.

After climbing through a band of subalpine forest, the trail enters a series of high mountain vales occupied by chuckling rivulets. The alpine tundra is a profusion of blooms, highlighted by pink heather, shooting star, and avalanche lily. Serrated ridges loom on all sides as the trail slogs up a series of switchbacks to reach Appleton Pass. The camping area lies to the east of the pass itself, commanding excellent views of Mount Appleton. The peak's folded strata are among the youngest rock formations in the park. A small tarn known as Oyster Lake lies on the ridgetop to the east and provides a water supply for campers. Mountain goats congregate in this area in a quest for the salt that is found in human waste; be sure to urinate on bare rock to avoid damage to the fragile vegetation.

The main trail then turns west along the forested ridgeline. An unmarked junction offers a faint spur path; continue straight to begin the descent into the Sol Duc Valley. Open meadows studded with beargrass blossoms offer an outstanding view of Mount Olympus and the ragged summits surrounding the Sol Duc basin. One mile beyond the pass, the trail crosses a series of level benches occupied by stagnant pools.

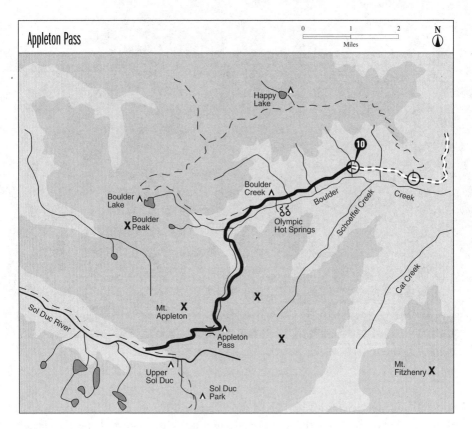

The subalpine forest soon gives way to a denser stand of hemlock and Douglas fir as the trail begins the final descent. A major stream is crossed just before the bottom of the grade, where the trail joins the High Divide Loop amid enormous old-growth conifers.

Key Points

0.0 Appleton Pass trailhead.

2.2 Junction with Olympic Hot Springs spur trail. Bear right.

2.3 Boulder Creek campground.

3.1 Junction with Happy Lake Ridge Trail. Bear left.

3.8 Footlog over North Fork Boulder Creek.

4.0 Spur trail to Lower Boulder Falls. Bear right.

4.2 Spur trail to Upper Boulder Falls. Bear right.

4.3 Trail crosses South Fork Boulder Creek to reach its east bank.

7.7 Appleton Pass camping area.

7.9 Unmarked junction with Oyster Lake way trail. Continue straight.

10.1 Junction with High Divide Loop along the Sol Duc River.

11 The Elwha River

A 29-mile backpack from the Whiskey Bend trailhead to the upper Elwha Basin or
31.2 miles to the Low Divide.

Difficulty: Moderate.
Trail type: Primary.
Best season: All year.
Elevation gain: 4,085 feet (to Low Divide).
Elevation loss: 1,675 feet (to Low Divide).

Maximum elevation: 3,580 feet (Lake
Margaret).
Topo maps: Hurricane Hill, Mount Angeles,
Mount Steel, Mount Christie; Custom Correct
Elwha Valley.

Finding the trailhead: From U.S. Highway 101, follow Olympic Hot Springs Road up the Elwha
Valley. Just beyond the ranger station, turn left onto Whiskey Bend Road. Follow this narrow, winding gravel road 4.4 miles to the trailhead at its end.

The Hike

This trail penetrates deep into the heart of Olympic National Park, following a valley
bottom with a grade gentle enough for novices. In 1889–90 an expedition of fools
and drunkards organized by the *Seattle Press* newspaper used this route to cross the
Olympic Mountains, a journey that took them almost six months. The same trip can
now be completed in a single week by an experienced backpacker. Watch for the rare
and colorful harlequin duck and the tiny water ouzel amid the churning, turquoise
waters of the Elwha River.

From Whiskey Bend the trail runs southward along a forested hillside high above
the valley floor. A spur path soon runs down to an overlook named the "Eagle's Nest"
by the Press Expedition. This spot commands a fine view of the Elwha Valley, and the
meadows of the former Anderson homestead can be seen across the river. Elk and
black bear are sometimes seen in this opening during the morning or evening. The
trail then makes its way across the several burns of the 1977 Rica Canyon fire. The
fire site is recovering naturally with a dense growth of shrubs and saplings. The Rica
Canyon Trail drops away in the middle of the first burn, and soon after the Elwha
River Trail returns to the forest, the Krause Bottom path splits away. Bear left, and the
trail soon arrives at Michael's Cabin, one of the many Geyser Valley homesteads. Trails
to Humes Ranch and Dodger Point depart from this spot. The path begins to climb
steadily as it pulls away from the Geyser Valley complex, and forest openings allow
views of Mount Fitzhenry at the northern end of the Bailey Range.

Atop a high bench burned at the turn of the century, a spur path to the left runs a
distance up the Lillian River valley. The main trail drops suddenly to reach the banks
of the Lillian River, which are forested in a lush growth of towering cedars and hemlocks underlain by a vigorous growth of ferns. The trail passes a number of campsites
as it runs downstream to a stock bridge, then climbs vigorously up the far side of the

valley. As it rounds the western side of the ridge, the sparse forest allows views of the mosaic of old burn scars on the eastern slope of Long Ridge. Many of the older trees survived in the moist swales, while the drier slopes burned entirely. The trail climbs high above the Elwha, avoiding its Grand Canyon, then descends into a thick forest as it returns to the valley floor.

The trail soon crosses tiny Prescott Creek and passes Mary's Falls Camp. This camp is located among tall red alders on the riverbank, and the waterfall that gives the camp its name breaches a feeder stream on the far side of the river. The trail climbs and falls through a mixed forest, reaching Canyon Camp 1.7 miles from Mary's Falls Camp. The tent sites are scattered up and down the river among enormous Douglas firs. A bit farther up the river is the Elkhorn patrol cabin, with its outbuildings scattered across a grassy meadow. Hikers may camp near the cabin or just around the bend at the Stony Point site. This riverbank camp is popular with horse parties and offers views up the Elwha of Mount Dana. Bigleaf maple and red alder interrupt the conifers as the trail makes its way to the Lost River, and the sturdy Remann's Cabin guards the east bank of the Elwha just beyond it. This structure was built as a fishing retreat in 1926; please do not camp here. The cutoff trail from Dodger Point fords the river just above the cabin and joins the Elwha River Trail.

There is a vigorous climb up the hillside as the river undercuts its steep eastern bank. The trail crosses a series of level benches planed by glaciers during the ice ages. The river has cut down through this old valley floor, leaving the terraces elevated high above the bottomlands. These terraces support old-growth Douglas fir with an understory of vine maple. After several miles the trail descends into the Press Valley, a rich bottomland named in honor of the Press Expedition. This broad, level basin is overgrown with alder and vine maple in the low-lying spots, while the higher ground supports mossy stands of ancient Douglas fir. Queen's cup bead lily and bunchberry brighten the forest floor in early summer. The trail swings near the river at Tipperary Camp, then crosses a low bench of forested country to reach the Hayes River patrol cabin and camping area. The main trail turns inland here, climbing moderately for 0.3 mile to pass a junction with the Hayden Pass Trail and reach a stock bridge over the turbulent waters of the Hayes River.

The trail soon returns to the Elwha, maintaining its altitude as it follows the watercourse. Openings in the trees allow glimpses of the rugged crest of Mount Dana. After dipping and rising through the riverside forest, the trail descends onto another wide bottomland occupied by Camp Wilder. There is a leaky shelter here and riverside campsites with views of Mount Dana. Granite cobbles found in the riverbed up to this point were brought in from the continental ranges on the great Cordilleran ice sheet, then floated here aboard icebergs on an ice-dammed lake 20,000 years ago. The trail then follows tiny Leitha Creek inland before a pack bridge spans the much larger course of Godkin Creek, which tumbles through a rocky canyon. After this crossing another long passage through the trees leads to the logjam-choked course of Buckinghorse Creek.

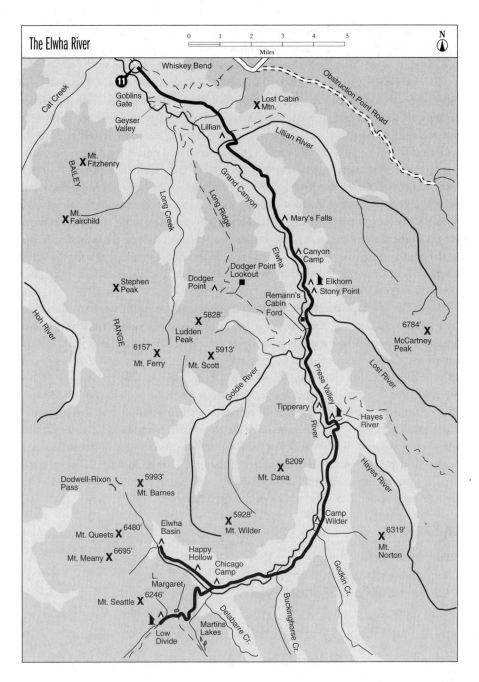

The Elwha River

0 1 2 3 4 5
Miles

N

Whiskey Bend

Obstruction Point Road

Cat Creek

Goblins Gate

Lost Cabin Mtn.

Geyser Valley

Lillian

Lillian River

Mt. Fitzhenry

BAILEY

Grand Canyon

Long Ridge

Long Creek

Mary's Falls

Mt. Fairchild

Elwha

Canyon Camp

Dodger Point Lookout

Stephen Peak

Dodger Point

Remann's Cabin Ford

Elkhorn
Stony Point

Hoh River

RANGE

5828'
Ludden Peak

6157'
Mt. Ferry

5913'
Mt. Scott

Goldie River

6784'
McCartney Peak

Lost River

Press Valley

Tipperary

River

Hayes River

Hayes River

Dodwell-Rixon Pass

5993'
Mt. Barnes

6209'
Mt. Dana

6480'
Mt. Queets

Elwha Basin

5928'
Mt. Wilder

Camp Wilder

6319'
Mt. Norton

6695'
Mt. Meany

Happy Hollow

Chicago Camp

Godkin Cr.

L. Margaret

6246'
Mt. Seattle

Martins Lakes

Delabarre Cr.

Buckinghorse Cr.

Low Divide

Shortly thereafter a knee-deep ford leads across the Elwha itself, and the trail runs level through the bottomlands on its west bank. Old flood channels choked with red alder allow occasional glimpses of Mount Queets' rocky dome, which dominates the head of the valley. The trail soon reaches Chicago Camp, where a trail junction set amid enormous western hemlocks offers the travelers a choice of trails. To the west a dead-end spur runs to the scenic Elwha Basin, while straight ahead a trail runs up to Low Divide, where it connects with the North Fork Quinault route.

Elwha Basin Option: This trail follows the Elwha west from Chicago Camp, crossing coniferous bottomland on a gentle uphill grade. Just before reaching Happy Hollow shelter, the trail approaches the rivercourse and becomes quite faint amid the wrack of flood-tossed debris. This condition persists beyond the shelter until the trail crosses two rivulets, whereupon it turns inland and enters the forest. There are several steep (but short) pitches, and il emerges at the confluence of two boulder-strewn torrents. Cross the first one for outstanding views of Mounts Meany and Seattle, robed in snowfields and adorned with numerous waterfalls. A primitive track makes a perilous crossing of the second stream and climbs along the steep bank of yet another tributary. Here, in a broad meadow of subalpine spiraea bounded by firs to the south and Alaska cedars to the north, lie the finest views of the Elwha Valley. Climbers can continue up the stream to ascend the Elwha snowfinger and access Dodwell-Rixon Pass.

Low Divide Option: After bridging the Elwha this trail crosses the valley floor on a southward bearing, then begins a steady and often steep ascent of the valley's headwall. A sparse forest gives way to open avalanche slopes spangled with the red and yellow blossoms of columbine. The trail ascends along a stream that is born in an unseen glacier on the flanks of Mount Christie and catapults over a 100-foot precipice. Views of the Elwha Valley feature Mount Norton at first, and later Mount Wilder as the path turns west for the final pitch. After rounding a lofty knob, the trail drops into the broad saddle occupied by lakes Mary and Margaret. The water of both lakes has a brownish tint that derives from tannins leaching from the fallen leaves of nearby shrubs. Lake Margaret is the larger of the two, and the Martins Lakes spur trail departs from its eastern shore. This trail and the remaining path over the Low Divide are discussed under The North Fork of the Quinault hike.

Key Points

0.0 Whiskey Bend trailhead.

0.9 Junction with spur path to "Eagle's Nest" overlook.

1.2 Junction with Rica Canyon Trail. Stay left.

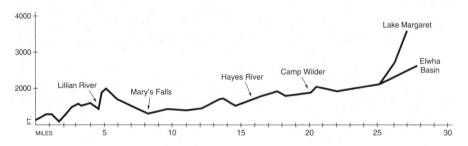

1.6 Junction with Krause Bottom Trail. Stay left.

1.9 Michael's Cabin. Junction with Humes Ranch/Dodger Point Trail. Bear left.

4.1 Junction with Lillian River Trail.

4.7 Trail crosses Lillian River. Lillian River Camp.

8.7 Spur path to Mary's Falls Camp.

10.4 Spur path to Canyon Camp.

11.4 Elkhorn Ranger Station and Camp.

11.5 Stony Point Camp.

12.4 Trail crosses Lost River.

12.9 Remann's Cabin. Junction with Dodger Point ford trail. Stay left.

16.4 Tipperary Camp.

16.7 Spur trail to Hayes River Guard Station and Camp.

17.0 Junction with Hayden Pass Trail. Bear right and cross Hayes River.

20.8 Camp Wilder spur trail.

21.1 Trail crosses Leitha Creek.

21.5 Trail crosses Godkin Creek.

23.3 Trail crosses Buckinghorse Creek.

23.8 Trail fords Elwha River.

26.2 Chicago Camp. Trail splits into Elwha Basin and Low Divide options.

Elwha Basin

26.9 Happy Hollow shelter.

29.0 Elwha Basin Camp.

Low Divide

28.6 Lake Margaret. Junction with North Fork Quinault and Martins Lakes Trails.

31.2 Low Divide and Camp.

12 The Geyser Valley Complex

A series of day hikes in the lower reaches of the Elwha River valley.

Difficulty: Moderate.
Trail type: Primary.
Best season: All year.

Topo maps: Hurricane Hill; Custom Correct *Elwha Valley*.

Finding the trailhead: From U.S. Highway 101, take Olympic Hot Springs Road up the Elwha Valley. Pass the ranger station, and turn left onto Whiskey Bend Road. Follow this narrow, winding gravel road 4.4 miles to the Whiskey Bend trailhead at road's end. Follow the Elwha River Trail.

Michael's Cabin

The Hikes

This collection of trails offers an assortment of day hiking options from the Whiskey Bend trailhead. The paths allow hikers to explore Geyser Valley, which is bounded to the north by the Goblins Gate and to the south by the Grand Canyon of the Elwha. The basin received its name when exploring members of the Press Expedition heard the drumming of grouse and saw wisps of cloud rising from the forest, leading them to the mistaken conclusion that there was geyser activity in the valley. The area was settled by homesteaders in the late 1800s, and these industrious pioneers carved small openings into the valley-bottom forest that persist to this day.

"Eagles Nest" overlook: This short path takes off from the Elwha River Trail at mile 0.9 and descends for 0.2 mile to reach an overlook that is also known as "Elk Overlook." A sweeping view of the Elwha Valley is highlighted by the snowy peaks of the northern Baileys as well as the rugged Goblin Gates far below. The spot was named "Eagles Nest" by Press Expedition members in the winter of 1889–90; they envisioned the site as a possible holiday retreat for Seattle residents. Across the river is a clearing that once held the Anderson homestead. Elk and black bear are sometimes seen in this meadowy opening. The path then makes a steep 0.1-mile ascent to return to the Elwha River Trail.

Rica Canyon Trail: This track departs the Elwha River Trail at mile 1.2, in the middle of a burn from 1977. It zigzags down to a forested river terrace, where it turns north for a short stretch. After 0.5 mile the path reaches the banks of the Elwha and

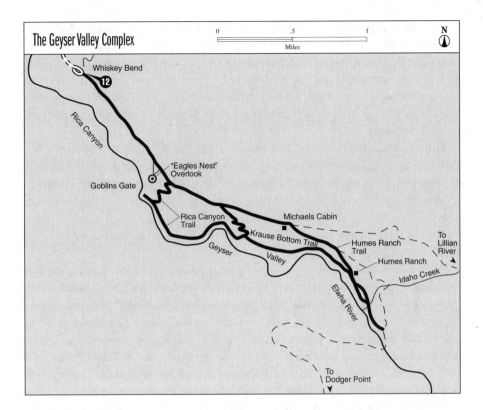

0   .5   1
Miles

N

Whiskey Bend
12

Rica Canyon

"Eagles Nest"
Overlook

Goblins Gate

Rica Canyon
Trail

Michaels Cabin

Krause Bottom Trail

Humes Ranch
Trail

To
Lillian
River

Geyser

Valley

Humes Ranch

Idaho Creek

Elwha River

To
Dodger Point

a junction with the Goblin Gates spur trail. This short path follows the river downstream for 0.1 mile to an outcrop of bedrock that overlooks the Goblins Gate. This interesting geological formation marks the entrance to Rica Canyon. It is an uplift of slate and sandstone that has been riven by the swirling turquoise waters of the Elwha over the course of centuries. The name reflects the imagination of early visitors who thought that they could discern the craggy faces of goblins amid the folds and crenellations of the rock walls.

The main trail turns south and enters Geyser Valley. In doing so it passes over an outcrop of unyielding stone that receives the full force of the Elwha River. The path soon disappears into a quiet riverbottom forest, where the murmur of the river provides a soothing background for the twittering of birds. A luxuriant undergrowth of moss, vanilla leaf, and sword fern suffuses the forest with a soft green light. As the flats come to an end, the trail climbs the hillside and reaches the site of the Krause homestead. Here, 1.4 miles from the Elwha River Trail, it meets the Krause Bottom route.

Krause Bottom Trail: From mile 1.6 on the Elwha River Trail, this path dives steeply through the timber. It levels off after 0.3 mile on a meadowy bench sprinkled with ornamental fruit trees that have reverted to a more or less wild state. These trees are the remnants of the Krause orchard. It was planted by a German couple who homesteaded here in the mid-1890s, but a fire burned them out and they were forced to abandon their pioneering efforts. The clearing and orchard trees are the only trace that remains of their labors. Upon reaching a junction with the Rica Canyon Trail, the Krause Bottom route turns sharply southward, descending to the lush river flats. Here clumps of gnarled vine maple are draped with mosses, and a mixed forest of red alder and Douglas fir provides a rather sparse canopy. The trail approaches the river, then climbs the hillside to reach the Humes Ranch junction, 1.1 miles beyond the Krause homestead.

Humes Ranch Trail: This trail begins at Michael's Cabin, at mile 1.9 on the Elwha River Trail. This sturdy dwelling was once the property of a colorful resident known locally as "Cougar Mike," a nemesis of mountain lions, noted for his sharpshooting ability. The next meadow to the north is the former site of Geyser House, a ramshackle hostelry that was run by a former Seattle policeman known as "Doc" Ludden. This self-proclaimed "Bee Man of the Elwha" kept hives of honeybees and made his own honey.

The trail descends obliquely through the trees, passing a junction with the Dodger Point Trail (bear right here). It then crosses diminutive Antelope Creek and descends sharply to reach the Humes Ranch at mile 0.4. The cabin found here was built in 1900 by Grant and Will Humes, who were among the earliest homesteaders in the Elwha Valley. This dynamic pair of brothers ran an outfitting operation in the Olympic Mountains, running pack trains for expeditions of climbers, hunters, and sightseers. A marked junction with the Krause Bottom Trail lies at the lower edge of the clearing; bear left for the remaining 0.6 mile along the Elwha.

The trail descends to a riverside meadow; backpackers can camp here or in the grove of red alder on the riverbank. The path splits into two tracks at this point, one running across the middle of the opening while the other skirts its lower edge. They converge again at the far edge of the field, only to split apart once more. A rough footpath follows the bare riverside bluffs, while the more substantial trail cuts a more direct path through the woods. These two trails unite for a crossing of Idaho Creek and then climb gently above a cutbank to reach a junction with the Dodger Point Trail.

13 Dodger Point

An 18.8-mile backpack from Whiskey Bend to Remann's Cabin on the Elwha River.

Difficulty: Moderately strenuous.
Trail type: Primary to Dodger Point; primitive from there to ford of the Elwha.
Best season: Late June to mid-October.
Elevation gain: 4,983 feet (to Dodger Point Lookout).

Elevation loss: 4,713 feet (including from Dodger Point Lookout).
Maximum elevation: 5,753 feet (Dodger Point Lookout).
Topo maps: Hurricane Hill, Mount Olympus, Mount Angeles; Custom Correct *Elwha Valley*.

Finding the trailhead: From U.S. Highway 101, follow Olympic Hot Springs Road up the Elwha Valley. Just beyond the ranger station, turn left onto Whiskey Bend Road. Proceed along this narrow, winding gravel road 4.4 miles to the Whiskey Bend trailhead at road's end. Follow the Elwha River Trail.

The Hike

This trail offers a long but rewarding hike to a vantage point with outstanding views of the Bailey Range and the Elwha Valley. The trek begins on the Elwha River Trail, which it follows as far as Michael's Cabin. Here the Dodger Point Trail splits away to the right, and the traveler is presented with two options. The most direct route runs along the forested hillside to reach a bridge over the Elwha at the mouth of its Grand Canyon. A longer but more interesting route runs past the old Humes Ranch, then follows the riverbank to the bridge. The river churns through a turbulent track of boulders here, making an impressive spectacle.

Once across the river the path runs westward to climb the toe of Long Ridge. As the valley floor falls away, red cedars are replaced by western hemlocks in the forest canopy. After surmounting the crest of the ridge, the trail makes a brief foray onto the western slope before re-crossing the ridgeline. It then makes the bulk of the ascent on the eastern face of the ridge, with long straight stretches punctuated by zigzagging climbs. The grade is rather shallow, but altitude is gained steadily as the path runs through a series of old burns dating from 1891 to 1941. A few old Douglas firs survived the blazes, but most of the trees are much younger and grew in the wake of the fires. Frequent openings allow views of the Elwha Valley. On its far side the Lillian River occupies the deep glacial cleft in its forested wall, overlooked by Hurricane Ridge.

The trail passes through a saddle in the ridgetop at the 3,500-foot level and completes the journey on the western slope of the ridge. Holes in the forest canopy yield tantalizing glimpses of the snow-clad Bailey Range. As the path continues southward, it passes two springs and an intermittent stream. In this vale, high soil moisture and

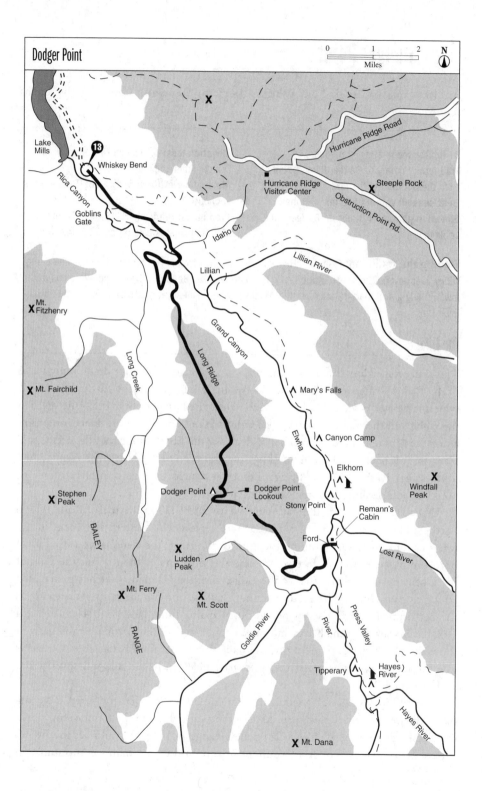

Dodger Point

0   1   2
Miles

N

Lake Mills

Rica Canyon

13

Whiskey Bend

Goblins Gate

Hurricane Ridge Road

Hurricane Ridge Visitor Center

Steeple Rock

Obstruction Point Rd.

Idaho Cr.

Lillian

Lillian River

X Mt. Fitzhenry

Long Creek

Long Ridge

Grand Canyon

X Mt. Fairchild

Mary's Falls

Elwha

Canyon Camp

Elkhorn

Dodger Point

Dodger Point Lookout

Stony Point

Remann's Cabin

Windfall Peak

X Stephen Peak

BAILEY

Ludden Peak

Ford

Lost River

X Mt. Ferry

X Mt. Scott

Goldie River

River

Press Valley

RANGE

Tipperary

Hayes River

Hayes River

X Mt. Dana

protection from the prevailing winds allow the trees to grow to an unusually large size. Just around the bend is a dry finger ridge; its rocky soil supports an assortment of rather stunted trees, white pine prominent among them. The larger forest openings found here offer stunning vistas of the Bailey Range from Mount Ferry in the south to Mount Fairchild in the north.

The path soon dives back into the forest, which gradually takes on a subalpine aspect. Snowfields often persist well into July from this point on, but the terrain is not steep enough for this to pose a real hazard. The trail soon rounds the southern end of Dodger Point, crossing a series of alpine meadows flecked with snowmelt tarns. The path climbs steadily through several flower-filled bowls, passing the Dodger Point camping area. It then climbs to a low spot on the ridgeline, where it reaches a marked trail junction.

To the left, a spur trail climbs the ridgecrest for 0.5 mile to reach the fire lookout atop Dodger Point. This structure is the last of its kind in the park, and it occupies a meadowy dome that is studded with stands of subalpine fir. Ironically, the best views are not from the lookout but from the meadows just below it on the south side. From here a sweeping vista is highlighted by Mounts Dana, Wilder, Christie, Scott, and Barnes to the south. To the southeast, one can look straight up the Hayes River valley to see Mount Anderson rising beyond it, with the Eel Glacier cupped between its two tallest spires. The regal massif of Mount Olympus rises huge and icebound to the southwest, dwarfing the much closer peaks of the Bailey Range.

Hikers who are willing to brave the steep and primitive trail and a difficult river

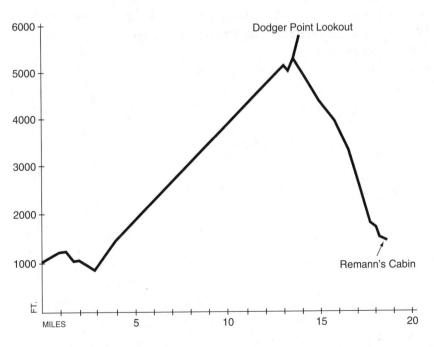

ford can complete the hike by turning right at the ridgetop junction. The trail follows the ridgeline down into a low saddle, where the Mount Ludden climber's path runs up into the Baileys. The main trail drops onto the eastern side of the ridge and runs northeast through ragged subalpine firs and clumps of beargrass. There are good views of the peaks above the Elwha as the trail loses altitude. As the trail winds onto the eastern buttress of Dodger Point, it crosses three extensive meadows that are frequented by elk, black-tailed deer, and bears. Watch for blaze-orange markers to indicate the location of the otherwise invisible route.

Upon leaving the meadows the trail becomes distinct again as it descends steadily through the timber. The grade is moderate at first, but after passing the NO FIRE marker at 3,500 feet, the drop becomes quite steep. Following a brief respite on a sunny glacial terrace, the path drops into the mossy inner sanctum of the river bottoms. The trail runs north for 0.5 mile between the massive boles of old-growth Douglas fir to reach the ford. The water varies from waist-deep in June to knee-deep in late August, but it is always swift and turbulent. The Elwha River Trail is joined on the far bank, just above Remann's Cabin.

Key Points

0.0	Whiskey Bend trailhead.
1.9	Michael's Cabin. Turn right onto Humes Ranch/Dodger Point Trail.
2.4	Dodger Point Trail splits away to the left.
3.2	Bridge over Elwha River.
13.2	Dodger Point camping area.
13.5	Junction with 0.5-mile spur trail (moderate) to lookout. Through traffic turn right.
14.0	Junction with Ludden Peak way trail. Turn left to start descent.
18.7	Ford of Elwha River.
18.8	Trail joins Elwha River Trail at Remann's Cabin.

14 Hayden Pass

An extended 10.7-mile trip from the Elwha River to Dose Meadows.

Difficulty: Moderately strenuous.
Trail type: Primary.
Best season: Mid-July to mid-October.
Elevation gain: 3,920 feet.

Elevation loss: 1,250 feet.
Maximum elevation: 5,700 feet.
Topo maps: Mount Angeles; Custom Correct *Elwha Valley.*

Finding the trailhead: From U.S. Highway 101, follow Olympic Hot Springs Road up the Elwha Valley. Just beyond the ranger station, turn left onto Whiskey Bend Road. Take this narrow, winding gravel road 4.4 miles to its end and the Whiskey Bend trailhead. From here, start down the Elwha River Trail. This trail leaves the Elwha River Trail 100 yards north of the Hayes River bridge, on the elevated terrace to the east of the patrol cabin. It joins the Dosewallips Trail at a signpost near the east end of Dose Meadows.

The Hike

This trail connects the Elwha and Dosewallips drainages over a high route that offers almost uninterrupted mountain vistas from end to end. Late-lingering snowfields on the east side of the pass are steep and often unstable. Early season travelers who use this trail will need an ice axe and proper training in avalanche safety. It departs from the Elwha River Trail on the north bank of the Hayes River and begins climbing along a tiny tributary stream. The path soon crosses the stream and emerges from the bottom-land forest onto a dry bench covered with lodgepole pines. After climbing straight up the shallow ridgetop, the route passes a tiny campsite as it crosses the stream again and runs north across the hillside. After a brief ascent across a slope of scattered Douglas fir, the trail finally sets its course in an easterly direction. Openings in the forest offer previews of the dazzling scenery to come: Mount Dana rises beyond the Elwha, and Mount Norton looms above the Hayes River to the south.

After the trail crosses several small streams, the surrounding forest becomes distinctly subalpine with a lush understory of grasses and forbs. Meadow pockets form around the numerous springs and rills that cross the trail, and these are lit by the blossoms of shooting

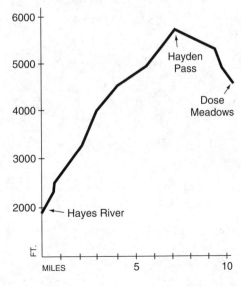

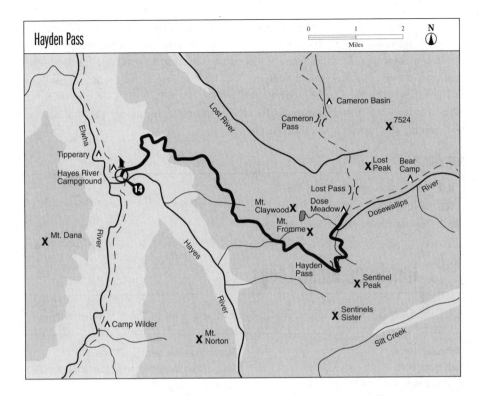

0   1   2   **N**
Miles

Cameron Basin

Cameron Pass

X 7524

Elwha

Lost River

Tipperary

Hayes River Campground

14

X Lost Peak   **Bear Camp**

River

Lost Pass

Mt. Claywood X   **Dose Meadow**

Dosewallips

X Mt. Dana

River

Mt. Fromme X

Hayes

Hayden Pass

Sentinel X Peak

River

Sentinels X Sister

Camp Wilder

X Mt. Norton

Silt Creek

star, bleeding heart, and avalanche lily. After about 5 miles of gentle climbing, the trail finally reaches a broad meadow that allows unimpeded vistas of Mount Anderson, Crystal Peak, and Mount Norton surrounding the glacier-carved trench of the Hayes River valley. The forest devolves into a gladed parkland where open meadows occupy the swales and subalpine firs are confined to the drier hummocks. Mounts Claywood and Fromme are soon visible to the northeast, rising above the meadows like rocky waves. The tops of the Bailey Range can be seen above the intervening ridges to the west.

Upon reaching a long finger ridge, the trail turns and climbs along the ridge's open spine. Look backward for a fine view of peaks to the west: the pointed mass of Mount Christie, Mount Seattle's slender spire, the rocky dome of Mount Meany cupping its tiny glacier, and the ice-bound mass of Mount Olympus. As the trail continues its climb, Mount Anderson rises from the lesser peaks with its towering pinnacles of dark rock thrust skyward around the Eel Glacier. The trail levels off after crossing a broad expanse of meadow and covers the final distance to the pass at a gentle pace. From the divide the Needles can be seen far to the east, and Mount Cameron dominates the tawny summits that line the Dosewallips valley.

After crossing Hayden Pass the trail drops into an open bowl overlooked by Sen-

◀ *Mount Cameron and the upper basin of the Dosewallips*

tinel Peak to the south and Mount Fromme to the northwest. A finger of Thousand Acre Meadows runs down toward the basin from the east. Although this open heath is much smaller than its name implies, it forms a critical summer range for the Dose-wallips band of elk. Black-tailed deer and Olympic marmots are commonly sighted in the fields of heather and blueberry bushes that border the trail. After a brief but vigorous descent through mountain hemlocks and open meadows, the trail reaches its terminus at a junction in Dose Meadows.

Key Points

0.0 Trail departs from the Elwha River Trail.

8.3 Hayden Pass.

10.7 Trail reaches junction in Dose Meadows.

15 Hurricane Ridge Loops

A series of day hikes atop Hurricane Ridge ranging from 0.2 to 1.5 miles in length.

Difficulty: Easy.
Trail type: Foot.
Best season: Mid-June to mid-October.
Elevation gain: 200 feet.

Maximum elevation: 5,500 feet.
Topo maps: Mount Angeles; Custom Correct *Hurricane Ridge.*

Finding the trailhead: From Port Angeles, drive 17.6 miles south on Hurricane Ridge Road to the visitor center atop the ridge. The trails depart from the northeast corner of the parking lot.

The Hikes

A network of walking trails wanders through the subalpine meadows atop Hurricane Ridge. This popular area receives more visitors than any other spot within the park, and because of the heavy foot traffic, most of the trails have been paved. The sole exception is the High Ridge Loop, which is graveled and has a more challenging grade than the other trails, which are quite easy. All of the trails offer outstanding views of the mountains, including Mount Olympus when the weather cooperates. A startling diversity of wildflowers offers a different combination of blossoms with each passing week. Mule deer and Olympic marmots are abundant here, and they are unafraid of humans. (Do not feed them!) There is a visitor center across the parking lot, and guided ranger walks are offered on a periodic basis. Each trail within the network will be discussed separately. The author's favorite routing follows the Cirque Rim Trail, with a side trip up the High Ridge Loop for an overall hike of 1.3 miles.

Big Meadow Loop: This short loop wanders through the lush meadows beside the parking lot. Though crowded, this trail offers the best opportunities to view

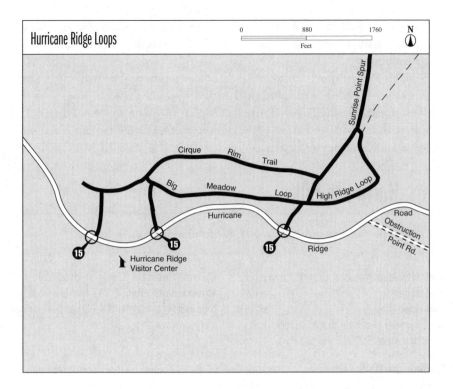

Hurricane Ridge Loops

0   880   1760   **N**

Feet

Cirque Rim Trail

Big Meadow Loop

High Ridge Loop

Sunrise Point Spur

Hurricane Ridge

Hurricane Ridge Visitor Center

Road

Obstruction Point Rd.

wildlife and alpine flowers. A broad panorama of the Olympic Mountains spans the horizon to the south.

Cirque Rim Trail: This trail follows the northern edge of Hurricane Ridge, passing through copses of subalpine fir and secluded glades. A spur path descends from its westernmost point to reach an overlook of the Little River valley, which is guarded by Hurricane Hill, Unicorn Peak, and Griff Peak. As the main trail follows the rim of a glacial cirque, openings reveal northward vistas that encompass the Strait of Juan de Fuca and Vancouver Island rising beyond it. During clear weather, both Port Angeles and Victoria, British Columbia, are visible. Mount Angeles is the prominent summit to the east, while below the trail is a ski lift that serves cross-country skiers during the winter months. Upon reaching it the Cirque Rim Trail turns south; follow it downward through the meadows to return to the parking lot.

High Ridge Loop: This 0.5-mile hike begins at the northeast corner of the Big Meadow Loop and ascends a steep ridgeline. It soon reaches a level overlook that commands excellent views. The Lillian River valley stretches southward, far below, with snow-dappled peaks on both sides. The next valley to the west bears the Elwha River, and beyond it are the Bailey Range and Mount Olympus itself. The pavement ends here, and now a gravel walkway completes the moderate ascent to the crest of a rocky knoll. The path then descends to a junction with the Sunrise Point and Mount Angeles Trails (see the Mount Angeles hike description). Take a hard left to continue the loop hike, which descends rather steeply through a subalpine woodland. Turn left at the top of the ski lift, where a paved path leads across the Big Meadow and back to the parking lot.

Sunrise Point Spur: This short side path ascends from the High Ridge Trail to the top of a stony knob. With a little jockeying for position, one can have views in all directions, featuring the Bailey Range and Mount Olympus to the southwest, Unicorn Peak to the west, and Steeple Rock to the southeast with the broad and snowy massif of Elk Mountain beyond it.

16 Hurricane Hill

A 7.4-mile day hike from Hurricane Ridge to the Elwha Valley.

Difficulty: Moderate east to west; strenuous west to east.
Trail type: Foot.
Best season: Mid-June to mid-October.
Elevation gain: 660 feet (to summit).

Elevation loss: 5,310 feet (from summit).
Maximum elevation: 5,757 feet (summit).
Topo maps: Hurricane Hill, Elwha; Custom Correct *Hurricane Ridge.*

Finding the trailhead: From Port Angeles, drive south 18.9 miles on Hurricane Ridge Road to its end, where a parking area marks the trailhead.

The Hike

This trail offers a scenic walk from Hurricane Ridge all the way down to the floor of the Elwha Valley. It begins as a paved nature trail that climbs gradually along a meadowy ridge-line. There are outstanding views of the Bailey Range here, and black-tailed deer and Olympic marmots are sometimes sighted. The trail soon reaches a saddle where the stark and forbidding heights of Mount Angeles can be seen to the east. The Little River Trail drops from this low pass into the valley to the north. The main path continues to climb the grassy flanks of Hurricane Hill, reaching a second junction near the top. To the right, the paved trail runs 0.2 mile to

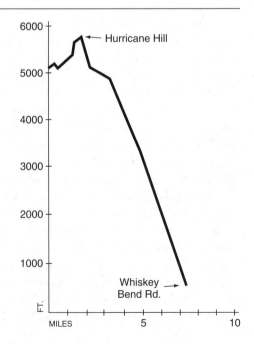

Mount Appleton from Hurricane Hill

the summit of the hill, which overlooks a shallow alpine tarn and provides good views of Unicorn Peak.

To the left the Hurricane Hill Trail descends along the spine of a lesser ridge, losing altitude in brief but steep spurts. The southern side of the ridge is a dry slope dominated by grasses and drought-resistant flowers such as yarrow and larkspur. The north-facing slope is covered in subalpine fir and mountain hemlock, and features water-loving plants like columbine and false hellebore. The trail begins to descend in earnest as it crosses a broad grassy meadow and drops into the trees for good at the lower edge of this opening. Before the forest closes around the trail, there are good views of the snow-clad summits that crowd the headwaters of the Elwha.

The forest is dominated by tall Douglas firs and much shorter western hemlocks that sprang up in the wake of a fire many years ago. The two species are the same age, and their different stature can be attributed to contrasting ecological strategies. Douglas fir grows quickly and attains a tall size, but its seedlings do poorly in the low light of the forest floor. The mature Douglas firs will always overtop the hemlocks, but this dominance will only last for one generation of trees. Western hemlock grows slowly and has shorter stature, but its seedlings thrive in the shade and grow readily in a closed-canopy forest. If this stand is undisturbed by fire for a number of centuries, the hemlocks will achieve a pure stand of climax forest.

After a long descent the trail rounds the western side of the slope, and an immediate change in vegetation is apparent. Under the influence of a moister microclimate,

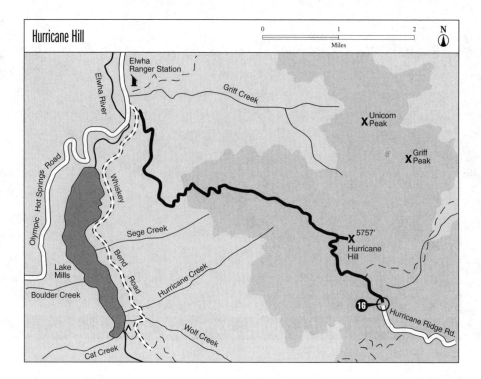

the understory changes from a sparse growth of vanilla leaf and false Solomon's seal to a rich assortment of ferns, mosses, and shrubs. As the trail makes the final descent to Whiskey Bend Road, it crosses several small rivulets. The largest of these streams supports its own miniature rain forest of red cedar and vine maple.

Key Points

0.0 Trailhead.

0.4 Junction with Little River Trail. Keep going straight.

1.4 Spur trail to summit of Hurricane Hill.

7.4 Whiskey Bend Road.

17 The Klahhane Ridge Loop

A 12.5-mile backpack loop from Heart o' the Hills.

Difficulty: Moderately strenuous to Lake Angeles; strenuous beyond.
Trail type: Foot.
Best season: Early July to mid-October.
Elevation gain: 4,735 feet.

Elevation loss: 4,735 feet.
Maximum elevation: 6,046 feet.
Topo maps: Port Angeles, Mount Angeles; Custom Correct *Hurricane Ridge*.

Finding the trailhead: From the park visitor center in Port Angeles, drive 6.4 miles south on Hurricane Ridge Road. Just past Heart o' the Hills, turn right onto the marked spur road to the trailhead.

The Hike

This trail offers a rigorous loop into the craggy country just south of Port Angeles. It can also be combined with the Mount Angeles Trail for two different point-to-point day hikes from Hurricane Ridge Road to Heart o' the Hills. Persistent snowfields on the western slope of Mount Angeles pose an extreme travel hazard until mid-July.

The trail begins in a dark forest of cedars on the lowlands bordering Lake Dawn. A lush growth of ferns and mosses grows between the massive boles, highlighted by the feathery fronds of fern moss. Just before reaching Ennis Creek, the trail passes an unmarked spur path that leads to a streamside campsite. Stay right and cross a footlog over the creek as the trail continues its gradual ascent. The climb stiffens after rounding the next finger ridge, and the forest is now a loose association of Douglas firs that sprang up in the wake of a fire that occurred around 1900. A handful of cedars populate the swales and depressions where ample groundwater can be found.

The trail runs along the side of the hill, then turns up the spine of the ridge. It soon works its way onto the eastern slope, where the grade eases off for the final approach to Lake Angeles. Another spur trail soon veers off to the left, ending at a set of crude, waterless campsites. Bear right to reach a marked intersection with the spur trail to Lake Angeles. This heavily used path runs down to a set of primitive campsites set among the large subalpine firs at the foot of the lake. The sheer walls of Klahhane Ridge rise majestically above its greenish waters, and a single island clad in firs rises in its center. Brook trout cruise the lake, and black bears roam its shoreline.

Travelers continuing the loop should bear right at the Lake Angeles junction; the trail climbs briskly above the western shore. The forest of subalpine fir and Alaska cedar thins progressively, allowing superb views of the jagged north face of Klahhane Ridge. Snowfields linger late in cool crevasses in the rock, dappling the dark stone with patches of white. Upon reaching the ridgetop, look west as the brittle spires of

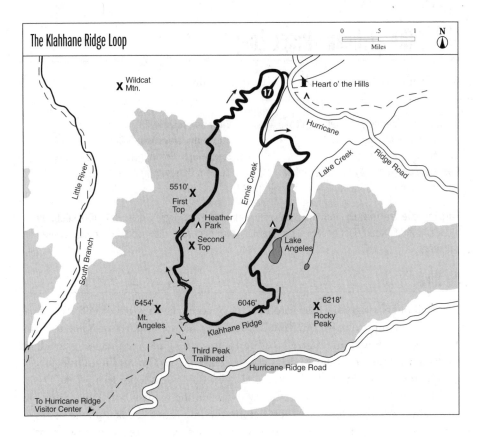

The Klahhane Ridge Loop

0   .5   1   N
Miles

Wildcat Mtn. X

Heart o' the Hills

Hurricane

Little River

Ennis Creek

Lake Creek

Ridge Road

5510' X
First Top

Heather Park

Second Top X

Lake Angeles

South Branch

6454' X
Mt. Angeles

6046'

Klahhane Ridge

6218' X
Rocky Peak

Third Peak Trailhead

Hurricane Ridge Road

To Hurricane Ridge Visitor Center

Second Top soar above the Ennis Creek basin. The path drops onto the western side of the ridge for a time, then climbs steeply to cross the ridgecrest. It then follows the foot of a rocky scarp all the way to the top of Klahhane Ridge itself.

The trail turns west here, tracking the ridgeline as it rises and dips. Outcrops of basalt punctuate its heights, providing escape terrain for the few remaining mountain goats. An alpine garden covers the gentler slopes, and flowers bloom from fissures in the rock. Spreading phlox, moss campion, and creeping penstemon are among the showier flowers. Elk Mountain and Maiden Peak rise to the southeast, across the deep gulf of the Morse Creek basin. This basin was once filled by a deep lake dammed by Pleistocene ice sheets. Upon reaching a saddle at the foot of Mount Angeles, the trail arrives at a junction with routes that run to Hurricane Ridge Road (discussed under the Mount Angeles hike). Stay right to complete the loop.

The path becomes little more than a goat track as it turns north, descending across a slope of loose scree. The descent is soon blocked by a jagged finger ridge, and the trail turns uphill to climb steeply through a narrow couloir. After crossing the saddle at its head, the trail undertakes an equally precipitous descent down the far side. This area retains snow well into July, and is extremely hazardous when snow is present. After a drop of several hundred feet, the trail turns east. It rises and falls to avoid outcroppings of pillow basalt, providing constant views of Griff and Unicorn Peaks to the west. A final uphill surge leads to the saddle north of Second Top.

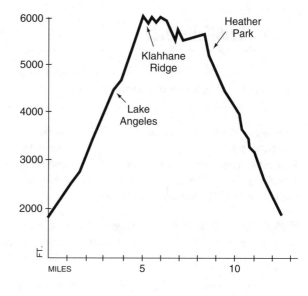

From this point the trail drops into a gentle meadow overlooked by the multiple spires of Second Top. The trail soon passes the foundation of an old shelter cabin and enters the Heather Park camping area. This spot lies in a delightful dell surrounded by tall subalpine firs. The trail then descends through widely spaced trees that offer a fine parting view of Rocky Peak, the summit that forms the eastern rim of Klahhane Ridge. The forest soon thickens as the trail descends across the eastern slope of First Top. Upon reaching the edge of this slope, a trailside boulder offers outstanding views of the Strait of Juan de Fuca and the snowy continental ranges far to the east. This is not Halfway Rock, which is a mile farther on and offers little in the way of views. Just below it is an unimproved camping area, which has water only during early summer.

The trail continues its descent into the rich bottomland forest that lies at the foot of the ridge. After crossing a series of level benches, the trail passes a moldering chimney that marks an old cabin site to the west of the trail. Just beyond it lies an extensive grove of mature red alder, thriving in a moist depression. In about 0.25 mile of gentle travel, the trail returns to the Heart o' the Hills trailhead.

Key Points

0.0 Heart o' the Hills trailhead.

1.1 Trail crosses Ennis Creek.

3.4 Junction with spur to Lake Angeles.

6.3 Junction with Switchback Trail. Turn right.

8.5 Heather Park camping area.

12.5 Heart o' the Hills trailhead.

18 Mount Angeles

A 5.2-mile day hike from the Hurricane Ridge visitor center to the Third Peak parking area, including a side trip to the crest of Klahhane Ridge.

Difficulty: Moderate (west to east).
Trail type: Foot.
Best season: Mid-June to mid-October.
Elevation gain: 1,270 feet (to ridgetop).
Elevation loss: 2,120 feet (includes ridgetop).

Maximum elevation: 5,850 feet (atop Klahhane Ridge).
Topo maps: Mount Angeles; Custom Correct *Hurricane Ridge.*

Finding the trailhead: From Port Angeles, drive 17.6 miles south on Hurricane Ridge Road to the visitor center atop the ridge. The trail departs from the northeast corner of the parking lot.

The Hike

This hike can be combined with the Klahhane Ridge Loop for a hike to Heart o' the Hills, or it can be taken as a semi-loop from the Hurricane Ridge visitor center to the Third Peak trailhead, midway down Hurricane Ridge Road. The trip begins in the complex of paved nature trails on Hurricane Ridge. Follow the High Ridge Trail

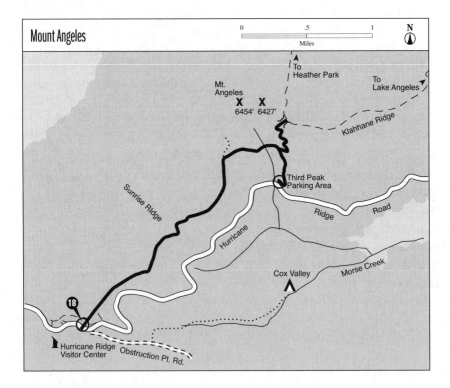

Looking along Hurricane Ridge toward Mount Angeles

northeastward as it climbs through alpine meadows. The junction with the Mount Angeles Trail is just beyond the first knob on the ridgetop. This path rises and falls, tracking the ridgetop northeastward through alpine meadows interrupted by stands of perfectly conical subalpine firs. There are wildflowers of all varieties here, highlighted by lupines, larkspurs, bistorts, and a magenta variety of paintbrush that is endemic to the Olympics. To the south lies a sea of snowcapped peaks. The rugged Bailey Range partially screens Mount Olympus to the southwest, while Steeple Rock rises in front of Elk Mountain farther east.

When the trail reaches the base of Mount Angeles, an unmarked climber's trail shoots straight up toward the summit. Bear right as the trail runs beneath the twisted basalt spires that guard the flanks of the peak. The path soon makes a shallow descent to intercept the Switchback Trail. Dedicated hikers will want to climb up to the saddle in Klahhane Ridge, which overlooks a nameless basin guarded by rugged ridges. There is a good possibility of sighting wildlife here: Marmots, chipmunks, mountain goats, and black bears are often seen in the basin or among the rocks above it. Hardy alpine plants like spreading phlox and creeping penstemon brighten the rockscape. Visitors who are pressed for time can hike

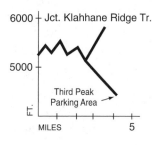

directly down the Switchback Trail to regain the road, cutting off the extra 1.9 miles of the spur trip to the ridgetop and back.

Key Points

0.0   Hurricane Ridge trailhead.

0.4   Mount Angeles Trail departs from High Ridge Trail.

2.2   Way trail toward summit. Bear right.

2.7   Junction with Switchback Trail. Turn left for Klahhane Ridge.

3.6   Junction with Klahhane Ridge Loop.

5.2   Trail reaches Hurricane Ridge Road at Third Peak parking area.

19 PJ Lake

A 0.9-mile day hike from the Obstruction Point Road to PJ Lake.

Difficulty: Strenuous.
Trail type: Foot.
Best season: Early June to mid-October.
Elevation gain: 150 feet.

Elevation loss: 620 feet.
Maximum elevation: 5,020 feet (trailhead).
Topo maps: Mount Angeles; Custom Correct *Hurricane Ridge.*

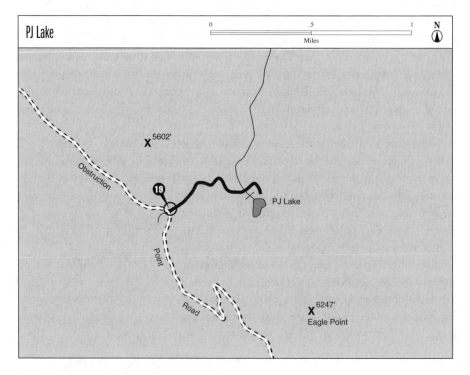

Finding the trailhead: From Port Angeles, drive 17.6 miles south on Hurricane Ridge Road to the visitor center. Then turn left onto the gravel Obstruction Point Road. Drive 3.7 miles to a large but unmarked parking area. The trail departs to the northeast.

The Hike

This trail descends from the top of Hurricane Ridge across an extremely steep grade to reach a subalpine lake. It begins by diving into a tributary valley of Morse Creek. The path crosses open avalanche slopes as it drops, and a lush growth of wildflowers is highlighted by paintbrush and tiger lily. At the bottom of the grade, the trail crosses several small rivulets, then reaches the base of a picturesque cascade. This marks the beginning of a short final uphill pitch. PJ Lake is at the end of the trail, a green pool set among the subalpine firs at the base of 6,247-foot Eagle Point. There is a camping spot on the lakeshore, and brook trout cruise the shallow waters.

Key Points

0.0   Trailhead.
0.9   PJ Lake.

Additional Trails

The **Foothills Trail System** is really for mountain bikers and can be quite muddy. Motorbikes may also be encountered here.

The **Peabody Creek Trail** is an interpretive walk that runs uphill from the Port Angeles visitor center.

The **Heart of the Forest Trail** runs east from the Heart o' the Hills campground. It passes through some nice silver firs before ending at the edge of a clear-cut.

The **Cox Valley Trail** is no longer maintained and can be hard to follow. It accesses some subalpine meadows in the head of the Morse Creek valley.

The **Madison Creek Falls Trail** is a barrier-free 0.1-mile spur from the Elwha entrance station to a scenic waterfall.

The **Cascade Rock Trail** begins at the Elwha Campground and climbs steeply up the valley wall to reach several rather uninspiring overlook points.

The **Griff Creek Trail** climbs to the top of the Elwha River Range from the Elwha Ranger Station. There are good views of the valley for those who make this strenuous climb.

The **Lake Mills West Shore Trail** runs through bigleaf maples along the shore of this reservoir. It is maintained and makes a nice autumn stroll.

The **Upper Lake Mills Trail** drops quickly from the Whiskey Bend Road to a camping spot at the head of the reservoir.

The **Wolf Creek Trail** follows the old Whiskey Bend Road to the top of Hurricane Ridge. It offers views only along the top mile or so. Power line boxes every 2,000 feet make a constant eyesore that detracts from the wilderness quality of the hike.

The **Ludden Peak Trail** is an unmaintained spur that runs for a little more than 1 mile from a junction on the Dodger Point Trail. It is mainly used by climbers bound for the Bailey Range.

The Rainshadow

This region of the park lies on the leeward side of the Olympic Mountains. Prevailing winds from the southwest are pushed upward by the mountains, and they dump their moisture on the western slopes as they cool. Little moisture remains for the northeastern corner of the range, which is known as a "rainshadow" area. The geology and ecology of the rainshadow is defined in many ways by this lack of precipitation. Glaciers that buried the central mountains filled only the valleys here, and the rounded ridgetops became refuges for alpine plants and animals amid a sea of glacial ice. An astonishing diversity of wildflowers can be found here to this day, occupying habitats that range from alpine tundra to semidesert.

Much of the area discussed in this section falls within the Buckhorn Wilderness. This extensive chunk of unspoiled land was created in 1984 and includes some of the highest peaks of the Olympic Mountains. It is the largest wilderness area administered

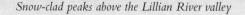

Snow-clad peaks above the Lillian River valley

by the Olympic National Forest. Machines of all sorts (including mountain bikes) are forbidden here. Permits are not required for camping in the wilderness area, but they are required on adjacent national park lands. Trailhead access is usually via a network of gravel logging roads. Be especially wary of logging trucks on these roads, and yield the right-of-way.

There are Forest Service campgrounds surrounding the mouth of the Gray Wolf River at Slab Camp, Dungeness Forks, and East Crossing. Most services can be found at the nearby towns of Sequim and Quilcene; the latter also has a Forest Service visitor center. The nearest National Park Service office is in Port Angeles.

20 Elk Mountain

A 7.4-mile day hike from Obstruction Point to Deer Park. (See map on page 87.)

Difficulty: Moderate west to east; moderately strenuous east to west.
Trail type: Foot.
Best season: Late June to mid-October.
Elevation gain: 1,260 feet.

Elevation loss: 2,120 feet.
Maximum elevation: 6,610 feet.
Topo maps: Mount Angeles; Custom Correct *Gray Wolf–Dungeness*.

Finding the trailhead: From Port Angeles, drive 17.6 miles south on Hurricane Ridge Road to the visitor center. Turn south onto the narrow, winding Obstruction Point Road. This route is too narrow for trailers and RVs. Drive 7.6 miles to road's end at Obstruction Point, where the trail begins.

The Hike

This trail offers a point-to-point hike across alpine ridges from Obstruction Point in the west to the Deer Park Campground in the east. Water is scarce along this route, so be sure to bring along a plentiful supply. The trail begins by crossing a grassy bowl that is home to a marmot colony; the engaging behavior of these social rodents can entertain for hours. The path drops across the steep headwall of the Badger Valley as it rounds Obstruction Peak, and the Badger Valley Trail drops away to the right. The path then begins to ascend onto the broad summit of Elk Mountain, with its endless rocky fells speckled with the blossoms of phlox and dwarf lupine. The rocky interstices support a sparse growth of hardy lichens that are close cousins to the ones that provide Arctic caribou herds with their winter forage. Take a glance backward for a grandstand view of the heart of the Olympic Mountains, from Mount Christie in the south to the Bailey Range in the north, and all surmounted by the ice-bound mass of Mount Olympus itself. To the south, the glacier-clad summit of Mount Cameron is partially hidden by the ridges that rise above the Grand Valley. The ragged spires of the Needles rise farther to the east.

As Elk Mountain peters out, the trail descends steeply to reach Roaring Winds Pass, then climbs high onto the flanks of Maiden Peak. The south slope of this peak is quite arid and supports a rather sparse flora of grasses and lichens interspersed with bistorts and dwarf lupines. A short trek to the ridgeline allows the traveler to look down into the basin containing Maiden Lake, a small, shallow pool of pale aquamarine. The slopes of Maiden Peak offer the park's finest view of the Needles,

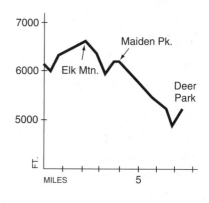

The Needles: Mounts Walkinshaw and Clark to the left, with Mount Johnson in the center. Mount Deception appears at the right.

which are, from north to south, Mount Walkinshaw, Mount Clark, and Mount Johnson. Mount Deception is the southernmost summit on this craggy ridge.

The path rounds the rocky eastern spur of Maiden Peak, then descends through rolling tundra as the subalpine firs close in around the ridgeline. Moist glades support white and pink heathers, avalanche lilies, and a deep lavender variety of paintbrush. As the trail drops onto the south slope of Green Mountain, it enters an arid forest of lodgepole pine. There is little in the way of understory vegetation here, and this habitat type is avoided by most species of wildlife. After a rather long and jolting descent into a low saddle, the trail picks up an old roadbed that climbs the remaining distance to the Deer Park Ranger Station.

Key Points

0.0 Obstruction Point trailhead

0.2 Junction with Badger Valley Trail. Keep going straight.

2.0 Junction with cutoff trail to Badger Valley. Bear left.

2.6 Easternmost summit of Elk Mountain.

3.2 Roaring Winds Pass.

3.9 Maiden Peak.

7.4 Deer Park Ranger Station.

21 Badger Valley

A 4.6-mile day hike or short backpack from Obstruction Point to Grand Lake.

Difficulty: Moderately strenuous.
Trail type: Foot.
Best season: Late June to mid-October.
Elevation gain: 720 feet.

Elevation loss: 2,110 feet.
Maximum elevation: 6,140 feet (trailhead).
Topo maps: Mount Angeles; Custom Correct *Gray Wolf-Dosewallips.*

Finding the trailhead: From Port Angeles, drive 17.6 miles south on Hurricane Ridge Road to the visitor center. Then turn left onto the gravel Obstruction Point Road. Drive 7.6 miles to a large but unmarked parking area. The trail departs to the northeast.

The Hike

This trail provides an alternate route to Grand Lake and can be combined with the Grand Valley route for a one-day loop trip. The trek begins by following the Elk Mountain Trail around Obstruction Peak, where the Badger Valley Trail splits away to the right. It switchbacks down a steep scree slope to reach the head of the Badger Valley, with its many snowmelt rivulets splashing down the mountainsides. The trail runs along the northern edge of this basin, passing alpine glades dotted with subalpine

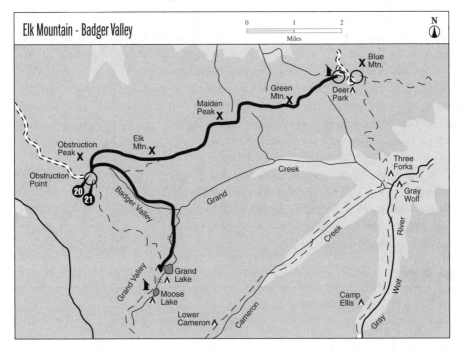

Looking down the Badger Valley

firs and Alaska cedars. A cutoff trail soon descends into the valley from Elk Mountain, after which the main trail dives into the subalpine forest for a time.

The path emerges at a low meadow, covered in some places by rank grasses and cow parsnip and in others by a well-groomed sward sprinkled with the pink and white spikes of elephant's head. After crossing this extensive opening, the trail descends steeply through a montane forest to reach the floor of the Grand Valley. Here it encounters an emergency camp where fires are permitted. The trail then turns south, climbing through the glades along Grand Creek and passing several impressive waterfalls. The path crosses a meadowy bench below the foot of Grand Lake where willows cluster in the poorly drained sites. The trail reaches a marked junction at the head of the lake; a path leading to the main camping area is to the left, and the Grand Valley Trail is a short distance uphill to the right.

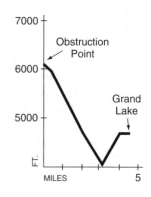

Key Points

0.0 Obstruction Point trailhead.

0.2 Junction with Badger Valley Trail. Turn right as trail descends.

1.2 Junction with Elk Mountain cutoff trail. Stay right.

3.0 Emergency camping area (fires allowed).

3.5 Trail crosses Grand Creek to reach east bank.

4.2 Trail returns to west bank of Grand Creek.

4.6 Junction with spur trail, head of Grand Lake.

22 Grand Valley

A 3.8-mile day hike from Obstruction Point to Grand Lake, or an 8.1-mile backpack to Cameron Creek.

Difficulty: Moderately strenuous north to south; strenuous south to north.
Trail type: Foot.
Best season: Early July to mid-October.
Elevation gain: 1,925 feet.

Elevation loss: 4,135 feet.
Maximum elevation: 6,400 feet.
Topo maps: Mount Angeles; Custom Correct *Gray Wolf-Dosewallips.*

Finding the trailhead:

From Port Angeles, drive 17.6 miles south on Hurricane Ridge Road to the vistor center. Then turn left onto the gravel Obstruction Point Road. Drive 7.6 miles to a large but unmarked parking area. The trail departs to the northeast. Obtain a camping permit at the park visitor center in Port Angeles.

The Hike

This outstanding hike combines the Lillian Ridge and Grand Pass Trails to link Obstruction Point with the Cameron Valley. Along the way the route runs alpine ridges, passes sparkling lakes, and offers sweeping views of the eastern Olympics. From Obstruction Point the trail climbs onto the rounded top of Lillian Ridge, clad in grassy meadows that are populated by colonies of playful marmots. The ridgetop is soon dominated by an arid alpine tundra, in which hardy flowers like dwarf lupine, phlox, and fleabane eke out a hardscrabble existence in the high winds, short growing seasons, and lack of water found here. Spectacular scenery abounds on all sides. To the east, the Needles rise sheer above the intervening ridgetops. To the south, McCartney Peak rises above the Lillian River valley amid a sea of equally spectacular (though nameless) summits, and the omnipresent mass of Mount Olympus hulks to the west.

After 1.6 miles of up-and-down travel, the trail drops into a low saddle. A climber's trail continues along the ridgeline to the south, while the main path bends east to descend into the Grand Valley. The alpine desert is particularly barren as the trail drops from the ridgetop: Low-growing krummholz fir huddle in small clumps amid wide expanses of bare, rocky soil. The blue mirror of Grand Lake can be seen far below

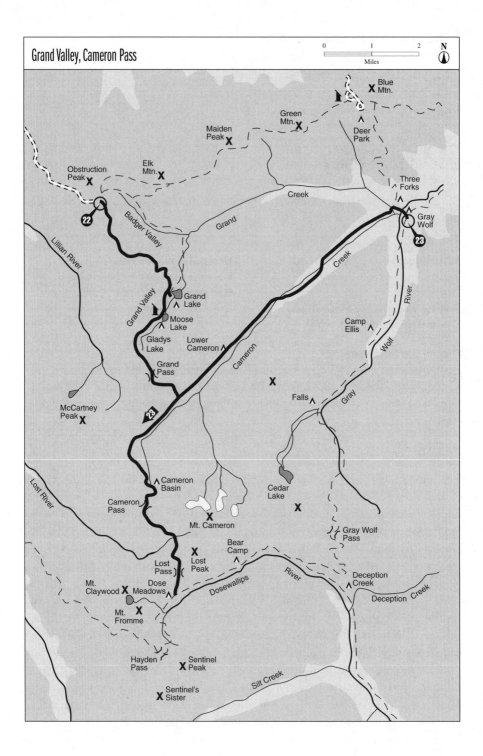

0   1   2

Miles

N

X Blue Mtn.

Green Mtn. X

Maiden Peak X

Deer Park

Three Forks

Obstruction Peak X

Elk Mtn. X

Gray Wolf

22

Creek

Badger Valley

Grand

23

Lillian River

Grand Valley

Grand Lake

Moose Lake

Creek

Camp Ellis

Wolf

River

Gladys Lake

Lower Cameron

Cameron

Grand Pass

23

X

McCartney Peak X

Falls

Gray

Cameron Basin

Cedar Lake

Cameron Pass

Mt. Cameron X

X

Lost River

Bear Camp

Gray Wolf Pass

X Lost Pass

Lost Peak

Deception Creek

Mt. Claywood X

Dose Meadows

Dosewallips

River

Deception Creek

Mt. Fromme X

Hayden Pass

X Sentinel Peak

Silt Creek

X Sentinel's Sister

Grand Lake

amid verdant forests on the valley floor. The path soon switchbacks down to the floor of a side valley, where it enters a lush subalpine basin of grassy glades and babbling brooks. It follows the floor of this valley for a time, then strikes off to the south to enter Grand Valley itself.

The trail passes through a subalpine forest above Grand Lake, then reaches a grassy avalanche slope where it meets a spur path descending to the lakeshore. After 0.2 mile it reaches a junction with the Badger Valley trail beside the still waters. The camping area lies straight ahead, set among the conical firs at the head of the lake. Black-tailed deer frequent the area, and a delightful waterfall is hidden a short distance up the inlet stream. The lake itself is a broad, placid affair, studded with fir-covered islets and harboring a large population of stunted trout that make for challenging angling.

The main trail runs south from the avalanche slope, cresting a low rise to reach the ranger tent at Moose Lake. This spectacular tarn sits at the foot of splendid snow-capped peaks and is surrounded by alpine parkland. Designated campsites are scattered at various points around the lake and are marked by small posts.

Beyond Moose Lake is a fairyland of meres and meadows. The largest of the pools is Gladys Lake, a shallow tarn in which the central peninsula is dominated by a cabin-size glacial erratic.

The path gets rougher as it crosses a rivulet near the head of the valley and turns southeast. The main part of the climb to Grand Pass lies ahead, a brief but sometimes steep ascent across barren scree slopes that often remain snow-covered through mid-July. The lofty pass boasts spectacular views, highlighted by the Needles, which rise in

craggy majesty beyond the intervening ridges. Mount Cameron
dominates the mountains to the
south, and the deep trough of the
Cameron Valley lies at their feet.
A short side trip to the top of the
summit to the west yields additional vistas that encompass Mount
Olympus and Mount Rainier.

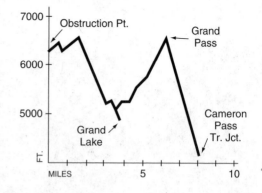

Beyond the pass the trail dives
steeply down to Cameron Creek,
passing through a succession of plant communities determined by the microclimates
of their altitude. Near the pass alpine tundra dominates an open bowl, and the moist
soil supports a sea of nodding avalanche lilies. Just below it a subalpine forest of fir
and Alaska cedar closes around the trail, occasionally interrupted by openings that
offer the special bonus of red columbines and orange tiger lilies. At the bottom of the
grade is a montane forest of silver and Douglas fir, as well as mountain hemlock. The
trail may be brushy as it drops the final distance to join the Cameron Pass route about
halfway between the Lower Cameron shelter and Cameron Basin.

Key Points

0.0   Obstruction Point trailhead.

1.6   Trail drops from Lillian Ridge.

3.6   Junction with trail to Grand Lake and Badger Valley.

4.2   Foot of Moose Lake. Ranger tent.

4.4   Head of Moose Lake.

4.9   Gladys Lake.

6.3   Grand Pass.

8.1   Junction with Cameron Pass Trail.

23 Cameron Pass

An extended 13.7-mile trip from Gray Wolf Camp to Dose Meadows. (See map on page 90.)

Difficulty: Moderately strenuous north to south; strenuous south to north.
Trail type: Foot to Cameron Basin; primitive beyond.
Best season: Late July to mid-October.
Elevation gain: 4,590 feet.

Elevation loss: 2,260 feet.
Maximum elevation: 6,450 feet (Cameron Pass).
Topo maps: Tyler Peak, Mount Angeles; Custom Correct *Gray Wolf-Dosewallips.*

Finding the trailhead: Taylor Cutoff Road leaves U.S. Highway 101 at mile 262, just west of Sequim. Follow it south for 2.7 miles to a junction with Fish Hatchery Road; turn right. This becomes lost Mountain Road, and after 2.8 miles, FR 2870 takes off to the left. Follow this gravel road for the remaining 6.8 miles (bearing left at junctions) to reach the marked Gray Wolf trailhead. The Cameron Pass hike begins at Gray Wolf Camp, at mile 9.8 on the Gray Wolf River Trail.

The Hike

This trail links the Gray Wolf and Dosewallips drainages, crossing Cameron and Lost Passes along the way. The grades to the passes are exceedingly steep when approached from the south, and travelers are advised to approach them from the much less strenuous northern side. This trail is well known for its late-lingering snowfields on the eastern approach to Cameron Pass, and an ice axe is often required. The trail begins at Gray Wolf Camp and runs downhill to cross a footlog over the river. It then follows the riverbank upstream to the Three Forks shelter, where a cutoff trail descends from the Deer Park auto campground. The camp occupies a grassy clearing in the gloomy forest beside the confluence of Grand and Cameron Creeks (the Gray Wolf enters some distance downstream from this point).

The Cameron Pass Trail then crosses a footlog over Grand Creek and follows the banks of Cameron Creek up into a glacier-carved valley. The path follows the streamside through a lush bottomland forest carpeted with a spongy layer of moss. It doesn't stay there long, though. There are plenty of vigorous ups and downs to keep the traveler breathless as the trail makes periodic forays onto the hillside to avoid cutbanks and washouts. A footlog spans the waters of Cameron Creek 2.1 miles above its mouth. The forest on this side of the creek receives less sunlight because of its northern exposure. As a result the closed-canopy stands are almost devoid of ground cover. When the trail returns to the northwest bank of the stream, note the vigorous growth of ferns, vanilla leaf, and trail-plant on the forest floor.

The path soon leaves the stream, climbing onto the first of many avalanche slopes that interrupt the forest from this point on. This is also the first chance to take in mountain scenery: Two sharp bulwarks of stone rise from the ridgetops across the valley. The lower spire is stout and pillarlike, while the upper one is as thin as a blade. Its triangular shape calls to mind the dorsal fin of some enormous shark, cleaving a green wave of forest. The trail continues to rise and fall as it crosses bands of timber and brushy clearings. One of the openings is occupied by the Lower Cameron shelter. Campsites are hard to come by here; campers may have to bushwhack through the tall grass to reach the creek bottom and find a spot suitable for pitching a tent.

The next major avalanche slope is 1.4 miles beyond the shelter. This opening is covered with subalpine spiraea, which bursts into lavender balls of tiny flowers in mid-July. From here hikers can look up a side valley at the summit of Mount Cameron, cradling its tiny glaciers between rocky spurs. The next broad opening allows views of the nameless peaks at the head of the valley. Just beyond its far edge, a trail descends from Grand Pass to join the Cameron Pass route. The trail then drops back to the valley floor, passing several good campsites as it follows Cameron Creek.

At the head of the valley, the trail bends gradually around to the south for the climb into Cameron Basin. Dense brushfields merge into subalpine parkland as the trail gains altitude, and nameless summits rise on all sides. The trail soon crests a rise and enters the basin, where a camping area occupies the top of a rocky knoll crowded with sparse-limbed subalpine firs. The paths get somewhat confusing here; the main trail follows the western edge of a wet alpine meadow. The path surmounts a low headwall of rock, then turns west to cross a broad plain of broken stones. Snow lingers so late in this upper part of the basin that no plant can complete its life cycle during a single snow-free season.

Follow the cairns as the trail begins to wind up steep slopes of loose scree. The trail is constrained to a rocky crest between lingering snowfields as it climbs. The long grade ends atop Cameron Pass, which at 6,450 feet is the highest major divide served by a trail in the Olympic Mountains. The peaks rise rank on rank to the west,

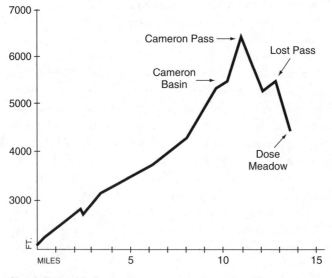

as numberless as waves on the sea. The distant peaks are highlighted by Mount Queets in the south, Mount Olympus in the center, and the Bailey Range in the north. Closer at hand the twin summits of Mount Claywood and Mount Fromme rear their somber heads above the basin of the Lost River. The noble summits of Mount Anderson cleave the sky beyond them, with pinnacles that guard the Eel Glacier.

Down goes the trail, following cairns through a barren waste where shrubby cinquefoils and alpine saxifrage cling tenuously to shale-covered slopes. Down farther it goes, across grassy slopes and among clumps of fir that cower as krummholz. Raptors of all kinds fill the skies, searching for the numerous rodents that in turn prey on the lush growth of grasses and forbs. The descent steepens as the trail goes downward through stands of tall firs, stately in their upright form on these more protected slopes. The path finally bottoms out in a luxuriant expanse of wet meadow that lies at the foot of Lost Peak. Marmots pipe their warning whistle in the basin. Several chuckling brooks wander through the grasslands, providing the extra moisture that is needed to sustain willows, monkeyflowers, and shooting stars.

The trail then climbs gradually through alpine parkland to reach Lost Pass. Looking south, the pointed crests of Wellesley and Sentinel Peaks guard the vast expanse of Thousand Acre Meadows. This high terrace of heath provides habitat for Roosevelt elk, black-tailed deer, and black bear. The brooding mass of Mount Claywood looms above the pass to the west. The path then dives headlong down the steep valley wall to the south, dropping through the timber at an insane rate. Watch out for loose rock that might roll underfoot; it is a serious safety hazard on pitches of this steepness. The trail deposits the traveler in Dose Meadows, where a pleasant camping spot provides a welcome respite. A trail ascends along the Dosewallips River to reach this point, and another climbs away to the southwest on its way to Hayden Pass.

Key Points

0.0   Gray Wolf Camp, junction with Gray Wolf River Trail. Bear north.

0.1   Trail crosses Gray Wolf River.

0.4   Three Forks shelter, junction with Three Forks cutoff trail. Turn left and cross Grand Creek.

2.5   Trail crosses Cameron Creek to reach its east bank.

3.6   Trail returns to northwest bank of Cameron Creek.

5.3   Lower Cameron shelter.

7.4   Junction with trail from Grand Pass. Keep going straight.

9.7   Cameron Basin camping area.

11.0   Cameron Pass.

12.1   Trail crosses headwaters of Lost River.

12.9   Lost Pass.

13.7   Junction with Dosewallips River Trail, Dose Meadows Camp.

24 The Gray Wolf River

A 22.7-mile backpack from Forest Road 2870 to the Dosewallips River.

Difficulty: Moderately strenuous.
Trail type: Secondary.
Best season: Late May to mid-October.
Elevation gain: 6,340 feet.

Elevation loss: 3,740 feet.
Maximum elevation: 6,180 feet.
Topo maps: Tyler Peak, Mount Angeles; Custom Correct *Gray Wolf-Dosewallips*.

Finding the trailhead: Taylor Cutoff Road leaves U.S. Highway 101 at mile 262, just west of Sequim. Follow it south for 2.7 miles to a junction with Fish Hatchery Road; turn right. This becomes Lost Mountain Road, and after 2.8 miles, FR 2870 takes off to the left. Follow this gravel road for the remaining 6.8 miles (bearing left at junctions) to reach the marked trailhead.

The Hike

The valley of the Gray Wolf penetrates deep into the northeastern Olympics, providing opportunities for long backpacks into remote territory. The trail is commonly accessed via three different routes. They are, in order of increasing length and decreasing steepness: the Three Forks Trail from Deer Park, the Slab Camp Trail, and the Gray Wolf River Trail itself. This last option will be discussed here, while brief synopses of the other two can be found at the end of the section.

The river derived its name from an abundance of timber wolves that were found here before extermination programs (to increase numbers of Roosevelt elk) drove them into extinction. The Olympic Peninsula would seem to be an ideal setting for reintroduction, with its protected core of mountains surrounded by timberlands rather than farms and ranches. Although there are no current plans for reintroducing the wolf to the Olympic Peninsula, it does not seem impossible that the howl of this magnificent creature may one day be heard again in the primeval depths of these mountains.

From the Gray Wolf trailhead, the path climbs briskly to a forested bluff that rises above the north bank of the river. It follows the hilltop westward and soon traverses a broad clear-cut logged in the early 1980s. Here, in a contest of quantity versus quality, plants of varying reproductive strategies meet on the battlefield of ecological succession. Sun-loving shrubs and weeds, such as thimbleberry, thistle, and fireweed, colonized first and formed a lush thicket of undergrowth. These plants depend on broadcasting millions of seeds, via wind in the case of thistle and fireweed, or through bird and mammal droppings as thimbleberry does. The shade-tolerant conifers produce fewer seeds and arise more slowly. These plants make up for their lack of reproductive prowess with long life spans and giant statures. They will ultimately overtop and shade out the shrubby colonizers that are currently so vigorous.

Rugged country near Gray Wolf Pass

After dropping into the forested bottomlands of the Gray Wolf, the trail enters the Buckhorn Wilderness. Campsites can be found all along the riverbank wherever the trail runs on the flats. The path winds along the river for a time, then climbs high above the water to pass behind a pair of rocky knobs. These high points afford several overlooks from which to contemplate the steep-walled valley of the Gray Wolf. After returning to the valley floor, the trail flattens out for a long stretch. A pack bridge ultimately leads to the south bank, as a sheer cliff of basalt blocks progress up the north bank of the river. Note the round nodule structure of the stone; it's called "pillow lava" and is formed when hot magma wells out of cracks in the seafloor and hardens quickly in the cold water of the ocean's depths.

After passing through this tight spot, the trail begins a long and steady climb to Slide Creek. It is soon joined by the Slab Camp Trail, and the ascent becomes more brisk. Near the top of the grade, openings in the trees reveal the tree-clad dome of Blue Mountain. The grassy point of Maiden Peak rises farther up the valley. The path passes beneath rocky brows of basalt, then drops down into the valley of Slide Creek. This entire drainage burned in 1953, and a dense stand of second-growth Douglas fir sprang up in its wake. After crossing the creek, with its gloomy campsites huddled in a wooded ravine, the trail maintains its altitude and returns to the slopes above the river.

The mature, unburned forest returns just beyond the boundary of Olympic National Park, and the trail descends steeply to reach the Three Forks area. A registration box lies at the bottom of the grade, and all overnight visitors must fill out a permit here. A trail to the right leads down through Gray Wolf Camp, then crosses the river and follows the far bank west to the Three Forks shelter. This spot marks the end of the Three Forks cutoff trail, and the Cameron Pass Trail ascends Cameron Creek from this point. Meanwhile, hikers bound for the Gray Wolf should turn left at the junction above Gray Wolf Camp.

This path follows the narrow valley bottom, picking its way among mossy hummocks as the river rushes noisily through boulders and logjams. After a mile the path crosses one of these logjams, which has been modified into a crude footbridge. It then follows the west bank upstream. The path ultimately climbs onto the hillside above the water but never strays far from the valley floor. The forest found here is a nondescript growth of red cedar, Douglas fir, and western hemlock. Several kinds of mosses thrive in the damp understory, and shelf fungi cling to downed logs and standing snags.

The valley widens a bit as the stream gradient lessens, and soon the trail reaches Camp Ellis. This camp is situated in a ragged stand of red cedars beside the streamcourse. A short distance beyond this point, the trail climbs vigorously up the side of the valley, attaining a height several hundred feet above the Gray Wolf. Several brushy openings are crossed, but only the wooded shoulders of Gray Wolf Ridge can be seen from them. After 2 miles of traveling through the forest, the trail glides gently back to the valley floor amid a wet forest of young silver firs that retain their conical form. The trail soon reaches the Falls shelter, which sits in a grassy meadow beside the much-reduced Gray Wolf. The name of this camp is a bit of a conundrum: The stream slides quietly through a dense growth of willow at this spot. There are tent sites among the trees at the edges of the meadow, and the Cedar Lake Trail departs from the south wall of the shelter. It is discussed in detail at the end of this trail description.

Beyond the shelter a footlog spans Cedar Creek. As the path continues up the valley floor, it makes numerous footlog crossings of the Gray Wolf. Old man's beard drapes the trees of the scraggly subalpine forest. After the third river crossing, the path switchbacks upward for a bit, then runs south for the final footlog over the waters. Open meadows offer the first views of the rugged mountain scenery before the trail disappears into the forest for a long, zigzagging climb. By the time the path reaches the first major opening, Mount Deception has disappeared behind an intervening knob. Mounts Walkinshaw and Clark, however, are revealed in their full glory.

The trail soon follows a chattering freshet into a high alpine basin, lavishly carpeted with heather and avalanche lily. Nameless peaks rise above the meadows, and a tangled skein of white water cascades across an outcrop to reach the valley floor. The landscape soon becomes more desolate as swards of grass give way to barren slopes of scree and talus. Look for Olympic marmots near the head of the basin, where boulder fields and swaths of grass intermix. As the trail climbs the final pitch across steep scree slopes, the brittle spires of Mount Clark can be viewed through a saddle to the east.

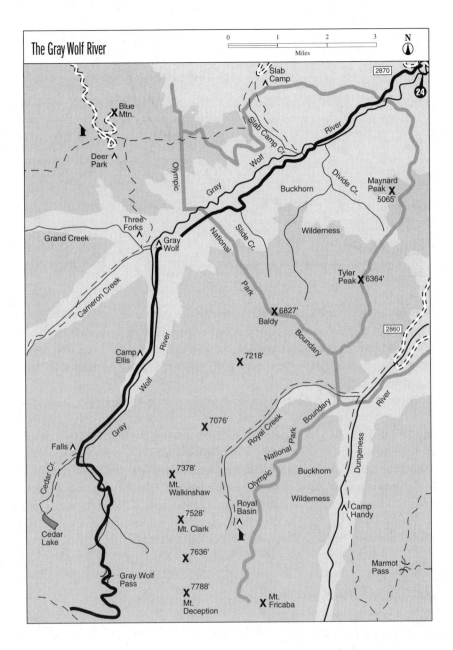

0　　　　1　　　　2　　　　3　　　N
Miles

Slab Camp

2870

24

Blue Mtn.

Slab Camp Cr.

River

Wolf

Deer Park

Gray

Buckhorn

Divide Cr.

Maynard Peak X 5065'

Olympic

Three Forks

Grand Creek

Gray Wolf

National

Slide Cr.

Wilderness

Tyler Peak X 6364'

Cameron Creek

Park

X 6827'
Baldy

Boundary

2860

Camp Ellis

River

X 7218'

Gray Wolf

X 7076'

Royal Creek

Boundary

River

Falls

Gray

National Park

Dungeness

Cedar Cr.

X 7378'
Mt. Walkinshaw

Olympic

Buckhorn

Cedar Lake

X 7528'
Mt. Clark

Royal Basin

Wilderness

Camp Handy

X 7636'

Gray Wolf Pass

X 7788'
Mt. Deception

X Mt. Fricaba

Marmot Pass

The view from the pass encompasses the entire Dosewallips Valley, with tawny teeth of sedimentary and metamorphic rock surrounding it. Wellesley Peak dominates the foreground, while Cameron Peak, Mount Fromme, and Mount Claywood rise above the valley's head. The views open up even more as the trail starts downward into the Dosewallips Valley. To the south the craggy spires of Diamond Mountain and Mount Elk Lick provide a foreground for the more distant summits of the Mount

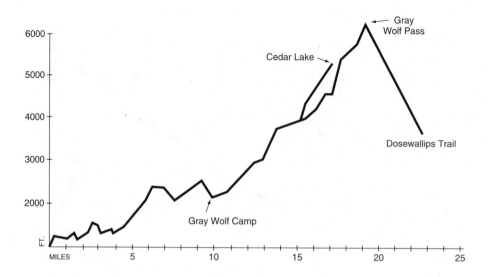

Skokomish group. Immediately to the southeast the steep rock face of Mount Mystery soars skyward almost 2,000 feet from its base. It is flanked on the left by the lofty heights of Mount Deception and on the right by the rugged crest of Little Mystery. Warrior Peak appears dwarfed by the closer summits of Mounts Mystery and Deception that frame it.

Outstanding views continue as the trail drops across the lush upper slopes of the ridge, which is covered in broad expanses of flowery meadows interrupted by pointed clumps of subalpine fir. The slope dries out farther down but is crossed by numerous mountain brooks. Along their banks water-loving plants like yellow monkeyflower and shooting star bloom literally within feet of desert parsley, which favors more arid soils. The trail is soon cloaked in conifers, but there are numerous openings for viewing the peaks all the way down the hill. As the path approaches the bottom of the grade, it makes a long dogleg to the west in order to intercept the Dosewallips River Trail about halfway between Deception Creek and Bear Camp.

Key Points

0.0   Gray Wolf River trailhead.

1.9   Trail enters Buckhorn Wilderness.

4.0   Bridge over Gray Wolf River.

4.9   Junction with Slab Camp Trail. Stay left.

7.4   Trail crosses Slide Creek.

7.7   Trail enters Olympic National Park.

9.8   Registration station above Gray Wolf Camp. Junction with trail to Cameron Pass. Turn left.

10.8   Trail crosses Gray Wolf River to reach its west bank.

12.5   Camp Ellis.

15.2 Falls Camp. Cedar Lake Trail departs to west.

15.3 Footlog over Cedar Creek.

15.4 Trail crosses Gray Wolf to reach its east bank.

16.0 Trail returns to west bank of Gray Wolf.

16.1 Trail crosses back to east bank of river.

17.2 Final crossing of the Gray Wolf.

19.2 Gray Wolf Pass.

22.7 Junction with Dosewallips River Trail.

Cedar Lake Option: From the Falls shelter this strenuous trail runs west across the meadow and soon crosses a small stream. It then begins a merciless ascent through the forest. Early on, a talus slope provides an opening for viewing the craggy pinnacles of Mount Deception. A better view can be had farther on, when the trail clears the forest into open alleyways between the drooping fronds of Alaska cedar. Overgrown avalanche slopes mark the top of the initial grade, and the openings provide a sneak preview of the nameless summits that crowd the head of the Cedar Creek drainage.

As the track approaches the timber, it veers downhill for a crossing of Cedar Creek. A scruffy forest of mountain hemlock clothes the valley floor, and the trail attacks numerous hillocks and terraces in relentless head-on fashion. Near the head of the valley, the path crosses several wide expanses of wet meadow dotted with alpine wildflowers. One final pitch remains to reach the shores of Cedar Lake. True to its name, Alaska cedars mingle with subalpine firs on the north shore of this large tarn. It was once stocked with rainbow trout, and fishing remains good despite the fact that stocking programs have been discontinued within the wilderness areas of the park. Across the greenish waters, steep talus slopes rise toward massive blocks of bedrock, mantled in snowfields that linger year-round.

25 The Upper Dungeness Trail

A 9.7-mile backpack from Forest Road 2860 through the Buckhorn Wilderness to Home Lake within the park.

Difficulty: Moderately strenuous.
Trail type: Foot.
Best season: Mid-June to mid-October.
Elevation gain: 3,320 feet.

Elevation loss: 520 feet.
Maximum elevation: 5,350 feet (Home Lake).
Topo maps: Tyler Peak; Custom Correct *Buckhorn Wilderness.*

Finding the trailhead: From Sequim, drive east on U.S. Highway 101 to mile 267.4 and turn south onto Palo Alto Road. The pavement ends after 6 miles, and the road becomes Forest Road 28. Drive another 3 miles to FR 2860. Turn left and drive 11.7 miles, avoiding Forest Road 2870, to the Upper Dungeness trailhead.

The Hike

This trail penetrates deep into the heart of the Buckhorn Wilderness, then enters Olympic National Park just before reaching Home Lake. The alpine country near the Boulder shelter makes a popular backpacking destination. Hikers can also connect with the Constance Pass, Marmot Pass, and Tubal Cain Trails for longer trips. The trek begins as a quiet woodland stroll through the mossy forest on the north bank of the Dungeness. The "river" is hardly more than a narrow mountain stream at this point, and it splashes noisily down a rocky course. A footlog spans the murky waters of Royal Creek, and the Royal Basin Trail takes off to the right. The Upper Dungeness Trail continues up the main valley, entering the Buckhorn Wilderness.

The trail passes quite close to the stream, revealing turbulent chutes and quiet eddies amid a jumble of mossy boulders. Before long a footlog crosses the Dungeness, and the trail moves inland as it follows the east bank of the stream. After crossing a gravelly tributary and passing across a landslide scar, a spur path descends to the Camp Handy shelter. Here tent sites occupy the edge of a valley-bottom meadow, and tan summits rise above the far side of the valley.

Another unmarked path soon splits away to the right, bound for the head of the valley. The main trail bears left and begins the long and steady ascent to the Boulder shelter.

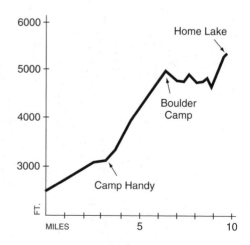

Warrior Peak and Home Lake

It is instructive to mark the changes in the forest with increasing elevation. Near the valley floor, hemlocks rise above a sparse understory of Pacific rhododendron and, later, vanilla leaf and Oregon grape. At the 4,500-foot level, this montane forest merges with a subalpine community dominated by silver fir and lit by the tiny blossoms of twinflower. Douglas fir and white pine make occasional appearances on the arid south-facing slopes. Steep washouts at these higher elevations allow fine views of Mount Fricaba rising amid a tawny sea of rocky ridgetops.

Around a final corner, the western buttress of Mount Constance looms ahead like a giant tooth as the trail bends east to enter a subalpine meadow. This grassy opening is filled with enormous chunks of rock and is overlooked by a blocky peak. The Marmot Pass Trail takes off at its northern margin, while a short spur trail runs into the trees from its southern edge to reach the Boulder shelter. This structure is perched atop an open knoll, and tent sites are scattered among the firs and Alaska cedars. Camp here rather than in the fragile meadows surrounding the stream.

The trail then swings uphill into the trees, bound for Home Lake. An unmarked way trail soon climbs away to the left, and the main trail begins a long and shallow glide downward. After crossing an open slope that affords fine views of Mount Mystery and the barren ridgetops that surround it, the trail returns to the subalpine forest for 1.2 miles. It emerges on the open slopes below Warrior Peak, with the jagged western bulwark of Mount Constance soaring skyward dead ahead. The opening soon

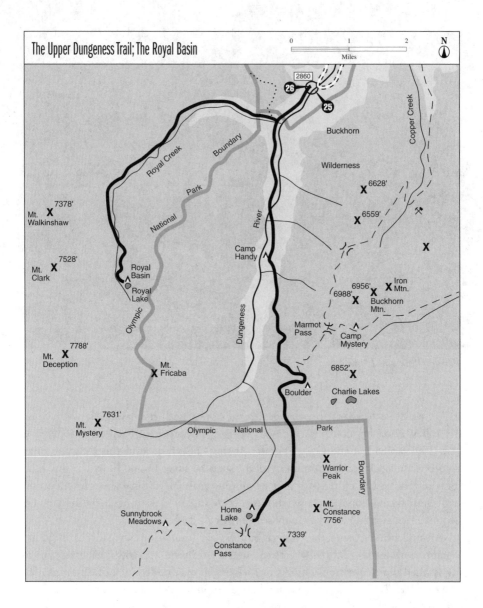

becomes overgrown with cow parsnip and Menzies larkspur, and the path crosses several streams. One of these crossings occurs in the midst of a tumbling cascade; be careful to avoid slipping on the algae-covered rocks.

The trail then picks its way across talus slopes of broken basalt; pinnacles and sheer walls of the same rock tower overhead. Isolated stands of subalpine fir rise from the midst of the rubble. After dropping to the boulder-lined floor of the drainage, the path mounts the narrow, fir-clad finger ridge that leads upward to Home Lake. This turquoise tarn occupies a rocky setting, overlooked to the south by moist, flower-strewn slopes. There are a few rocky tent spots here, but they are not level. The route becomes the Constance Pass Trail at this point, climbing over the divide and then dropping into the Dosewallips Valley.

Key Points

0.0 Trailhead.

1.0 Junction with Royal Basin Trail. Bear left and cross Royal Creek. Trail enters Buckhorn Wilderness.

2.6 Trail crosses Dungeness to reach its east bank.

3.3 Spur path to Camp Handy.

3.7 Unmarked junction with Home Creek way trail. Bear left.

6.3 Junction with Marmot Pass Trail. Stay right.

6.4 Spur trail to Boulder shelter.

6.5 Junction with Charlie Lakes way trail. Stay right.

7.3 Trail enters Olympic National Park

9.7 Home Lake.

26 The Royal Basin

A long (7-mile) day hike or backpack from Forest Road 2860 to Royal Lake. (See map on page 104.)

Difficulty: Moderate.
Trail type: Secondary.
Best season: Late June to mid-October.
Elevation gain: 2,570 feet.

Maximum elevation: 5,120 feet (Royal Lake).
Topo maps: Tyler Peak; Custom Correct *Buckhorn Wilderness.*

Finding the trailhead: From Sequim, drive east on U.S. Highway 101 to mile 267.4 and turn south onto Palo Alto Road. The pavement ends after 6 miles, and the road becomes Forest Road 28. Drive another 3 miles to FR 2860. Turn left and drive 11.7 miles, avoiding Forest Road 2870, to the Upper Dungeness trailhead.

The Hike

This trail provides one of the gentlest grades to an alpine lake in the Olympic Mountains. The trek begins on the Upper Dungeness Trail, which it follows for the first mile along the noisy course of the headwaters of the Dungeness River. A dense forest of young hemlocks is underlain by a carpet of duff and moss. After 1 mile a footbridge marks the spot where the Royal Basin Trail splits off to the right, climbing gently beside the rather milky waters of Royal Creek. As the valley bends to take on a southwesterly orientation, the trail leaves the stream to wander up a series of

Royal Lake

forested benches. Undergrowth plants such as vanilla leaf and bracken fern begin to invade the understory.

At last the trail climbs into the first of several avalanche slopes that are choked with thimbleberry and ocean spray. This opening offers a fine first view of Mounts Clark and Walkinshaw. The path begins to climb steadily as the conifers become increasingly scarce. Stately silver firs, some of them quite stout, take shelter from avalanches on the rocky knobs. The trail makes its way through stands of subalpine fir and Alaska cedar on its way into the hanging upper valley of Royal Creek. In doing so, the trail passes within earshot of the roaring cataract that pours over the steep headwall.

The flat basin above is filled with subalpine vegetation: Silver and subalpine firs cluster on the higher ground, while grassy meadows and clumps of willow surround the myriad streams that wander the valley floor. Here a few blocky boulders were deposited far from their origins by the glaciers that once filled the valley. Mount Deception and its lesser companions can barely be glimpsed above the next rise, while the craggy faces of Mounts Clark and Walkinshaw tower to the west. On the opposite side of the valley, the steady slope of an arid ridge rises from fir-clad shoulders to tawny peaks. Sedge meadows near the head of the basin offer a few tent sites.

After a footlog crossing of Royal Creek, the trail makes a rocky and washed-out passage up the next rise to enter the Royal Basin. It soon arrives at Royal

Lake, a tiny pool surrounded by firs and over-looked by Mounts Deception and Fricaba and a retinue of lesser snow-mantled peaks. There are a few campsites at the head of the lake and more in the meadow beyond it. Stunted brook trout cruise the waters of the lake, which are tinted green by suspended microscopic algae. The maintained trail ends at a huge overhanging boulder known as "Shelter Rock." Beyond this point the upper part of the basin invites exploration by map and compass, featuring additional tarns, permanent snowfields, and abandoned glacial moraines.

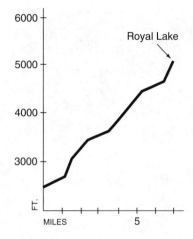

Key Points

0.0   Upper Dungeness trailhead.

1.0   Junction with Royal Basin Trail. Turn right.

1.2   Junction with Lower Maynard Burn way trail. Bear left.

1.5   Trail enters Olympic National Park.

6.4   Lower camping area

6.5   Trail crosses Royal Creek to reach east bank.

7.0   Royal Lake.

27 The Tubal Cain Trail

An 8.7-mile backpack from Forest Road 2860 to Marmot Pass in the Buckhorn Wilderness.

Difficulty: Moderately strenuous.
Trail type: Secondary.
Best season: Early July to mid-October.
Elevation gain: 2,920 feet.

Elevation loss: 240 feet.
Maximum elevation: 6,170 feet.
Topo maps: Tyler Peak; Custom Correct *Buckhorn Wilderness.*

Finding the trailhead: From Sequim, drive east on U.S. Highway 101 to mile 267.4 and turn south onto Palo Alto Road. The pavement ends after 6 miles, and the road becomes Forest Road 28. Drive another 3 miles to FR 2860. Turn left and drive 11.7 miles, avoiding Forest Road 2870, to the Upper Dungeness trailhead. From the Upper Dungeness trailhead, continue south 3.7 miles on FR 2860 to the Tubal Cain trailhead (a total of 24.4 miles from US 101). The trail runs southwest from the road.

Looking east from Marmot Pass

The Hike

This trail runs past an old mine site on Copper Creek, then crosses a high divide at the head of the valley and descends to meet its end at Marmot Pass. Hikers will have to do some off-trail exploring to find evidence of mining activity; the forest has healed itself well and now presents as pristine a valley as can be found in the Buck-horn Wilderness.

This trail begins by descending past a shelter to a footlog over Silver Creek with its bottomland forest of red cedar and western hemlock. The trail registration station is on the far bank, and the path soon rounds the hillside to enter the valley of Copper Creek. The plant community changes markedly here: A rather open forest of silver fir and hemlock rises above a dense growth of Pacific rhododendron. Early openings allow views of Tyler Peak and Baldy on the end of Gray Wolf Ridge. The trees thicken as the trail climbs gently up the valley, but periodic openings are provided by stream washouts from the hillside above the trail. The ridge across the valley rises, tawny and pointed, above a narrow band of firs. Brief glimpses of Iron and Buckhorn Mountains are proffered up on an occasional basis.

A doghair stand of young silver fir crowds the trail as the Tull Canyon way trail splits away to the left. This faint track is easily missed and climbs steeply up the wooded slopes to the old Tull City mining camp. A faint spur to the left runs to the wreckage of a World War II vintage B-17 bomber. The main trail soon boulder-hops

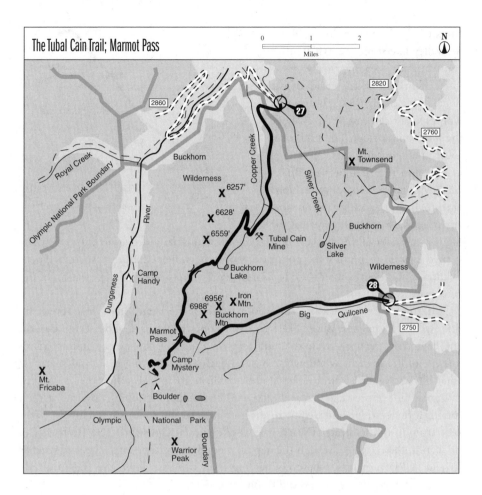

0   1   2
Miles

N

2820

2860

Royal Creek

Olympic National Park Boundary

Buckhorn

Wilderness

Copper Creek

Silver Creek

2760

Mt.
X Townsend

X 6257'

River

X 6628'

X 6559'

⚒ Tubal Cain
Mine

Buckhorn

Silver
Lake

Dungeness

∧ Camp
Handy

⊘ Buckhorn
Lake

Wilderness

6956'
6988' **X** **X** Iron
Mtn.

28

X
Mt.
Fricaba

X Buckhorn
Mtn

∧

Marmot
Pass

∧

Camp
Mystery

∧

Boulder ◍ ⬭

Olympic   \ National Park

X
Warrior
Peak

Boundary

Big   Quilcene

2750

across Copper Creek near the former site of the Tubal Cain Mine, and there are a
number of good campsites on the streambank.

The path then zigzags upward onto broad expanses of grassy meadows that are
dotted with wildflowers. These open hillsides allow excellent vistas of Iron and Buckhorn Mountains rising above the head of Copper Creek, as well as views of the
massive block of basalt that looms directly across the valley. The trail climbs steadily
westward as it traverses the northern wall of the valley. A spur trail to Buckhorn Lake
soon drops away to the left. This path drops to the valley floor, then climbs and falls
abruptly as it negotiates a series of small streams. Several prominent trails depart to
the west along the way; always take the left fork to get to the lake. Buckhorn Lake lies
deep in a forested depression below a spur of Iron Mountain. Its still waters harbor a
healthy population of rainbow trout, and there are tent sites near the inlet stream and
on the heights above the head of the lake.

The main trail switchbacks upward from the junction, alternating between open
hillsides and dense stands of subalpine fir. From a nearby vantage point, Iron and

Buckhorn Mountains loom above the valley like stone giants. The path gains altitude steadily, finally cresting a high pass at the head of the drainage. Looking west, the tops of The Needles can just be seen above the intervening ridge. The trail turns south and continues its zigzagging ascent onto the shoulders of Buckhorn Mountain. According to Nelsa Buckingham, the authority on botany in the Olympics, this area has the

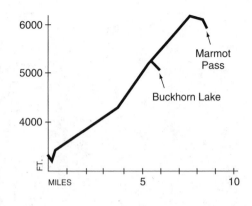

highest diversity of wildflowers on the entire peninsula. Indeed, the efforts of concerned citizens to protect the populations of indigenous wildflowers such as Piper's bellflower and Flett's violet were to a large degree responsible for the creation of the Buckhorn Wilderness.

The trail then curves onto the western face of the ridge, 3,000 feet above the floor of the Dungeness Valley. Note that the slopes that face slightly south are arid and devoid of greenery, while the hillsides with a north-facing aspect support a lush growth of grasses and wildflowers. Golden eagles soar the thermals, and marmots and chipmunks scurry from cover and utter shrill alarm calls when the shadow of this great bird of prey falls across the slopes. The trail begins sloping downward, then rounds a finger ridge and begins to drop rapidly. To the south sheer cliffs of basalt mount up to the summits of Warrior Peak and Mount Constance. The Brothers can be seen in the distance through the gap formed by Constance Pass. The trail reaches its end at Marmot Pass, where connecting trails run east down the Big Quilcene drainage and southwest toward the Boulder shelter.

Key Points

0.0   Trailhead.

0.1   Trail crosses Silver Creek.

0.5   Trail enters Buckhorn Wilderness.

3.6   Trail crosses Copper Creek and begins to climb.

5.6   Spur trail to Buckhorn Lake. Bear right.

7.0   Copper Creek–Dungeness River divide.

8.7   Marmot Pass. Junction with Marmot Pass Trail.

28 Marmot Pass

A 7.1-mile day hike or backpack from Forest Road 2750 to the Upper Dungeness Trail. (See map on page 109.)

Difficulty: Moderately strenuous.
Trail type: Secondary.
Best season: Late June to mid-October.
Elevation gain: 3,580 feet.

Elevation loss: 980 feet.
Maximum elevation: 5,980 feet.
Topo maps: Tyler Peak; Custom Correct *Buckhorn Wilderness.*

Finding the trailhead: From mile 296.1 on U.S. Highway 101 (just south of Quilcene), turn west onto Penny Creek Road. It becomes Forest Road 27, a paved, one-lane trunk route. Drive 11.2 miles from US 101 and turn left onto FR 2750 at a poorly marked junction. This dirt road splits three ways; follow the middle road 4.9 miles to the Upper Big Quilcene trailhead.

The Hike

This trail offers a brief climb to a windswept pass in the Buckhorn Wilderness. It is centrally located to connect with other trails in the area, providing longer trips to Constance Pass or the Copper Creek valley. This trail is officially known as the Upper Big Quilcene River Trail, even though the "river" is no more than a small mountain stream at these elevations. The hike begins in the mature forest that cloaks the north bank of the Big Quilcene. This small woodland brook splashes and tumbles through a gauntlet of mossy stones and fallen logs. After leaving the water's edge, the climb stiffens and the path crosses several breaks in the forest. It is too early in the trek for mountain scenery, but showy wildflowers thrive in these patches of sunlight.

The trail approaches the stream once more at Shelter Rock Camp, named for an enormous boulder that hulks amid the trees just to the east. After passing the tent sites, the trail makes a sharp bend to the north and climbs vigorously beside a feeder stream. It then turns west again as the ascent slackens, and the montane forest is interrupted by openings that provide the first scenic views. Still climbing, the path crosses an open slope of broken basalt surrounded by spectacular scenery. Alaska cedar, ocean spray, and serviceberry grow amid the rocky waste, while Olympic daisies and mountain asters bloom on the verdant slopes beyond. Across the valley rise the towers and pinnacles of Warrior Peak, while the angular spires of Buckhorn Mountain protrude from the slopes above the trail.

The route soon crosses moister slopes clothed in elegant silver and subalpine firs, through which it climbs the final pitch to reach Camp Mystery. The tent sites are sheltered amid the firs atop a level shelf. A chuckling brook runs past the camp, providing a last reliable supply of water on the trail (be sure to treat it). The path then makes its way up through a charming vale where wildflowers thrive on the moisture provided by the rill. It then climbs around a brow of rock and enters a small, grassy bowl just below Marmot Pass. Once on top, the trail reveals the summits of the Needles rising above the ridgetops to the west: Mount Deception in the south, Mount Clark in the center, and the tip of Mount Walkinshaw just visible to the north. The rounded summits of Mounts Mystery and Fricaba rise farther to the south.

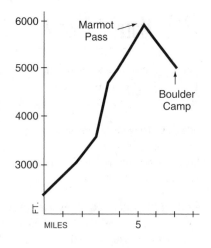

The Tubal Cain Trail descends into the pass from the north, while the Marmot Pass route departs on a southwesterly tangent. It crosses meadowy slopes splashed with clumps of wildflowers. Olympic daisies, rockslide larkspurs, spreading phlox, lupines, yarrow, and paintbrushes all intermix in a dazzling display of color that peaks in midsummer. Watch for Olympic marmots on these verdant hillsides, and keep an eye out for golden eagles that hunt along the open ridgetops. As the trail descends, the slopes become more arid, and a few whitebark pines are scattered amid broad expanses of bare ground. Magnificent views of Warrior Peak and a western spur of Mount Constance unveil themselves as the path rounds a finger ridge and begins to switchback down its spine. The trees thicken as the trail sheds altitude, finally reaching its end at a junction with the Upper Dungeness Trail, just north of the Boulder shelter.

Key Points

0.0 Upper Big Quilcene trailhead.

0.1 Trail enters Buckhorn Wilderness.

2.6 Trail leaves valley floor near Shelter Rock.

4.6 Camp Mystery.

5.3 Marmot Pass. Junction with Tubal Cain Trail. Turn left.

7.1 Junction with Upper Dungeness Trail.

29 Mount Townsend–Silver Lake

A 4.5-mile day hike to the summit of Mount Townsend, or 5.5 miles to Silver Lake.

Difficulty: Moderately strenuous.
Trail type: Secondary.
Best season: Early July to mid-October.
Elevation gain: 3,000 feet (to Mount Townsend).

Maximum elevation: 6,250 feet (Mount Townsend).
Topo maps: Tyler Peak; Custom Correct *Buckhorn Wilderness*.

Finding the trailhead: From mile 296.1 on U.S. Highway 101 (just south of Quilcene), turn west onto Penny Creek Road. It becomes Forest Road 27, a paved, one-lane trunk route. Some 14.3 miles from the highway is a sign for the Mount Townsend Trail; keep going straight. Take the next road to the left, 0.7 mile beyond the sign, and follow it 1.3 miles to the upper trailhead.

The Hike

This trail climbs to the top of Mount Townsend for sweeping views of the leeward Olympics. The route also offers an outstanding diversity of wildflowers throughout the summer, including several species found only in the Olympic Mountains. An optional side trip to Silver Lake is well worth the extra effort.

The trail begins by climbing through a montane forest underlain by Pacific rhododendrons. These shrubs light up the forest with enormous pink blossoms in early July. A few avalanche chutes crisscross the forest and host a timberline community of plants normally found at much higher elevations. The reason behind this phenomenon is twofold: Snow lingers late in these protected gullies, and cooler air tends to settle here, reducing the annual degree-days experienced by the plants that grow here.

Near the head of the valley, the woods open up into subalpine meadows dotted with a diverse array of flowers. The trail zigzags upward to reach a forested bench, where Camp Windy guards a meltwater pond populated by frogs and tadpoles. A brief climb beyond this terrace leads to a junction with the Silver Lake spur. The right-hand trail is the Mount Townsend route, and the left-hand path goes to Silver Lake (see the end of this trail description); bear right. The subalpine firs soon dwindle into a few scattered clumps of krummholz, and a handful of shrubby lodgepole pines are scattered across the meadowy slopes of Mount Townsend. The trail soon reaches the flattened ridgetop and follows it eastward through shrubby cinquefoil and harebells toward the summit.

A short spur path runs to the top of the peak, which commands outstanding views in all directions. The Brothers and Mount Mystery rise in plain view to the west, while the craggy tops of Mount Constance, Warrior Peak, and the Needles rise behind the intervening ridges. Looking to the east, Mount Rainier thrusts its lofty dome high above the Cascade Range. Looking northeast along the ridgeline, a rocky knob of pil-

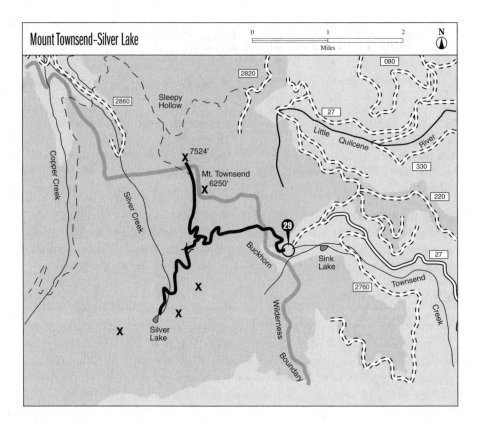

low basalt rises half a mile away. This former lookout site is reached by the main trail and offers additional views of Port Townsend and the Canadian city of Victoria to the northwest. The trail begins to drop steadily from this point on, reaching a junction with the Dirtyface Ridge Trail on a wooded ridgetop above Sleepy Hollow.

Key Points

0.0 Upper trailhead.

3.0 Junction with Silver Lakes Trail (2.5 miles). Turn right for Mount Townsend.

4.0 Spur path to the summit of Mount Townsend.

4.5 Old lookout site on north summit.

Silver Lake Option: This trail offers a 2.5-mile side trip to a stunning alpine tarn set among the jagged peaks that surround the head of Silver Creek. From the junction above Camp Windy, this trail climbs briefly through subalpine forests to reach a low saddle to the south of Mount Townsend. As the path drops gently over the far side of the ridge, rocky meadows are dotted with larkspur and harebells. With decreasing altitude these flowery openings are gradually replaced by stands of subalpine fir, and white rhododendron becomes a prominent component of the understory.

Upon reaching the floor of the Silver Creek valley, the trail begins an equally gradual ascent. It crosses tiny Silver Creek several times before entering a narrow vale that leads to the lake. Silver Lake is a pool of transparent emerald, cupped in a cirque valley of glacial origin. Rugged spires of rock tower nameless on all sides; these have contributed numerous large boulders to the lakeshore over the course of time. Flowery meadows adorn the southern and eastern shores of the lake, while subalpine firs rise in tall, slender spires to the north and west. There are brook trout in Silver Lake; the smaller tarn 0.2 mile to the north is barren of fish.

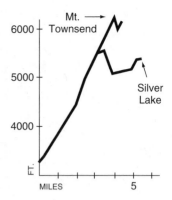

30 Tunnel Creek

A day hike or short backpack 3.9 miles to Harrison Lake, or 7.7 miles to the Dosewallips Valley.

Difficulty: Moderately strenuous north to south; strenuous south to north.
Trail type: Secondary to Harrison Lake; foot beyond.
Best season: Late June to mid-October.

Elevation gain: 2,550 feet.
Elevation loss: 4,500 feet.
Maximum elevation: 5,050 feet.
Topo maps: Tyler Peak, The Brothers; Custom Correct *Buckhorn Wilderness*.

Finding the trailhead: From mile 296.1 on U.S. Highway 101 (just south of Quilcene), turn west onto Penny Creek Road. It becomes Forest Road 27, a paved, one-lane trunk route. Follow it for 4.8 miles from the highway to a junction with Forest Road 2740. Turn left and drive 7.1 miles to the trailhead.

The Hike

This trail climbs over a subalpine ridge in the southern lobe of the Buckhorn Wilderness. Tiny Harrison Lake sits atop the ridge, and there are fine views of the surrounding country. The hike is not difficult when approached from the north, but from the south it presents one of the longest sustained grades in the Olympics.

The trail begins by ascending the wooded ravine of Tunnel Creek. This forest rivulet splashes through mossy logjams as the path climbs in spurts beside it. After about 1 mile the valley widens into a forested basin, and looming masses of basalt can be glimpsed to the south. The forest here is quite distinctive: A sparse overstory of mature hemlocks rises high above a rather dense growth of saplings. The result is a forest with two distinct canopy layers, which are separated by ranks of smooth, clean boles belonging to the older trees.

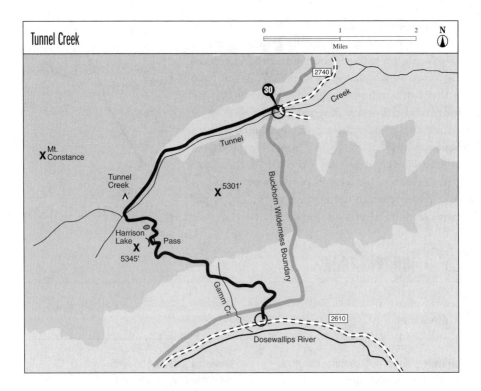

The trail continues to climb, ultimately leveling off in a forested flat of some size. At its west end lies the Tunnel Creek shelter, set amid a sparse forest where the mossy stream gurgles across its stony bed. The valley constricts sharply beyond this point, and the trail turns south to ford the creek. There is a footlog a short distance upstream, but the path associated with it is so steep and poorly built that hikers are better off to take the horse trail with its rock-hopping crossing.

The trail zigzags rather steeply up the wooded hillside, then runs onto a high bench containing a small frog pond. The track then turns west for the short remaining climb to Harrison Lake. This shallow tarn is set among mountain hemlocks, and a rocky tower rises above its western shore. There is a marginal campsite at the head of the lake, and both the lake and the nearby frog pond support populations of rainbow trout.

The trail beyond the lake is narrow and extremely steep, and is not passable to horses. It climbs vigorously through the subalpine forest to reach a rocky knob that commands an outstanding view of the sheer east face of Mount Constance. As the path rises higher through the folds and rises of the ridgetop, the craggy summits surrounding Buckhorn Mountain can be seen to the north. After crossing the crest of the ridge, the trail passes several grassy sinks where water seeps down through chinks in the bedrock and leaves a dry depression in the hilltop. It then winds onto a spur ridge clothed sparsely in subalpine fir and carpeted with a vigorous growth of huckleberry bushes. From this spot the traveler can get a clear view to the south and east, featuring the lone massif of The Brothers and the more distant peaks surrounding Mount Skokomish. Mount Jupiter rises to a much lower peak straight across the Dosewallips Valley.

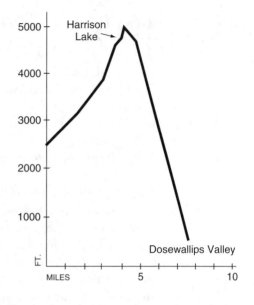

The trail descends sharply from the heath-fir community of the ridgetop into the montane forest below. Pacific rhododendrons abound in the understory, enlivening the woods with their enormous pink blossoms in mid-July. The foot-pounding pace abates a bit as the path approaches its crossing of Gamm Creek. A steep washout just before the stream may provide treacherous footing. The trail passes beneath the braided cascades of the creek, then continues to sidehill eastward at a level grade for a short distance. It then resumes its brutal descent, diving steeply down the remaining slope to reach the floor of the Dosewallips Valley. Here it meets Dosewallips Road 100 yards west of a large parking area.

Key Points

0.0 Tunnel Creek trailhead. Trail enters Buckhorn Wilderness.

2.7 Tunnel Creek camp.

2.9 Trail crosses Tunnel Creek.

3.9 Harrison Lake.

4.3 Tunnel Creek-Dosewallips divide.

7.5 Trail leaves Buckhorn Wilderness.

7.7 Dosewallips Road.

Additional Trails

The **Three Forks cutoff trail** descends for 4.4 miles from the Deer Park auto campground to the Three Forks shelter, which is near the intersection of the Gray Wolf River and Cameron Pass Trails.

The **Elk Mountain cutoff trail** is an extremely steep path that connects Elk Mountain with the Badger Valley.

The **Deer Ridge Trail** connects Deer Park and Slab Camp via a ridgetop route.

The **Slab Camp Trail** descends from Forest Road 2875 down a steady grade to reach the Gray Wolf River Trail at mile 4.9.

The **Mount Zion Trail** rises from the clear-cuts near Bon Jon Pass to reach the top of a summit that stands apart from the rest of the range. There are good displays of rhododendron blossoms in early July and views of Puget Sound and the Cascade Range through the vegetation.

The **Maynard Burn way trail** is an abandoned route up Mount Baldy. It is hard to find early on and is extremely steep throughout.

The **Gold Creek Trail** was built to motorbike standards and has lots of rhododendrons. Horse parties can combine this trail with the Lower Dungeness Trail, which follows clear-cut bottomlands, for a loop trip.

The **Dirtyface Ridge–Little Quilcene Trail** provides an alternate trek to Mount Townsend and is well suited to hiking.

The **Lower Big Quilcene Trail** is a favorite with horseback riders and traverses logged bottomlands.

The Hood Canal Country

An abundance of short rivers penetrates the rugged outer ranges of the Olympic Mountains on their way to Hood Canal. These offer travel corridors into the interior of the park, where a high alpine country of rugged, glacier-clad peaks is interspersed with lush meadows filled with wildflowers. The climate here is a transition between the temperate rain forest of the west and the rainshadow forests

of the northeast. Valley bottoms harbor a lush growth of vegetation, while the nearby slopes may have dry montane forests. Lake Cushman, which lies outside the park on private lands, is a prime attraction of the area. Its close proximity to Seattle translates into weekend crowds when the weather is sunny.

The interior of the region falls within Olympic National Park, while the outer ranges and foothills are managed by the Forest Service. The Mount Skokomish Wilderness is the prime hiking area within Forest Service jurisdiction, although few trails penetrate its interior. A small National Park Service ranger station can be found at Staircase. There are Forest Service campgrounds on the Dosewallips, Duckabush, and Hamma Hamma Rivers, and also at Big and Lilliwaup Creeks. In Olympic National Park there are campgrounds at Staircase and on the Dosewallips River, and the state of Washington maintains heavily developed campgrounds at Dosewallips and Lake Cushman State Parks. Some services and facilities can be found along U.S. Highway 101 in the villages of Hoodsport, Eldon, and Brinnon.

◀ *Staircase Rapids on the North Fork of the Skokomish River*

31 The Dosewallips River

A 12.7-mile backpack from the Dosewallips Ranger Station to Dose Meadows.

Difficulty: Moderate.
Trail type: Secondary.
Best season: Mid-May to mid-October.
Elevation gain: 3,026 feet.
Elevation loss: 176 feet.

Maximum elevation: 4,450 feet (Dose Meadows).
Topo maps: The Brothers, Tyler Peak, Mount Angeles; Custom Correct *Gray Wolf-Dosewallips*.

Finding the trailhead: From mile 306.1 on U.S. Highway 101 in the north part of Brinnon, turn west onto Dosewallips Road (Forest Road 2610). Drive 15.5 miles to the trailhead at road's end. Recently, Dosewallips Road was washed out at Gamm Creek, about 3 miles short of the trailhead. Check at a ranger station for current conditions.

The Hike

This trail is a major access corridor for the eastern Olympics. Along its gentle ascent to Dose Meadows are junctions with the Constance Pass, Anderson Pass, and Gray Wolf River Trails. At its terminus it is joined by the Hayden Pass and Cameron Pass routes. The valley is broad and U-shaped, with tawny summits lining either side that become visible when the forest peters out about halfway up the Dosewallips (pronounced "doh-see-WAHL-ips") River.

The trek begins by climbing the hillside behind the Dosewallips Ranger Station. The Dose Terrace Trail soon loops away to the left, running along the riverbank only to return to the main trail 0.4 mile farther on. Meanwhile the Dosewallips Trail climbs through a mature forest of tall, slender hemlocks and Douglas firs. After crossing Pass Creek the climbing eases, and the surrounding ridges can be seen through gaps in the thinning canopy. The trail crosses a second woodland stream before reaching a major junction. The trail that runs to the Dose Forks camping area and on to Anderson Pass drops down to the left, while the Dosewallips Trail ascends to the right.

The track climbs rather vigorously through the dry forest high above the forks of the rivers. An overlook offers rather limited views down the valley; Mount Constance can be glimpsed through the treetops. The trail follows the valley of the Dosewallips River as it makes a bend to the northwest. Soon after this bend is a junction with the Constance Pass Trail, after which the main route levels off considerably. The trees become sparser beyond the junction, allowing a vigorous growth of Pacific rhododendron to thrive amid the Douglas firs. A ragged crest of Diamond Mountain can barely be seen above the curve of its forested shoulders. There are several significant ups and downs as the trail crosses the Twin Creeks. Lower Twin Creek pours through a mossy

An Olympic marmot in Dose Meadows below Mount Fromme

bed amid a gloomy growth of conifers. Upper Twin Creek showcases Calypso Falls, a delicate streamer of water that drops onto mossy boulders overhung by a handful of red alders. The hiker's trail passes below the foot of the cascade; horse parties can dismount and take a 50-yard detour for a better view.

Beyond Upper Twin Creek a dense stand of young conifers closes around the trail and blocks sunlight from reaching the forest floor. Only mosses can make a living in this light-deprived environment, and they grow abundantly here. At mile 5.1 a trail sign marks the spot where a break in the canopy allows a glimpse of Hatana Falls as it tumbles through a cleft in Diamond Mountain. Beyond Burdick Creek the steep hillsides give way to a series of flat benches forested with widely spaced conifers. The trees, mostly Douglas fir, are much older than the previous stand. A vigorous growth of huckleberry and blueberry bushes chokes the understory.

The path climbs briskly for some distance, then levels off again as the terraces come to an end. In an opening created by numerous blowdowns, the tip of Wellesley Peak makes its first appearance. The trail then passes through heavy timber above a roaring waterfall that is obscured by the trees. Soon after, the rushing torrent of Deception Creek tumbles down from the Deception Basin, a lofty and hidden bowl surrounded by Mounts Mystery, Deception, and Fricaba. There are several camping spots along the stream and on the alluvial bench above its north bank.

Beyond the camp the trail continues to maintain its height above the river. There is a second camp on a forested terrace 0.5 mile beyond Deception Creek. A spring

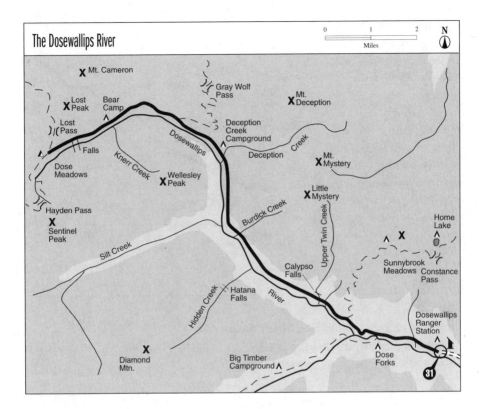

at the base of the slope provides a trickle of water in early summer. The trail passes above the horse camp and begins ascending steadily across this slope. A small stream soon provides an opening with fine views of Wellesley Peak. After traversing some wet forestland, the trail works its way across a series of broad openings filled with rank grasses and forbs. These gaps in the conifers offer an unobstructed view of Wellesley Peak and glimpses of Diamond Mountain to the south. The second such opening bears a signpost where the Gray Wolf Trail descends to the valley floor.

The path soon climbs high into a brushfield to reach the grassy meadow that marks a great bend in the valley. This meadow commands views of Mount Deception, Mount Mystery, and Little Mystery to the east, as well as Mount Fromme rising above the head of the valley. A gentle descent leads back into a forest of silver fir and mountain hemlock as the trail settles into its new southwesterly heading. The next major break in the forest is at Bear Camp, located across from the confluence of Knerr Creek and the Dosewallips. A shelter and campsites occupy a grove of trees between overgrown meadows that allow fine views of Mount Deception and a western bulwark of Wellesley Peak.

The forest then closes around the trail yet again, shading a steep reach of the Dosewallips that is punctuated by small waterfalls. Beyond this pitch the valley levels off again, and avalanche slopes flanked by Alaska cedars let in the sun. At the head of

the valley is Dose Mead-
ows, a grassy expanse that
rests at the foot of Mount
Fromme. A colony of
Olympic marmots thrives
on the greenery provided
by this lush opening.
There are campsites along
the river, while trails to
Hayden Pass and Cam-
eron Pass (see respective
hike descriptions) depart
from a signpost near the
foot of the meadows.

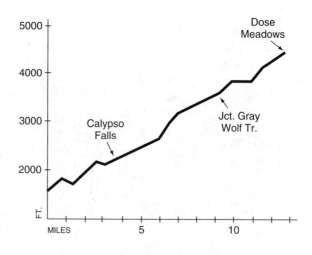

Key Points

0.0 Trailhead.

0.1 First junction with Dosewallips Terrace Trail. Stay right.

0.5 Second junction with Dose Terrace Trail.

1.4 Junction with Anderson Pass Trail. Bear right.

2.5 Junction with Constance Pass Trail. Keep going straight.

3.2 Trail crosses Lower Twin Creek.

3.5 Trail crosses Upper Twin Creek at Calypso Falls.

6.5 Burdick Creek.

7.8 Pack bridge over Deception Creek. Deception Creek Camp.

8.4 Waterless camping spot.

9.3 Junction with Gray Wolf Trail. Stay left.

11.0 Bear Camp.

12.7 Dose Meadows camping area. Junctions with Hayden Pass and Cameron Pass Trails.

32 Anderson Pass

A 10.5-mile backpack from the Dosewallips Ranger Station to Anderson Pass.

Difficulty: Moderately strenuous.
Trail type: Primary.
Best season: Late June to mid-October.
Elevation gain: 3,346 feet.
Elevation loss: 482 feet.

Maximum elevation: 4,464 feet (Anderson Pass).
Topo maps: The Brothers, Mount Steel; Custom Correct *The Brothers–Mount Anderson.*

Finding the trailhead: From mile 306.1 on U.S. Highway 101 in the north part of Brinnon, turn west onto Dosewallips Road (Forest Road 2610). Drive 15.5 miles to the trailhead at road's end. Recently, Dosewallips Road was washed out at Gamm Creek, about 3 miles short of the trailhead. Check at a ranger station for current conditions.

The Hike

This popular hike follows the West Fork of the Dosewallips to Anderson Pass, connecting there with a spur trail to Anderson Glacier as well as the Enchanted Valley Trail. The hike begins by following the Dosewallips River Trail through a lowland forest of western hemlock and Douglas fir. After 1.4 miles the trail reaches a major fork; the left fork is the Anderson Pass Trail, which immediately descends to the Dose Forks Camp. The tent sites are set amid a grove of immense Douglas firs beside the swirling turquoise waters of the Dosewallips. Just beyond the camp is a sturdy bridge to the south bank of the river. Once there, the trail ascends briskly onto forested slopes high above the water. The actual "forks" of the Dosewallips lie 0.6 mile above the camp, and the trail skirts to the edge of a steep bluff to overlook the converging waters of the west and main forks of the Dosewallips River.

A second bridge spans the deep chasm of the West Fork, and the waters churn through a turbulent passage far below it. The trail then climbs steadily through the dry forests above the West Fork. Western hemlocks are underlain by a sparse growth of salal, which thrives under the rather arid conditions of this south-facing slope. After passing opposite the valley of Hungry Creek, the trail finally tops the rise and begins to descend toward Big Timber Camp. Huge boulders and outcrops of bedrock lie beneath a thick second growth of conifers as the path loses altitude. The camp itself is situated in a gloomy grove of old-growth Douglas fir, with the tiny West Fork tumbling as a mossy white water beside it.

Beyond this spot the valley begins to take on a moister aspect, with ferns and devil's club choking the seeps that interrupt the forest. Enormous Douglas firs grow in extensive stands on the better-drained soils. Most of these clean-limbed giants are in the 250- to 300-year class, while some are even older. Silver firs begin to appear along the trail as it approaches Diamond Meadows. Here a campsite occupies a grassy

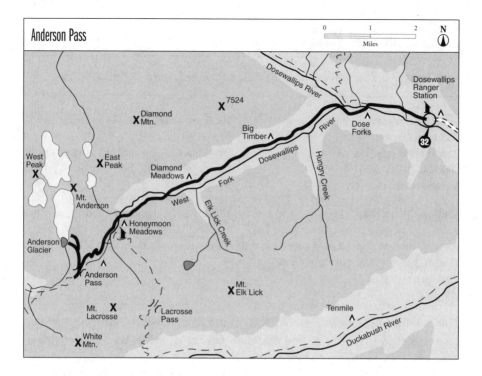

glade surrounded by tall Douglas firs that block out views of the surrounding mountains. Across the river, Elk Lick Creek joins the West Fork of the Dosewallips. This stream is named for a warm springs that has been appropriated by local wildlife as a mineral lick.

Beyond Diamond Meadows the path passes through a flooded woodland before crossing the West Fork with the aid of a footlog. Pause midway in the crossing for an early view of Mount Anderson's East Peak. Openings in the forest are frequent as the trail hugs the south bank of the stream, allowing additional views of East Peak. The summit of Diamond Mountain remains hidden above its bulky lower pediment of rock. The trail ultimately leaves the streamside and climbs vigorously, topping out on a heavily timbered terrace. It weaves among the miniature hillocks of this mature forest for a time, then returns to the stream. The West Fork now tumbles down a steep course strewn with boulders; look for water ouzels that flit among the rocks and dive into the torrent in pursuit of aquatic insects.

The path tracks the turbulent waters up into the flat valley above. Here the chuckling waters form a fitting complement for views of Mount Lacrosse. Honeymoon Meadows Camp lies in a stand of timber on the south bank of the stream; pitch camp here and not in the fragile meadows themselves. At the camp the trail turns north to cross the West Fork, then turns upstream to enter Honeymoon Meadows itself. This gorgeous expanse of grasses and wildflowers derives its name from the nuptial adventures of several couples who visited the area early in the twentieth century. Fine views of the surrounding peaks are highlighted by Mount Lacrosse to the south and the East Peak and Diamond Mountain along the northern rim of the valley.

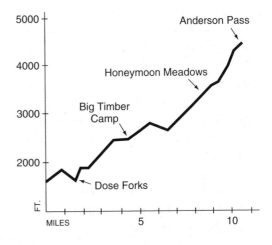

The trail continues west along the stream, passing through stands of fir and dense thickets of willow, to a junction with the Lacrosse Pass Trail. There is a horse camp here that can be used if the Honeymoon Meadows Camp is crowded. The Anderson Pass Trail continues up the valley, mounting a considerable incline as it passes among mature mountain hemlocks. The Anderson Pass camp, also known as Camp Siberia, lies at the top of the grade. The shelter and tent sites are situated just inside a stand of old hemlocks at the edge of an alpine basin. Beyond them the trail ascends steadily for the remaining 0.5 mile. Pause awhile to look around; there are spots along the final ascent that offer fine vistas down the Duckabush Valley as well as an unobstructed view of Mount Lacrosse. The pass itself is screened by trees, but a short jaunt down the Enchanted Valley Trail yields views of the headwaters of the Quinault.

Anderson Glacier Option: A steep track leaves Anderson Pass bound for the high country to the north, gaining 750 vertical feet in 0.8 mile on its way to an overlook of the mighty Anderson Glacier. As it climbs, the path leaves the mountain hemlocks behind and enters an expanse of low-growing spiraea and blueberry bushes. Views open up on all sides, featuring the glacier that is perched high among the spires of White Mountain. Upon cresting a high knoll, the path splits. Straight ahead lies a direct route to the top of the terminal moraine overlooking Anderson Glacier, while a more circuitous path winds around a snowmelt pool and provides access onto the toe of the glacier.

This long river of ice, scored with fissures and crevasses, inches downward year by year as it carves a deep trench into the mountainside. Winter snows build up its head while summer heat erodes its foot, so that the glacier is continually being torn down and made new again. The balance of forces shaping the glacier currently favors the heat, and the glacier appears to be "retreating" over the years, even though it is always moving downhill. Beneath its toe is a large lake fed by meltwater from the ice; its waters are stained gray by suspended particles of finely ground silt (called "glacial flour" or "gletschermilch"). Tread carefully on the terrain surrounding the glacier— pioneering plants that have taken root here live on the razor's edge of survival and are easily killed by disturbance.

Key Points

0.0 Trailhead.

0.1 First junction with Dosewallips Terrace Trail. Stay right.

0.5 Second junction with Dosewallips Terrace Trail.

1.4 Junction with Anderson Pass Trail. Turn left.

1.6 Dose Forks Camp. Trail crosses Dosewallips River.

2.4 Bridge spans West Fork Dosewallips River to reach north bank.

4.2 Big Timber Camp.

6.6 Diamond Meadows camping area.

6.9 Trail crosses West Fork to reach its south bank.

8.6 Honeymoon Meadows Camp. Trail returns to north bank of West Fork.

8.8 Honeymoon Meadows.

9.1 Horse camp. Junction with Lacrosse Pass Trail. Stay right.

9.9 Anderson Pass camping area.

10.5 Anderson Pass.

33 Constance Pass

A 7.9-mile day hike or backpack from the Dosewallips Ranger Station to Home Lake.

Difficulty: Moderately strenuous.
Trail type: Foot.
Best season: Mid-July to mid-October.
Elevation gain: 5,044 feet.

Elevation loss: 1,344 feet.
Maximum elevation: 6,500 feet.
Topo maps: The Brothers, Tyler Peak; Custom Correct *Buckhorn Wilderness.*

Finding the trailhead: From mile 306.1 on U.S. Highway 101 in the north part of Brinnon, turn west onto Dosewallips Road (Forest Road 2610). Drive 15.5 miles to the trailhead at road's end. Recently, Dosewallips Road was washed out at Gamm Creek, about 3 miles short of the trailhead. Check at a ranger station for current conditions.

The Hike

This trail climbs into the verdant bowls of Sunnybrook Meadows, then climbs high onto a ridgecrest before dropping through Constance Pass. Scenery is nothing short of spectacular along the upper portion of the route, featuring the basaltic crags that crowd the eastern rim of the Olympic Mountains. The trail reaches its terminus at Home Lake in the headwaters of the Dungeness River. The Upper Dungeness Trail runs north into the Buckhorn Wilderness from this point.

The trek begins by following the Dosewallips River Trail as it climbs from the lush

The western buttress of Constance Peak towering above Constance Pass

lowland forest near the trailhead to the drier montane stands beyond Dose Forks. The Constance Pass Trail splits away from the Dosewallips Trail some 1.1 miles beyond its junction with the Anderson Pass route. This trail soon begins a stiff climb through the progressively thinning forest. Higher on this south-facing slope, the microclimate becomes drier as Douglas fir and kinnikinnik replace the hemlock-salal community found on the lower slopes. The wrinkled bedrock dome that rises above the forested ridgetops across the valley is an eastern buttress of Mount Elk Lick. Its summit will be unveiled in all its glory farther up the trail. After 2.8 miles of climbing, the trail arrives at an overlook atop the ridgeline. The upper valley of the Dosewallips can be viewed through the rhododendrons, and the tilted ridges surrounding Gray Wolf Pass rise above it. A dependable spring flows from the forest floor east of the trail, providing an isolated water source in the midst of dry slopes. Mountain hemlocks soon close ranks about the trail, offering welcome shade as the trail continues upward at a steady pace.

The track works its way into a steep side valley and then breaks out onto an open slope. An old forest fire has long since cleared away the timber, and water-loving grasses and forbs now occupy the seep-saturated slope. Look to the southeast for an early view of The Brothers. The trail bends around the narrow valley that bears Sunny Brook, crossing numerous rivulets and then continuing the ascent onto a set of level terraces beyond it. Here the flower-strewn expanses of Sunnybrook Meadows occupy

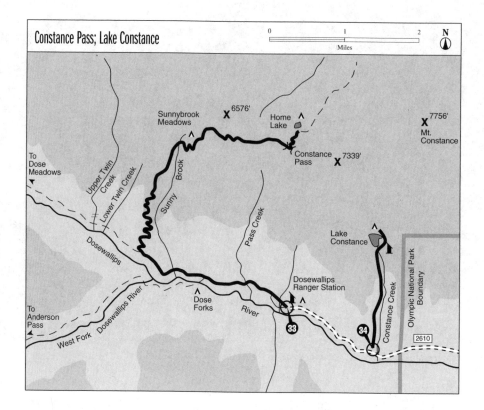

0   1   2   **N**

Miles

a rolling country of knobs and vales. There are no hardened campsites here; use zero-impact techniques while pitching camp on the grassy hillocks that rise beyond a collection of shallow meltwater ponds. A tiny rivulet crosses the hillside above the camp, providing a source of fresh water. The meadows command spectacular vistas to the south and west. Mount Elk Lick, Mount Lacrosse, and White Mountain rise to the southwest beyond the West Fork of the Dosewallips. Far to the west, the peaks of Mount Anderson hide behind the rugged mass of Diamond Mountain.

The trail soon mounts the hillside above the Sunnybrook Meadows camp, alternating between barren slopes of gravel and swards of alpine tundra. The mountainside is pocked with the tunnels and mounds excavated by Olympic marmots; watch for these rotund balls of animated fur as they forage and stand sentinel against predators. Views continue to expand until the trail crests a high, grassy ridgetop that commands a spectacular panorama of the major Olympic peaks. Mount Constance and Warrior Peak dominate the scene, their stark pillars of basalt soaring naked into the sky. In the opposite direction, the cliffy cockscomb of Little Mystery rises to the south of the taller horns of Mount Mystery and Mount Deception. Mounts Olympus, Anderson, Skokomish, and The Brothers round out the roll of dominant peaks that rise above the countless ridges and basins of the Olympic Mountains.

A short scramble to the top of the hill ends at a stonework observation post that provides protection from the wind. Winds are a dominant force in the shaping of these alpine plant communities. The stouter firs that send their leaders above the snowline have their windward branches shorn away by the winter blasts. Windblown snow abrades away the growing points of the less fortunate trees; the result is a ground-hugging shrub form called krummholz. The warm winds of summer desiccate these high slopes, drawing off the already scant moisture deposited here by snowmelt. Only the hardiest of alpine plants can grow in the extremes of this environment, achieving most of their annual growth in the few weeks following snowmelt.

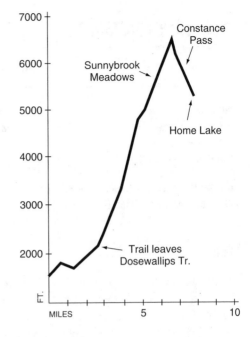

Having crested the heights of the ridgetop, the trail turns east and dives headlong down the ridgeline. The path makes a faint and rugged trace among meadows, bare gravel, and windblown firs. The low saddle in this ridge is Constance Pass, which looks out onto the barren ranges that loom above the upper Dungeness Valley. The trail turns north here, dropping across a barren bowl before zigzagging downward across wet meadows to reach Home Lake. This small tarn occupies a rather desolate basin that boasts views of the western buttress of Mount Constance as well as Warrior Peak. There is a scattering of primitive tent sites along its shore, and the Upper Dungeness Trail runs north from this point toward the Boulder shelter.

Key Points

0.0 Trailhead.

0.1 First junction with Dosewallips Terrace Trail. Stay right.

0.5 Second junction with Dosewallips Terrace Trail.

1.4 Junction with Anderson Pass Trail. Bear right.

2.5 Junction with Constance Pass Trail. Turn right to begin the ascent.

5.1 Trail crosses headwaters of Sunny Brook.

5.9 Sunnybrook Meadows camping area.

6.7 Top of grade. Trail starts descending.

7.4 Constance Pass.

7.9 Home Lake.

34 Lake Constance

A 2.2-mile wilderness route to Lake Constance. (See map on page 130.)

Difficulty: Strenuous.
Trail type: Primitive.
Best season: Early June to mid-October.
Elevation gain: 3,300 feet.

Maximum elevation: 4,750 feet.
Topo maps: The Brothers, Tyler Peak; Custom Correct *Buckhorn Wilderness.*

Finding the trailhead: From mile 306.1 on U.S. Highway 101 in the north part of Brinnon, turn west onto Dosewallips Road (Forest Road 2610). Drive 14 miles to the trailhead. The trail begins from a hard-to-see trail sign beside the cascade of Constance Creek.

The Hike

This "trail" is little more than a climbing route and is typified by brutal uphill pitches choked with roots and exposed boulders. Surfaces are often slippery when wet, and the route should not be attempted during rainy weather. There are campsites on the north shore of the lake that require reservations, but only a mountaineer would be crazy enough to haul a full pack up this grade. Camping is restricted to a limited number of permits, which are issued at the Dosewallips Ranger Station.

From the trailhead the route wastes no time in heading straight up the steep mountainside. It makes its way up among mature hemlocks that spread networks of exposed roots across the boulders and bedrock. Constance Creek soon disappears, leaving a stony bed beneath which the waters seek an underground passage. House-size boulders litter the forest floor. After 0.8 mile the path levels off, and the splashing of the stream can be heard once more.

The respite is brief, however, as the trail enters a narrow valley choked with brush. The trail plunges relentlessly up the cleft, following the streambank. Take a backward glance early in this pitch for a fine view of The Brothers. Upon reaching an impassable scarp of bedrock, the trail turns west to climb straight up the valley wall. Some scrambling skill is useful here as the path ascends along chinks in the basalt; travelers should keep three of their four limbs solidly on the rock at all times.

After a long and grueling ascent, the traveler arrives at the foot of Lake Constance. At this point the hiker is rewarded with dazzling views of the sheer spires of basalt that soar skyward above the turquoise waters of the lake. The main mass of Mount Constance rises above the eastern shore of the lake, while the rugged

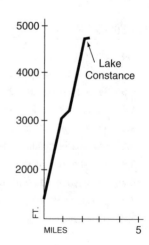

peak above its head to the west is known to climbers as "Inner Constance." Brook trout cruise the depths, and mountain goats are frequently seen from the lakeshore. A few small tent pads occupy a stand of fir on the north shore of the lake; camping is prohibited elsewhere. Because of heavy human impacts around the lakeshore, visitors should stay on the designated trail and avoid areas marked for revegetation.

Key Points

0.0 Trailhead.

2.0 Foot of Lake Constance.

2.2 Camping area, head of lake.

35 Lacrosse Pass

A 6.4-mile trip from the West Fork of the Dosewallips to the Duckabush River.

Difficulty: Moderately strenuous.
Trail type: Secondary.
Best season: Mid-July to mid-October.
Elevation gain: 1,939 feet.

Elevation loss: 2,889 feet.
Maximum elevation: 5,566 feet.
Topo maps: Mount Steel; Custom Correct *The Brothers–Mount Anderson.*

Finding the trailhead: The trail begins at a marked junction at mile 9.1 on the Anderson Pass Trail (see the Anderson Pass hike). To reach the Anderson Pass trailhead, turn west onto Dosewallips Road (Forest Road 2610) from mile 306.1 on U.S. Highway 101 in the north part of Brinnon. Drive 15.5 miles to the trailhead at road's end. Recently, Dosewallips Road was washed out at Gamm Creek, about 3 miles short of the trailhead. Check at a ranger station for current conditions. In any case, follow the Anderson Pass Trail description to mile 9.1 where this hike begins.

The Hike

This trail links the West Fork Dosewallips and Duckabush Valleys and is a popular component for loop trips that encompass O'Neil and Anderson Passes. Although the trail gradient is no steeper on the south side of Lacrosse Pass, the elevation gain is almost twice as great. With the complete lack of water on the southern slope factored into the equation, it is easy to see why most hikers prefer to approach the route from the north.

This trail leaves the Anderson Pass Trail in a willow-choked opening, 0.3 mile west of Honeymoon Meadows. There is a horse camp at this junction, which offers additional campsites when the Honeymoon Meadows camp is full. The trail follows the West Fork of the Dosewallips downstream for a short distance, then crosses it and climbs into the forested hills. It ascends steadily through mature mountain hemlocks for about a mile, then shoots southward as the gradient becomes gentler. The forest

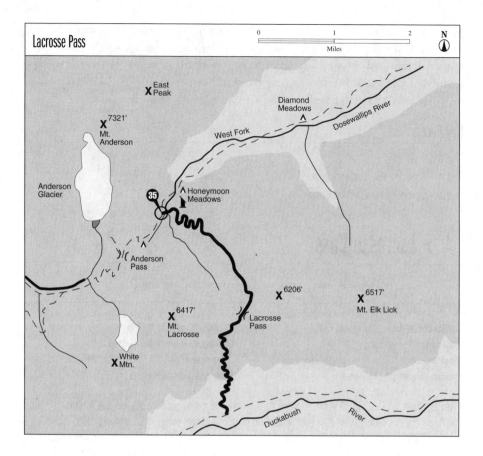

is soon replaced by meadows of tall grass, offering unobstructed views of Mount Lacrosse on the far side of a rounded basin. Later the folded and compressed sandstone strata of Mount Anderson rise to sharp spires in the north. Watch for marmots, bears, and elk as the trail climbs high above an open cirque then skirts the bases of bleached pinnacles. These outcrops shelter snow catchment basins; sometimes water is available here.

Lacrosse Pass is no more than a notch in the spine of rock that links Mount Lacrosse with Mount Elk Lick; it offers little in the way of scenic vistas. After a brief descent, however, flowery meadows offer a sweeping panorama of the northern peaks in the Mount Skokomish group. Skokomish itself hides behind Mount Hopper, while the reeflike wall of Mount Stone protrudes to the east of it, crowned by needlelike spires. Farther west, Mounts Steel and Duckabush hulk above the head of the Duckabush Valley. To the east is Lena Peak and beyond it the sharp point of Mount Bretherton. The trail descends through the meadows, pocked with shapely stands of subalpine fir and filled with low-bush blueberries. The fruit ripen in mid-August, providing a connoisseur's smorgasbord that is attended by black bears and many species of birds. The solitary peaks of The Brothers become visible far to the east as the path continues downward.

Within a mile beyond the pass, the trees close ranks and cloak the trail in a subalpine forest. Views of the mountains are now restricted to small, windowlike openings in the canopy. It is interesting to track the life zones that the trail crosses as it loses elevation. Subalpine forest of mountain hemlock and huckleberry is soon replaced by a montane stand with no understory. Salal begins to intrude lower down, and the dominant conifers are Douglas fir and mountain hemlock. Near the bottom of the grade is a wet-ter lowland forest of silver fir and hemlock; ferns, devil's club, and vine maple form a rich understory. The path reaches its end on a dry riverside terrace, where old-growth hemlocks rise above its junction with the Duckabush Trail.

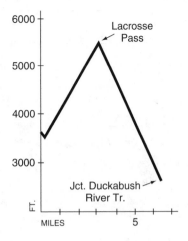

Key Points

0.0 Junction with Anderson Pass Trail. Horse camp.

3.1 Lacrosse Pass.

6.4 Trail joins Duckabush Trail.

36 Jupiter Ridge

A 7.1-mile day hike to the summit of Mount Jupiter.

Difficulty: Moderately strenuous.
Trail type: Foot.
Best season: Mid-June to mid-October.
Elevation gain: 4,000 feet.

Elevation loss: 350 feet.
Maximum elevation: 5,701 feet.
Topo maps: Mount Jupiter, Brinnon; Custom Correct *The Brothers–Mount Anderson*.

Finding the trailhead: From Brinnon, drive north on U.S. Highway 101 to mile 309.5 (across from the small bulldozer on the tall stump). Turn west onto Mount Jupiter Road. Stay on the widest road through confusing forks, following signs where available. Bear left at two forks of equal magnitude as the road gains altitude and narrows. The trailhead is 6 miles from the highway.

The Hike

This trail follows a high ridgetop into The Brothers Wilderness, arriving at an old lookout site that commands excellent views of the eastern Olympics. It is the only

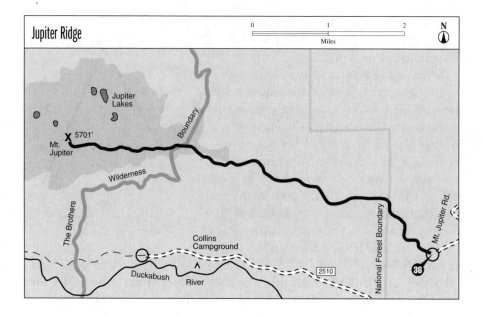

relatively level trek in the southeastern part of the range that visits the high country. There is no surface water along the route, so be sure to bring a plentiful supply for drinking. The road to the trailhead runs across Weyerhauser timberland, and a gate along the way may be locked, barring public access. Before driving up here, call the Quilcene Ranger District to ask about the status of this gate and to encourage the Forest Service to keep this access route open to the public.

The trail begins by zigzagging upward at a steady clip, passing through a forest of spindly Douglas firs. The path soon levels off as it turns west along the ridgeline. The trees become a bit sparser here, and a vigorous growth of salal and Pacific rhododendron chokes the understory. After 2.1 miles the trail reaches a tiny campsite on a rocky spur; there is, of course, no water available. As the path continues its level westward trek, openings in the canopy allow early views of The Brothers and Mount Jupiter.

After dropping onto the Dosewallips side of the ridge, the trail begins a long and shallow descent through a rather dense stand of young conifers. Just before the bottom of the grade is a second campsite carpeted with a soft layer of duff. After the path climbs over the next high point, exposed knobs of bedrock begin to protrude from the ridgetop. At mile 3.9 a spur path leads to an overlook of the Dosewallips Valley. A checkerboard of clear-cuts covers the sharp walls near its mouth, and the tip of Mount Constance peeks out above the next fold in Jupiter Ridge. A short distance farther, an exposed finger of bedrock juts out over the Duckabush Valley. The twin summits of The Brothers can be plainly seen here. They were named for Arthur and Edward Fauntleroy, whose sisters, Ellinor and Constance, also have peaks named in their honor. This overlook spot makes a good destination for hikers who are looking for a shorter trip.

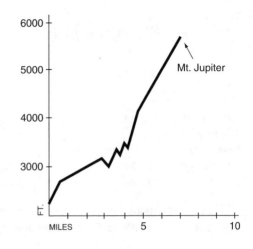

The trail drops into the next saddle and then begins climbing heartily as it enters The Brothers Wilderness. Upon emerging from the timber into a vigorous heath-beargrass community, the path works its way onto the south face of the ridge and thus avoids the first towering outcrops of Mount Jupiter. It soon begins to switchback upward, bound for the first of many false summits that raise the hopes of hikers only to dash them upon revealing a still-higher peak. The trail works its way among the broken slabs and fingerlike pinnacles of basalt. These display the pillow formation that bespeaks their undersea origins. The grade steepens somewhat as the path, often chiseled into the rock itself, makes its final ascent toward the summit of Mount Jupiter.

The trail reaches its terminus at an old fire lookout site atop the peak. A crude path runs onto the spur of rock to the north, allowing a fine view of the deep blue Jupiter Lakes, set in a flat basin corrugated with bedrock. The views from the summit are sweeping: The islands and channels of Puget Sound are spread in a watery tableau to the east, with the regal summit of Mount Rainier rising in solitary majesty beyond them. The Brothers seem but a stone's throw away to the south and are flanked by the more distant Mount Washington and Mount Skokomish. Mounts Duckabush and Anderson rise above the ridges to the west, and to the north Mount Constance dominates the scene with its reddish crest of basalt.

Key Points

0.0 Trailhead.

3.9 Spur path to Dosewallips overlook.

4.2 Duckabush overlook.

7.1 Summit of Mount Jupiter.

37 The Duckabush River

A 21.1-mile backpack from Forest Road 2510 to Marmot Lake.

Difficulty: Moderately strenuous.
Trail type: Secondary.
Best season: Late May to mid-October.
Elevation gain: 5,000 feet.
Elevation loss: 1,067 feet.

Maximum elevation: 4,300 feet (Marmot Lake).
Topo maps: Mount Jupiter, The Brothers, Mount Steel; Custom Correct *The Brothers–Mount Anderson.*

Finding the trailhead: From Brinnon, drive north on U.S. Highway 101 to mile 310. Turn west onto Duckabush Road (FR 2510) and drive 6 miles to the marked trailhead.

The Hike

The Duckabush River follows a long and remote valley deep into the heart of the southeastern Olympics. Its lower reaches flow through The Brothers Wilderness, and the upper part of the valley lies within Olympic National Park. Near the headwaters there is a collection of beautiful alpine lakes in a meadowy expanse that is critical summer range for small bands of Roosevelt elk. The upper end of the drainage offers connecting routes into the Quinault, North Fork Skokomish, and West Fork Dose-wallips basins.

The trail begins on an old road grade that climbs steadily through the forest to reach the top of Little Hump. It enters The Brothers Wilderness here, then constricts into a narrow path as it descends onto the flats that border the north bank of the Duckabush. The forest that occupies these floodplains is the lowest-elevation plant community in the eastern Olympics to be protected from logging, and it displays an astonishing diversity of species. Silver fir, Douglas fir, and red cedar mix freely with such hardwoods as bigleaf maple and red alder. Rain forest understory plants such as sword fern and vine maple can be found in close proximity with shrubs like kinnickinnick and salal that prefer more arid soils. The trail swings close to the water's edge, then crosses a series of gravel washes to reach the base of Big Hump.

The trail turns inland here to begin the long and grueling climb of this unusual terrain feature. The trail snakes northward through the forest, then steepens into a series of tight hairpins that drive relentlessly up the hillside. There are several openings during the course of the climb that allow views of the Duckabush Valley. The best view is from a dome of bedrock high on the shoulder of Big Hump, which faces the craggy buttresses of St. Peter's Dome. The trail continues upward for a short time, then begins a long and foot-pounding descent through a dense second-growth of Douglas fir and hemlock.

At the bottom of the grade, a rather steep spur path drops to the riverside tent sites of Fivemile Camp, which is set amid tall red cedars and Douglas firs. A handful

Mount Duckabush rising beyond Lake Lacrosse

of campsites are available 0.2 mile farther on, just over the next hill. Here the clear waters of the Duckabush swirl lazily through a boulder-strewn course. The trail passes the foot of a talus slope and then reaches the base of an enormous outcrop of metamorphic rock. At the foot of this outcrop, a short spur track runs to a rocky overlook at the water's edge. The Duckabush, fresh from a tumultuous passage through the rocky cleft, pours into a deep and quiet pool where small trout can be seen finning in the turquoise depths.

The trail then surmounts the rocky obstacle, with its wall of rock soaring 100 feet overhead and a mossy, rounded face sloping away to the river below. Upon returning to the bottomlands, the trail follows the river, which slides lazily amid bars of bleached cobbles. The silence of the forest contributes a general ambience of tranquility to the scene. The forest becomes quite brushy some distance beyond the park boundary, and this condition persists all the way to Tenmile Camp. The spacious tent sites are set in a grove of lofty, widely spaced Douglas firs at a sharp bend in the Duckabush.

Beyond this spot the trail continues to climb moderately through the forest, sticking close to the river. At mile 11.5 there is an overlook spot above a roaring falls in the river. The bluish stratum of phyllite that produced the waterfall is exposed here; note the direction of its tilt. After climbing high onto the hillside to avoid a washout, the trail returns to the riverbank. A spur trail runs to an overlook of the river's confluence with Crazy Creek, which joins the flow with a picturesque little waterfall. There are

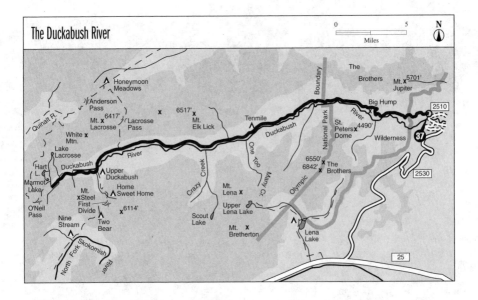

several tent sites here for travelers who cannot make it to Upper Duckabush Camp. The main trail follows the lip of a rocky gorge, then soars upward through an eerily silent stand of Douglas fir and red cedar. The path soon levels off, crossing several alder-choked streams that descend from the slopes of Mount Elk Lick. The forest found here is a hodgepodge of widely different habitats: Hoary alders grow in moist openings, red cedars rise in dense groves around seeps and streams, and Douglas fir and hemlock stands of varying ages occupy the well-drained slopes.

The path soon rises to meet the Lacrosse Pass Trail, then drops a bit as it continues its journey through the forest. At mile 16.9 the forest is interrupted by an opening studded with the snags of dead silver firs. After crossing this barren spot, the trail follows lush avenues through a forest of enormous Douglas firs. These natural openings, 100 feet wide and filled with ferns and underbrush, are in fact old flood channels that the river has abandoned. The path soon reaches the first of several braided channels that bear the flow of the Duckabush. A knee-deep ford in June, a rock hop in August, this ford deposits the traveler at Upper Duckabush Camp. Here a breezy stand of tall hemlocks and spruces shelter a number of pleasant tent sites. A short distance beyond the camp is a junction with the North Fork Skokomish Trail.

The main trail then makes a footlog crossing of a major feeder stream and continues the gradual ascent along the south bank of the Duckabush. Brushy avalanche slopes make frequent interruptions in the forest during the next 2 miles; several of them feature streams that tumble from the flanks of Mount Steel in breathtaking cascades. Just after crossing the first such stream, the trail climbs vigorously to reach a forest opening that faces down the Duckabush Valley. The trail soon makes a second ford of the Duckabush and then climbs along the far bank for a short time.

Before long the trail begins the climb to Marmot Lake, zigzagging upward

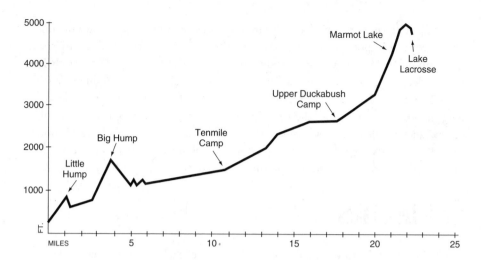

through open slopes of slide alder and groves of Alaska cedar. The openings allow increasingly spectacular views of Mount Steel and Mount Duckabush, a pair of towering crags that guard the head of the valley. The path crests a rise and crosses the outlet stream of Marmot Lake, then arrives at a junction on the lakeshore. Marmot Lake is cupped in a shallow basin and is surrounded by alpine meadows. Clumps of mountain hemlock, Alaska cedar, and subalpine fir grow from rocky knolls surrounding the lake and from the single island in its center. Campsites are scattered around the south shore, and a ranger tent lies just east of the lake. A spur trail runs northeast from the junction toward the upper lakes, while the O'Neil Pass Trail runs west beside the greenish waters.

Key Points

0.0 Trailhead.

1.1 Top of Little Hump. The Brothers Wilderness boundary.

4.0 Top of Big Hump.

5.1 Spur path to Fivemile Camp.

6.7 Trail enters Olympic National Park.

10.7 Tenmile Camp.

16.0 Junction with Lacrosse Pass Trail. Keep going straight.

17.5 Trail fords Duckabush River to reach south bank.

17.6 Upper Duckabush Camp.

17.7 Ford of nameless creek.

19.8 Trail fords Duckabush to reach north bank.

21.1 Marmot Lake. Junction with O'Neil Pass Trail.

Upper Lakes Option: A rough trail climbs onto the alpine shelves above Marmot Lake, giving access to Hart Lake and Lake Lacrosse. It climbs aggressively for 0.5 mile to reach a trail junction amid a rocky moorland clothed in heather and punctuated by outcrops. This spot commands a fine view down the Duckabush Valley, with snow-clad summits rising all around it. A spur path runs level for 0.3 mile to reach Hart Lake, a deep blue tarn six times as large as Marmot Lake and surrounded by rocky walls. The trail to Lake Lacrosse runs 0.8 mile due north from the intersection, dropping slightly as it approaches the lake. This elongated, shallow pool rests on the floor of a meadowy vale that is overlooked by the western buttresses of White Mountain. Both lakes offer outstanding views of Mount Steel and Mount Duckabush, whose massive crowns tower majestically on the far side of the Duckabush basin.

38 Lena Lakes

A 3.3-mile day hike to Lena Lake, or a 6.9-mile backpack to Upper Lena Lake.

Difficulty: Moderate to Lena Lake; strenuous to Upper Lena Lake.
Trail type: Foot/bike to Lena Lake; foot to Upper Lena.
Best season: Early July to mid-October.

Elevation gain: 3,965 feet.
Elevation loss: 150 feet.
Maximum elevation: 4,500 feet.
Topo maps: The Brothers, Mount Washington; Custom Correct *The Brothers–Mount Anderson.*

Finding the trailhead: From Quilcene, drive south on U.S. Highway 101 to mile 318. Turn west onto Hamma Hamma Road (Forest Road 25) and drive 8 miles to the trailhead.

The Hike

This trail is a wide and easy track as far as the lower lake, but then it turns into a steep and rough track upon entering the park. Upper Lena is by far the more scenic of the two lakes, and its alpine setting is dominated by the rugged peaks of Mount Bretherton. The path to it is very steep and has an unstable bed; it is not recommended in wet weather.

The trail begins by zigzagging lazily upward from the floor of the Hamma Hamma Valley. A lowland forest of Douglas fir, Sitka spruce, and bigleaf maple filters the sunlight. The path soon turns north, following the hillside high above Lena Creek. There is a well-built footbridge over the streambed at mile 1.9. Water flows here, but only on the surface during spring runoff and in wet weather. For much of the summer the water runs unseen through underground passageways. After another 0.8 mile the trail passes above the foot of Lena Lake, but the water lies far below the trail and cannot be seen through the timber.

As the trail nears the head of the lake, a heavily traveled path leads to a rocky overlook of this large lowland pool. A rockslide dammed the exit centuries ago, and water flows from the lake through subterranean gaps in the old rubble. There are 23 campsites scattered around the head of the lake, each with its own built-in fire ring.

Upper Lena Lake and Mount Bretherton

The Brothers Trail bears north from the head of the lake, bound up the East Fork of Lena Creek to a climber's base camp.

From the junction above the lake, the much smaller path to Upper Lena Lake splits away to the left and begins to climb at a moderate clip. The valley soon bends westward as the trail follows the chattering waters of Lena Creek. This moist, north-facing slope is covered in a dark forest populated by deer fern and dwarf raspberry, with mosses covering all other surfaces. A registration station marks the national park boundary, and the valley levels off into a broad basin. An avalanche slope graces an eastern spur of Mount Lena, and the recurrent snowslides have also cleared the valley floor. The resulting opening has been invaded by an impenetrable mass of willow and slide alder, whose supple limbs bend with the force of the tumbling snow.

The trail then crosses a substantial tributary stream and begins to climb the imposing headwall of the basin. The track soars upward at a killing pace, crossing tangled roots and brushy slopes, scaling boulder-choked chutes, and traversing treacherous outcrops of bedrock. When the summit is finally attained, the path levels off and enters a gladed vale. This is not the end of the climbing, but rather a brief respite before the final pitch. The trail soon zigzags even more steeply up the north wall of the valley, avoiding a frontal assault on the next headwall. The gradient is greater, but the trail bed is in better shape and so the traveling seems easier. After working its way up through meadowy slopes, the trail levels off and runs west across an open expanse that offers fine views of Mount Bretherton.

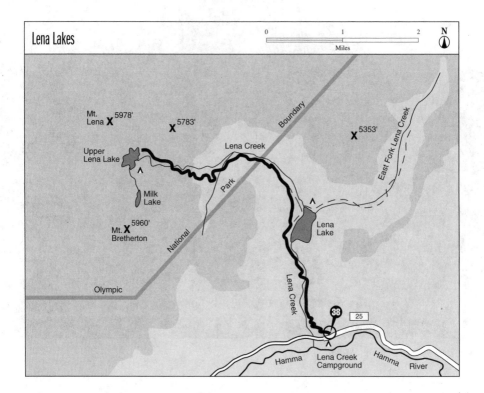

An easy grade leads to an intersection above the foot of Upper Lena Lake, and a map posted here shows the locations of the designated campsites. Heavy use has led to damage on this fragile subalpine lakeshore; be sure to avoid spots where restoration efforts are being pursued. This stunning alpine tarn fills the basin between Mount Lena and the pinnacles of Mount Bretherton. Flower-studded meadows are punctuated by stately copses of subalpine fir along the lakeshore. Several rocky peninsulas extend into the blue-green water, providing the growing space for miniature conifers. The low divide at the head of the lake leads to the Boulder Creek drainage and provides a popular access route for cross-country explorations.

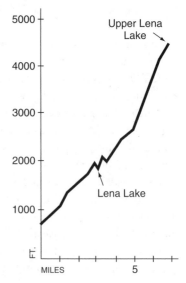

Key Points

0.0 Trailhead.

3.0 Junction with trail to Lena Lake and The Brothers. Turn left for Upper Lena Lake.

4.2 Olympic National Park boundary and registration station.

6.9 Upper Lena Lake.

39 Mildred Lakes

A 4.4-mile wilderness route from Forest Road 25 to the Mildred Lakes.

Difficulty: Strenuous.
Trail type: Primitive.
Best season: Early July to mid-October.
Elevation gain: 2,500 feet.

Elevation loss: 400 feet.
Maximum elevation: 4,150 feet.
Topo maps: Mount Steel; Custom Correct *Mount Skokomish–Lake Cushman.*

Finding the trailhead: From Quilcene, drive south on U.S. Highway 101 to mile 318. Turn west onto Hamma Hamma Road (FR 25) and drive 14.1 miles to the trailhead at road's end.

The Hike

This route is not a designed trail but rather a track worn into the mountains by the passage of countless hikers. It is extremely steep, and some climbing ability will be required at several points along the route. Check the weather report before going; if there is a possibility of rain, choose another hike. This unstable trail bed becomes quite slippery in wet weather.

The trek begins in a second-growth stand of Douglas fir; the original forest was logged off. The path is choked with boulders and tree roots from the very beginning and only gets worse as it proceeds. There are several brushy openings in the trees, and beyond the second of these lies the virgin forest. It consists principally of silver fir and western hemlock, with a few old Douglas firs overtopping them all. A tangled web of roots forms the trail bed here, looking to snare the foot of an unwary traveler. The path soon arrives at a steep pitch covered with boulders. The climb is brief, though, and rewards the hiker by landing on an open overlook. There are fine views of the surrounding mountains from this point, highlighted by the rugged crag of Mount Pershing rising sheer to the south.

The route then turns southwest, descending steadily through an open stand of mountain hemlock. It bottoms out beside a substantial stream, and here the route becomes a bit vague. Follow the streambank upward for about 50 yards to reach a footlog, and after crossing bear west through downed timber. A hundred yards of traveling brings the hiker to a second stream crossing, and the path becomes distinct again on its far bank. The route then begins ascending the hill on the far side of the valley and soon reaches a steep-walled ravine. A tricky crossing of this gulch marks the beginning of the second (and much steeper) grade. Hikers will scramble straight uphill amid giant hemlocks, whose roots form handholds and footholds for the ascent.

The forest thins out at the top, and the hill is revealed to be an enormous scarp of tilted sandstone. Its summit reveals the first views of Mount Cruiser and the other peaks that surround the basin. A hemlock-heath community offers heather blossoms

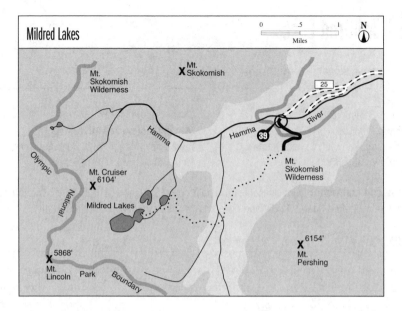

Mildred Lakes

in midsummer and huckleberries in early fall. The trail then descends past a number of shallow ponds. It turns west at the bottom of the grade and soon reaches the foot of the easternmost of the Mildred Lakes. This teardrop-shaped pool of 6.5 acres is hemmed in by a dense forest of hemlock and contains a vigorous population of smallish rainbow trout. Although the parent rock of the basin is sandstone, a number of house-size boulders of pillow basalt are scattered about the lakeshore. These are glacial erratics, carried down from the heights of Mount Cruiser in past millennia by the flowing ice.

The route to the upper lake follows the east shore of this tarn, rounding its head and crossing the inlet stream on the south shore. Here it turns inland, following the streamcourse for a time before climbing out of the forest into an open heath parkland punctuated by sandstone outcrops and small ponds. The route runs fairly level as it heads southwest to the foot of the uppermost of the Mildred Lakes. This giant reflecting pool is six times larger than the previous lake, making it the largest alpine lake in the Olympics. It sits at the base of Mount Cruiser in an open parkland of mountain hemlocks. It shares a common shape with the eastern lake and is likewise inhabited by rainbow trout. A third lake, lying to the northeast, boasts both rainbow and cutthroat trout.

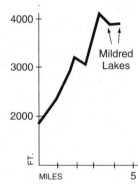

Key Points

0.0 Trailhead. Trail enters Mount Skokomish Wilderness.

1.8 Top of first grade.

2.5 Trail fords two major streams.

3.2 Top of second grade.

3.7 Foot of easternmost of Mildred Lakes.

4.0 Trail leaves easternmost of Mildred Lakes.

4.4 Uppermost of the Mildred Lakes.

40 Mount Ellinor

A 1.7-mile day hike to the summit of Mount Ellinor.

Difficulty: Strenuous.
Trail type: Foot.
Best season: Early July to mid-October.
Elevation gain: 2,424 feet.

Maximum elevation: 5,944 feet.
Topo maps: Mount Washington, Mount Steel; Custom Correct *Mount Skokomish–Lake Cushman.*

Finding the trailhead: From Eldon, drive south on U.S. Highway 101 to mile 321.3. Turn west onto Jorsted Creek Road. Drive 7.5 miles, following signs for Forest Road 24, to a junction with Forest Road 2419. Take FR 2419 past the first trail sign for Mount Ellinor to an unmarked junction with Forest Road 2419-014 (the first road on the left). Turn left and drive to the upper trailhead at road's end.

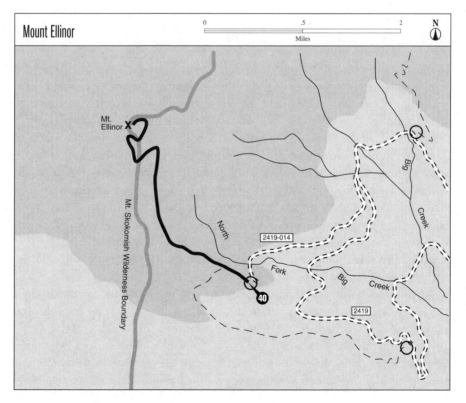

Mounts Pershing (foreground) and Stone as seen from Mount Ellinor

The Hike

This steep trail seems much longer than its 1.7 miles but rewards those who reach the summit with the finest views to be had in the southeastern Olympics. The trail begins in a clear-cut but soon climbs onto a wooded finger ridge, which it ascends via a natural staircase of tree roots. The path from the lower trailhead soon joins it, and thus bolstered the trail continues up the ridgetop beneath an open canopy of Douglas fir.

Within a mile an open subalpine forest dominates the landscape, and a mat of heather provides splashes of color in midsummer. The first views are of Mount Ellinor itself. Later the trail passes rocky knobs that command an unimpaired vista of Lake Cushman and the southern end of Puget Sound, with Mount Rainier looming ghostlike beyond it. The forest falls away altogether as the trail picks a rocky path up through the outcrops. A dazzling display of wildflowers greets the traveler from chinks and swards among the boulders. Anemones are prominently displayed, and harebells bloom everywhere.

An unmarked spur path soon runs east to a tent site, while the main trail shoots steeply across a slope of loose scree to reach the ridgeline. The view from this spot is dominated by Sawtooth Ridge, with Mount Lincoln at its south end and Mount Cruiser rearing its vertical spires to the north. The trail turns north and switchbacks up a meadowy slope, then winds onto the rocky eastern face of Mount Ellinor. The ragged tooth of Mount Washington rises boldly beyond a rocky saddle in the ridge, and Mount Constance and The Brothers can be seen beyond it. The trail then doglegs back and picks its way to the summit for even finer vistas. Mount Pershing rises above a nameless lake to the north, and the spires of Mount Stone loom just beyond it. Mount Skokomish hulks to the west of Stone on the same ridgeline, and Mount Anderson peeks out behind its summit. Mount Olympus is now visible above Sawtooth Ridge, completing a splendid panorama of rocky upheaval.

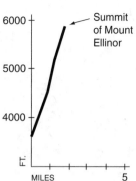

Key Points

0.0   Upper trailhead.
0.3   Junction with path from lower trailhead. Bear right.
1.4   Unmarked spur to campsite. Turn left.
1.7   Summit of Mount Ellinor.

41 Mount Rose

A 6.4-mile loop day hike to the summit of Mount Rose.

Difficulty: Strenuous.
Trail type: Foot.
Best season: Early June to mid-October.
Elevation gain: 3,500 feet.

Elevation loss: 3,500 feet.
Maximum elevation: 4,301 feet.
Topo maps: Mount Steel; Custom Correct
Mount Skokomish–Lake Cushman.

Finding the trailhead: From Hoodsport, drive west on Lake Cushman Road past Lake Cushman State Park. Turn left onto Forest Road 24 and drive 2.7 miles to a sign for the Mount Rose Trail. It is easiest to follow an unmarked path that leaves the road to the west of the nameless feeder stream that descends here.

The Hike

This trail has been recently rebuilt with new switchbacks and erosion control structures. A direct route to the summit allows a loop hike. The trek begins with a tedious, switchbacking ascent through a loose forest of Douglas fir. Thin spots in the canopy allow tantalizing glimpses of Lake Cushman, but the view never broadens into any kind of panorama. As the trail ascends, it passes outcrops of bedrock that rise from the forest like mossy whale backs. Conifers cannot take root on this thin, arid soil, and the resulting sunny spots provide footholds for the shade-intolerant Pacific madrone. This broadleaf tree has a distinctive bark that peels away from the trunk, giving the tree an appearance of nudity.

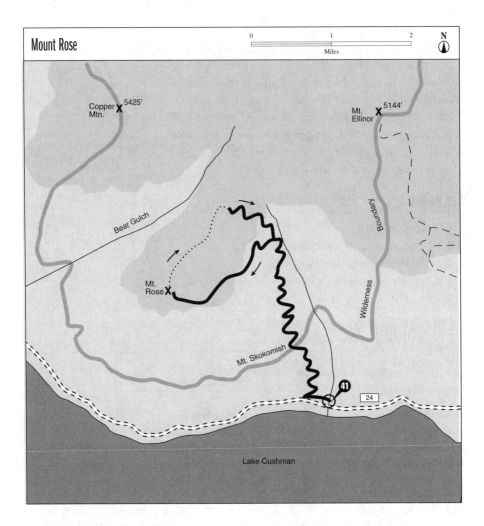

0   1   2   N

Miles

Copper **X** 5425'
Mtn.

Mt. **X** 5144'
Ellinor

Bear Gulch

Mt.
Rose **X**

Boundary

Wilderness

Mt. Skokomish

41

24

Lake Cushman

High up on the mountainside, the trail splits. The left fork climbs directly to the summit. This path zigzags up the mountainside in tight turns, then unexpectedly reaches a flat bench. It then winds into a natural amphitheater of rock that resembles a long-abandoned quarry. An intermittent stream runs through it and may offer water following wet weather. Ascending gradually, the trail passes through a maze of hillocks covered in silver fir and beargrass. As it climbs higher, rounded upwellings of stone support a growth of heather, which brightens the forest with its pink and white blooms in early summer.

The final pitch to the summit is steep and culminates in a fingerlike outcrop of stone that rises above the trees. Lake Cushman lies far below like a giant mirror. Forested ridgetops, dominated by Lightning Peak and Wonder Mountain, stretch away to the southern horizon. Looking through the charred snags of an old fire, it is possible to look straight up the North Fork of the Skokomish at the sharp points of Six Ridge.

Hikers can then follow the "ridge loop" route down the ridgeline to the north. At the time of this writing, the track was faint and prone to blowdowns but could be followed by watching for plastic flagging marking the way. The route descends gradually along the rocky ridgetop, with occasional views of Copper Mountain to the west and Mount Ellinor to the east. Mountain hemlocks rise from chinks in the bedrock and are hung with banners of old man's beard (a type of epiphytic lichen). Upon reaching a low saddle, the trail turns east and drops from the ridgeline and into a loose grove of mature hemlocks. The path, now more distinct, passes through several spots of catastrophic winter blowdown as it veers southward. The descent picks up speed, and the trail crosses a small stream before zigzagging

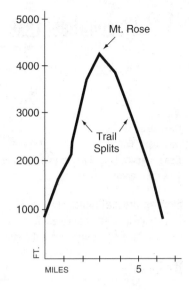

down to return to the main trail junction. From this point, a foot-pounding descent of 1.8 miles returns the hiker to the road.

Key Points

0.0 Trailhead, shore of Lake Cushman.

1.1 Trail enters Mount Skokomish Wilderness.

1.8 Junction of summit and ridge loop trails. Bear left.

2.9 Summit of Mount Rose.

3.7 Ridge loop trail drops from ridgeline.

4.6 Trail returns to junction.

6.4 Trailhead.

42 Wagonwheel Lake

A 2.8-mile day hike from the North Fork Skokomish trailhead to Wagonwheel Lake.

Difficulty: Strenuous.
Trail type: Foot.
Best season: Early June to mid-October.
Elevation gain: 3,240 feet.

Maximum elevation: 4,100 feet.
Topo maps: Mount Steel; Custom Correct *Mount Skokomish–Lake Cushman.*

Finding the trailhead: From Hoodsport, drive west on Lake Cushman Road past Lake Cushman State Park. Turn left onto Forest Road 24 and drive 6.6 miles to the Staircase Ranger Station. Follow the paved street uphill from the station to the North Fork trailhead.

The Hike

This trail is a laborious climb across wooded slopes with limited views, ending at a woodland lake. The trail begins by running north through a dry forest of young Douglas fir underlain by a dense mat of Oregon grape. It soon crosses the moist bottom of a side valley and begins the long ascent by switchbacking up the steep hillside. When it finally reaches the top of a finger ridge, the grade eases a bit before becoming even steeper as it follows the ridgeline upward. There are several overlooks as the path alternates between doghair stands of young hemlocks and open groves of more mature trees. These vantage points offer views of Lightning Peak, which rises on the far side of Lake Cushman.

After a brutal climb the trail levels off as it swings onto the western side of the ridge. Here the trail offers a new challenge in the form of dense brush that clogs an open avalanche slope. The craggy summit that rises above the forest to the north is Mount Lincoln, and good views of it can be had from the midst of the shrubbery. Soon after returning to the forest, the path crosses a small outlet stream and arrives on the bluffs above Wagonwheel Lake. This pool of deep aquamarine occupies an oval pocket in the timber. Mountain hemlock, Alaska cedar, and subalpine fir are the principal overstory species, while willows and devil's club crowd the shores of the lake. There are several campsites above the western shore, and they offer limited views of the rocky crest of Copper Mountain.

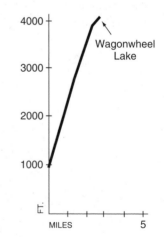

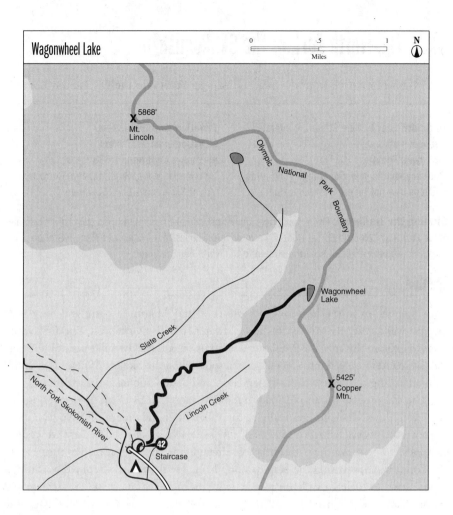

Wagonwheel Lake

0 .5 1

Miles

N

5868'
Mt.
Lincoln

Olympic National Park Boundary

Wagonwheel
Lake

Slate Creek

North Fork Skokomish River

Lincoln Creek

5425'
Copper
Mtn.

42
Staircase

Key Points

0.0 North Fork Skokomish trailhead.

2.8 Wagonwheel Lake.

43 The North Fork of the Skokomish

A 15.1-mile backpack from the Staircase Ranger Station to the Duckabush River.

Difficulty: Easy to Nine Stream; moderately strenuous beyond.
Trail type: Primary.
Best season: All year. Some higher elevation sections may not be open until mid-June.

Elevation gain: 3,908 feet.
Elevation loss: 2,078 feet.
Maximum elevation: 4,688 feet.
Topo maps: Mount Steel; Custom Correct *Mount Skokomish–Lake Cushman.*

Finding the trailhead: From Hoodsport, drive west on Lake Cushman Road past Lake Cushman State Park. Turn left onto Forest Road 24 and drive 6.6 miles to the Staircase Ranger Station. Follow the paved street uphill from the station to the North Fork trailhead.

The Hike

This trail begins in the lush lowland forests of the Skokomish basin and ultimately climbs over a lofty pass to reach the headwaters of the Duckabush. The first white man to explore the area was Melbourne Watkinson, a local sawmill operator. His initials were found carved into trees at several spots along the Skokomish by Lt. Joseph P. O'Neil during the course of his much later (and better-publicized) expeditions.

The trek begins on an old road grade and soon climbs to an open overlook of the river. It then descends gradually to the valley floor and enters a lush lowland forest unrivaled in its richness and diversity. Ancient Douglas fir, red cedar, and western hemlock tower above the path, and moss-draped vine and bigleaf maples thrive amid the conifers. After passing the Rapids Loop bridge trail, the main trail passes through a pure stand of bigleaf maple on its way to a crossing of Slate Creek. This stream and others like it experienced floods in the wake of the Beaver Fire of 1985, and the waters brought down vast quantities of rubble and deposited them in great heaps on the valley floor. The trail soon enters the burn itself, where the mournful skeletons of once-mighty conifers still rise above a growth of pioneering shrubs. The blaze was ignited by an illegal campfire during a period of drought, burning more than 1,300 acres of old-growth forest. This charred landscape accompanies the hiker to the Flapjack Lakes junction, where the road grade ends and the living forest returns.

The valley soon constricts, and the trail finds itself hugging the hillside above the river bottoms. A signpost marks the spot where a spur trail descends to Big Log Camp. The tent sites are situated among enormous Douglas firs and red cedars, one of which has a hollow base that can be explored by people of small build. The Black and White way trail descends to meet the trail opposite the camping area spur. A pack bridge soon spans the waters of the river, which flows through a shady canyon of stone overhung by stately trees. On the far bank is a junction with the Six Ridge Trail; the main path turns right to continue upriver.

A rushing cascade near Eight Stream

The valley soon opens up into a broad alluvial plain, and the conifers are replaced by groves of red alder and bigleaf maple. Such broadleaf trees do well in this environment of gravelly soils and periodic flooding. Large openings in the trees are choked with salmonberry, thimbleberry, and (watch out!) stinging nettle. The old Darky Mine site is inland from the trail; it was worked for copper, iron, and manganese around the turn of the century. Camp Pleasant lies at the northern edge of this disturbed area, half in a grove of bigleaf maple and half in a stand of old conifers.

After passing the stairstep cascade of a nameless stream, the forest again closes around the trail. A pack bridge crosses the mossy torrent of Eight Stream, shaded by tall and stately conifers. The trail soon climbs 100 feet above the riverbank, then works its way across several brushy avalanche slopes. The summit of Mount Steel is just visible through the tops of the alders at this point. Beyond the second opening the forest is gladed with sun-dappled swards of grass, and the trail rises gently before crossing the footlog over Nine Stream. A camp occupies an opening in the mixed forest of the far bank.

The trail continues along the river for a short distance beyond the camp, then crosses a small tributary and begins the climb to First Divide. The grade is fairly rigorous in the beginning as the track switchbacks upward through a silent forest of hemlock. The pace slackens a bit after 1 mile, and the route crosses brushy openings

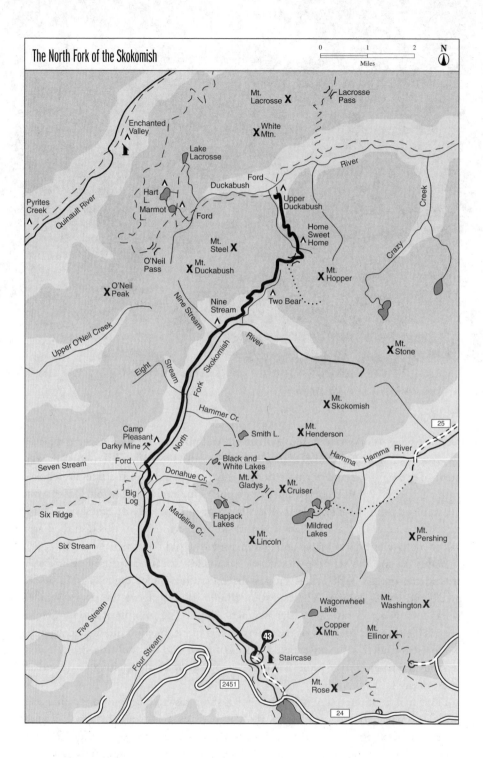

The North Fork of the Skokomish

0   1   2
Miles

N

Mt. Lacrosse X

Lacrosse Pass

X White Mtn.

Enchanted Valley

River

Lake Lacrosse

Ford Duckabush

Upper Duckabush

Pyrites Creek

Hart L.

Marmot L.

Ford

Home Sweet Home

Crazy

Creek

Quinault River

Mt. Steel X

O'Neil Pass

X Mt. Duckabush

Mt. Hopper X

Two Bear

O'Neil Peak X

Nine Stream

Nine Stream

Mt. Stone X

Upper O'Neil Creek

North Fork Skokomish

River

Eight Stream

Hammer Cr.

Mt. Skokomish X

Mt. Henderson X

25

Camp Pleasant
Darky Mine

Smith L.

Seven Stream

Ford

Donahue Cr.

Black and White Lakes

Hamma   Hamma   River

Big Log

Mt. Gladys X

Mt. Cruiser X

Six Ridge

Madeline Cr.

Flapjack Lakes

Mildred Lakes

Mt. Pershing X

Six Stream

Mt. Lincoln X

Five Stream

Wagonwheel Lake

Mt. Washington X

Copper Mtn. X

Mt. Ellinor X

Four Stream

43

Staircase

2451

Mt. Rose X

24

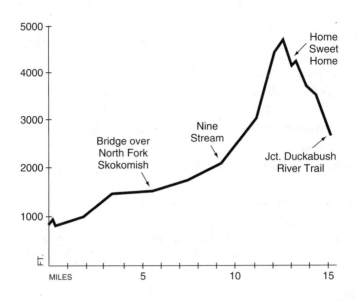

with views of Mount Skokomish. Salmonberries and thimbleberries grow densely here, providing an abundance of wild fruit in late August. The trail reaches Two Bear Camp at the end of a long jog to the east. This camp occupies a stand of conifers beside a rushing stream.

The ascent picks up again as the trail climbs beside the western bank of this brook. The forest soon gives way to subalpine meadowland overgrown with berry bushes and columbines. The ascent continues up the narrow vale to reach the pass at its head. The trail jogs east here and keeps climbing toward a higher crossing of First Divide. Just before the summit is a junction with the Mount Hopper way trail, a primitive route used by climbers to access the upper basin of Crazy Creek. A swale below the summit holds a flowery alpine meadow interrupted by stands of mountain hemlock and highlighted by a placid meltwater pool. Trees block the view from the top of First Divide, but excellent views of White Mountain and Mount Lacrosse await the traveler a short distance down the north slope. The descent is steady as the trail drops down to the floor of a magnificent alpine basin. The trail crosses a rushing stream and climbs onto a rise from which the summits of Mount Steel and Mount Hopper are plainly visible. A spur path leads up into the meadows to the east.

From this point the main trail descends steadily into a brushy montane forest that blocks out views of the mountains. A landslide opening offers one last glimpse of the lesser peaks that line the head of the Duckabush Valley. Soon afterward the trail drops into a stand of old-growth conifers to meet the Duckabush River Trail just above Upper Duckabush Camp.

Key Points

0.0 North Fork Skokomish trailhead.

1.0 Junction with Rapids Loop bridge trail. Bear right.

3.5 Junction with Flapjack Lakes Trail. Keep going straight.

5.3 Junction with Big Log Camp spur and Black and White way trail. Keep going straight.

5.6 Bridge over North Fork of the Skokomish. Junction with Six Ridge Trail. Turn right.

7.5 Trail crosses Eight Stream.

9.2 Trail crosses Nine Stream. Nine Stream Camp.

11.3 Two Bear Camp.

12.4 Junction with Mount Hopper way trail. Stay left.

12.6 Trail crosses First Divide.

13.2 Junction with spur to Home Sweet Home meadows. Through traffic bear left.

15.1 Junction with Duckabush River Trail.

44 Flapjack Lakes

A 7.4-mile backpack from the Staircase Ranger Station to Flapjack Lakes.

Difficulty: Moderately strenuous.
Trail type: Foot.
Best season: Early June to mid-October.
Elevation gain: 3,120 feet (to Flapjack Lakes).
Elevation loss: 60 feet (to Flapjack Lakes).

Maximum elevation: 3,900 feet (Flapjack Lakes).
Topo maps: Mount Steel; Custom Correct *Mount Skokomish–Lake Cushman.*

Finding the trailhead: From Hoodsport, drive west on Lake Cushman Road past Lake Cushman State Park. Turn left onto Forest Road 24 and drive 6.6 miles to the Staircase Ranger Station. Follow the paved street uphill from the station to the North Fork trailhead.

The Hike

This popular route climbs to a series of alpine lakes that sprinkle the high shelves around Mount Gladys. The Flapjack Lakes camping area has received such heavy use that rehabilitation efforts have been undertaken to revegetate the trampled spots, and the limited permits required for camping here are issued at the Staircase Ranger Station. Gladys Divide makes a fine side trip from the Flapjack Lakes, and the Black and White Lakes Trail offers a more wild and remote destination.

The trek begins in the lush bottomland forest of the North Fork of the Skokomish and follows the trail of the same name along the river. After 1.5 miles the forest is replaced by the mournful landscape created by the Beaver Fire in 1985. The Flapjack Lakes Trail departs from the valley bottom at a junction just beyond the northern

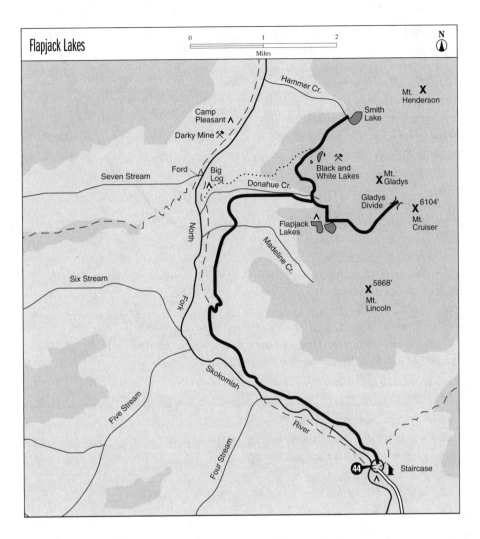

edge of the burn. It ascends through a montane forest underlain by a dense growth of shrubbery. Its chief component is salal, whose berries were once considered by some coastal tribes to be food fit for chieftains. Salal is largely ignored by berry pickers these days, as is the sour red huckleberry that also grows here.

After a few upward switchbacks, the trail levels off for a long dogleg to the north. The forest here is a sparse collection of Douglas fir and western hemlock, allowing ample views of the serpentine ridges that surround Six Stream. As the trail continues north, the hillside becomes quite marshy. Maidenhair fern shares space with bunchberry in the shady spots, while bracken fern dominates the sunnier areas. The trail then dips into the gully containing Madeline Creek, and a footbridge spans its mossy cascades. Numerous deadfalls crisscross the waters, providing runways for small rodents that would otherwise find the stream impassable.

Beyond this creek the trail begins climbing again and soon turns east into the deep cleft carved by Donahue Creek. The climb is often quite steep as the trail makes its way to the streamside then zigzags sharply upward. There are several good campsites just below the junction with the trail to Black and White Lakes (discussed in detail at the end of this trail description). Turn uphill at the signpost and follow the initially rough trail through a forest of silver fir to reach Flapjack Lakes. This pair of green subalpine tarns is bisected by a narrow isthmus, and the basalt pillars of Sawtooth Ridge rise above them. There are campsites scat-

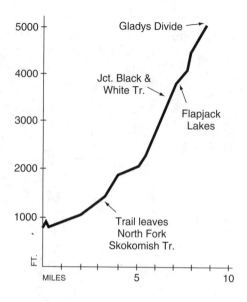

tered among the mountain hemlocks of the lakeshores; check the map at the campground and be sure to use a designated site. Black bears are particularly abundant here; be sure to keep food items out of reach at all times.

Key Points

0.0 North Fork Skokomish trailhead.

1.0 Junction with Rapids Loop bridge trail. Bear right.

3.5 Junction with Flapjack Lakes Trail. Turn right.

5.2 Trail crosses Madeline Creek.

6.9 Junction with Black and White Lakes Trail. Turn right for Flapjack Lakes.

7.4 Flapjack Lakes camping area.

Gladys Divide Option: For excellent views of the pinnacles of Sawtooth Ridge, follow the Gladys Divide Trail east from Flapjack Lakes. This well-built path climbs moderately through the timber before emerging onto a grassy meadow on the south slope of Mount Gladys. The pillars of basalt that make up Mounts Lincoln and Cruiser rise in spectacular fashion above a tiny vale that cups an alpine pond. The trail continues upward at a steady pace, crossing numerous openings on the slopes above the valley floor. Enormous slabs of rock have tumbled down from Mount Cruiser, littering the landscape with fractured boulders of gargantuan proportions. They form ideal escape cover for the rodents that are often sighted near Gladys Divide. The pass itself looks out over a spectacular vista of the headwaters basin of the Hamma Hamma River, with Mounts Henderson and Skokomish soaring above it.

Black and White Lakes Trail Option: This old trail has fallen into disuse, but it can still be navigated without difficulty. From the junction below Flapjack Lakes, this path crosses Donahue Creek and then zigzags upward to pass beneath a slender waterfall on a tributary stream. It then bears north, climbing across a burned slope. A fire raged here in 1936, and the burn is being slowly repopulated by mountain maple, elderberry, and conifer seedlings. The trail passes through a stand of mountain hemlock that survived the blaze as it turns uphill and climbs onto level benchlands. Here the burn site is a solid carpet of huckleberry and blueberry bushes, a feast for travelers and bears alike when the berries ripen in early September.

A signpost marks the junction with the Black and White way trail, and the Black and White Lakes are 0.2 mile beyond this point. They are easily missed by oncoming hikers because they sit in a low depression in the burn that is visible only from above. The lakes got their name from a brand of whiskey that was found carved into a tree by a presumably well-lubricated elk hunter during the early part of the century. An old manganese mine occupies the hillside below the lakes, and tailings and tunnels can still be found. The trail then continues to ascend on a northeast bearing across berry-covered terraces. Just beyond the edge of the burn, it dives down an incredibly steep pitch that is extremely dangerous when wet. At the bottom of the grade is Smith Lake, a round pool that is set among mountain hemlocks at the foot of Mount Henderson. A primitive campsite lies on the far side of the outlet stream at the foot of the lake.

45 Six Ridge

A 10.6-mile trip on a wilderness route from the North Fork of the Skokomish to Lake Sundown.

Difficulty: Strenuous.
Trail type: Primitive.
Best season: Early July to mid-October.
Elevation gain: 4,736 feet.

Elevation loss: 2,336 feet.
Maximum elevation: 4,680 (Six Ridge Pass).
Topo maps: Mount Steel, Mount Christie; Custom Correct *Enchanted Valley–Skokomish*.

Finding the trailhead: This trail begins at mile 5.6 on the North Fork Skokomish Trail. To get to the trailhead: From Hoodsport, drive west on Lake Cushman Road past Lake Cushman State Park. Turn left on Forest Road 24 and drive 6.6 miles to the Staircase Ranger Station. Follow the paved street uphill from the station to the North Fork trailhead.

The Hike

This route can be followed without difficulty as far as Belview Camp, but open meadows swallow the path· beyond this point, making map and compass work a necessity. The trek begins on the banks of the North Fork of the Skokomish and follows the river south through an ancient forest of red cedar and Sitka spruce. After

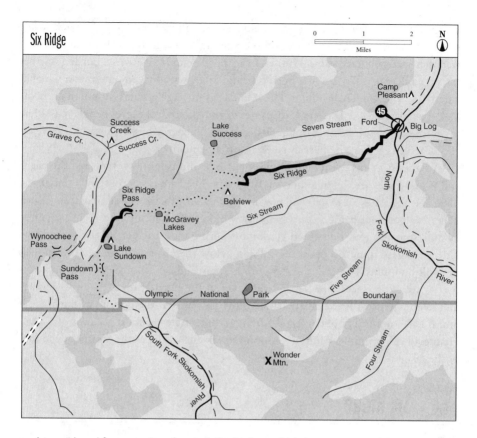

passing a riverside campsite, the trail fords the ankle-deep waters of Seven Stream. This stream is so named because it marks the seventh camp of the O'Neil expedition during its crossing of the southeast Olympics in 1890. It is the last spot where water is available before Belview Camp.

The trail continues south for a time, then strikes west to begin the long ascent to the crest of Six Ridge. The grade is never unreasonably steep but seems interminable by virtue of its countless switchbacks. The ferns and cedars fall away in short order and are replaced by a montane stand of Douglas fir and salal. Early openings in the sparse canopy allow limited views of Mount Lincoln to the east. As the trail climbs into the subalpine zone, mountain hemlock becomes the dominant tree, with lesser components of noble and silver firs. Huckleberry and blueberry bushes crowd the understory. The trail tops out on a high, wooded point, then begins a roller-coaster journey along the ridgeline. The path rises and falls steeply through a forest that allows only limited views of the surrounding mountains.

As the trail nears the highest point on Six Ridge, a burn dating from 1992 interrupts the trees. The trail passes through it and climbs through the more extensive 1962 burn with its snags bleached white by the sun. Six Ridge receives more than its share of lightning strikes because it lies directly across the storm track of the prevailing southwesterly winds. The trail mounts a bald knob, and outstanding views open up in all directions. To the north, the tops of Mounts Duckabush, Steel, and Hopper peek out over the wooded crest of the intervening ridge. Mounts Skokomish and Henderson, along with the entire length of Sawtooth Ridge from Mount Cruiser to Mount Lincoln, rise in plain view along the eastern skyline. To the south lies Lake Cushman and range upon range of twisted ridgetops. The trail weaves among the various points atop the ridge, sticking to low hollows that serve as catch basins for winter snow. After a short distance the trail reaches a signpost in a ridgetop saddle. From this point it is possible to run the ridgeline west and then north to reach tiny Lake Success.

The main trail drops from the junction onto the south face of the ridge, descending without interruption to reach Belview Camp. This tent site is set on a knoll screened by young subalpine firs and mountain hemlocks. A flowery meadow beside the camp has its own cold spring. Views from the camp are blocked by trees, but a little jockeying for position yields fine views of Sawtooth Ridge as well as the wooded hogback that lies to the south. From this point on, the trail becomes faint with alarming frequency. Hikers will often find it necessary to navigate through overgrown meadows and tangles of downed timber by the use of blazes, cairns, flagging, and orange markers.

Beyond the camp the trail descends through loose forest and soon crosses a meadowy stream basin. It then begins to climb, passing through a forest choked with deadfalls. Upon reaching the top of the spur ridge, the faint path meanders westward. A large opening reveals several ponds in the basin below and the first glimpse of Wonder Mountain to the south. The trail makes its way across the next spur and traverses onto an avalanche slope that requires careful navigation. The trail climbs beside the trees, then crosses the open slope and returns to the forest. A short distance farther on is a second avalanche path, this one strewn with boulders that are overgrown by grasses and wildflowers. The trail makes a direct crossing, then follows the forest edge downhill before resuming its westward course.

After climbing steadily to surmount another spur ridge, the trail drops precipitously into the meadowy basin containing McGravey Lakes. These shallow ponds are surrounded by low, rounded hillocks covered with heather and blueberry bushes. The trail continues west for another 0.6 mile, then starts a brief but rather grueling climb across open slopes to reach Six Ridge Pass. The pass offers one last look at the ranges

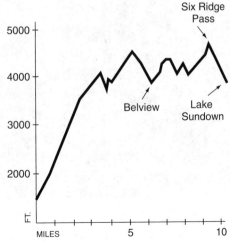

to the east before dropping into the drainage of Graves Creek. In doing so, the trail drops steadily across open slopes that allow distant views to the northwest of Mounts Olympus, Tom, and Seattle. The path clings to a steep hillside as it runs southward for the final mile to Lake Sundown. The trail reaches its terminus at a marked junction with the Lake Sundown route beside the outlet of the lake.

Key Points

- **0.0** Junction with North Fork Skokomish Trail.
- **0.2** Trail fords Seven Stream.
- **2.4** Trail reaches crest of Six Ridge.
- **5.6** Junction with Lake Success route. Turn left and begin descending.
- **6.3** Belview Camp.
- **8.4** McGravey Lakes.
- **9.4** Six Ridge Pass.
- **10.6** Trail joins Lake Sundown Trail. Lake Sundown Camp.

Looking east from Six Ridge Pass

Additional Trails

The **Dose Terrace Trail** makes a 1.2-mile loop through the bottomland forest beside the Dosewallips River.

The **Ranger Hole Trail** is a 0.8-mile spur from the historic Interrorem Ranger Station to a pretty pool on the Duckabush River. A short nature trail loops out from its beginning and identifies some of the more common plants found here.

The **Brothers Trail** is an access route for climbers bound for The Brothers. It ends at a base camp on the East Fork of Lena Creek.

The **Putvin way trail** makes a brutal and brushy climb from the Hamma Hamma River to Lake of the Angels within Olympic National Park. It is not maintained, and travelers should expect problems finding the route at the higher elevations.

The **Mount Washington Trail** runs up to a saddle in the ridge, then disappears. It is mainly a climber's access route.

The **Dry Creek Trail** runs southwest from the head of Lake Cushman, offering a little-used path into the forested hills. It is popular with stock parties.

The **Black and White way trail** is a steep route from Big Log Camp to the Black and White Lakes. It is brushy at both ends but is in good shape in between. Hiking this trail in the uphill direction is not recommended.

The **Mount Hopper way trail** is a rough track that runs from the First Divide to the upper basin of Crazy Creek. Expect a route-finding challenge.

The **Lake Success way trail** is extremely difficult to follow but roughly tracks the ridgeline west and then north from Six Ridge to a small alpine tarn.

The Western Approaches

The westward-flowing rivers of the Olympic Peninsula rise from massive glaciers at the crest of the range and churn through braided channels to reach the Pacific Ocean. Deep, U-shaped valleys receive more than 150 inches of rain each year, giving rise to the ancient temperate rain forests for which the region is famous. Here trees may be more than 1,000 years old, and every surface—living and dead—is covered with smaller forms of plant life. A few of the western trails penetrate all the way up into alpine regions, offering views of active glaciers that receive up to 20 feet of snow each winter.

The Hoh and Quinault valleys have the best access and receive the greatest attention from tourists. The Hoh Rainforest has a full visitor center and campground, and a fee station at the park entrance. There are also several campgrounds outside the park entrance. Lake Quinault is a particular focus of attention in this area, with several resorts along its southern shore. There are campgrounds and ranger stations at Graves Creek and on the North Fork of the Quinault, and the district ranger station is on North Shore Road. The Forest Service has a visitor center and several campgrounds on the south shore of Lake Quinault.

The other river valleys are wilder and more remote, offering a more primitive wilderness experience. There is a National Park Service campground at the end of Queets River Road, which has been washed out in recent years, while various state agencies administer campgrounds on the South Fork of the Hoh and the Bogachiel River. Supplies can be procured at Lake Quinault or in the town of Forks, and there are also a few stores along the Hoh Rainforest Road.

46 Colonel Bob

This is a 4.2-mile day hike from Forest Road 2204 to the summit of Colonel Bob, or a 7.8-mile backpack to the Lake Quinault South Shore Road.

Difficulty: Moderately strenuous (through hike); strenuous (Colonel Bob spur).
Trail type: Secondary.
Best season: Early July to mid-October.

Elevation gain: 3,522 feet (Pete's Creek to Colonel Bob summit).
Maximum elevation: 4,492 feet (Colonel Bob).
Topo maps: Lake Quinault East, Colonel Bob; Custom Correct *Quinault-Colonel Bob.*

Finding the trailhead: From Neilton, drive 10.3 miles south on U.S. Highway 101 to mile 112.7. Turn left (east) onto paved Forest Road 22 and drive 8.6 miles to FR 2204. Turn left and drive 11 miles on FR 2204 to the well-marked Pete's Creek trailhead.

The Hike

This trail climbs into a fragment of mountainous wilderness above Lake Quinault. There are camping opportunities at the Mulkey shelter and Moonshine Flats, or the trek can be done as a day hike. The easiest road access is from the north, but the hike gains much less elevation when the trail is approached from the Pete's Creek side.

The trek begins in a damp lowland forest in the valley of the West Fork of the Humptulips. Scattered conifers rise above a luxuriant undergrowth of ferns, shrubs, and mosses. This diverse forest has been undisturbed for centuries: The largest trees die from disease and windthrow at odd intervals, creating openings that allow seedlings to get started in the understory. The result is a mixed forest of many different canopy heights, and this creates a wide spectrum of ecological niches for birds and mammals.

The trail soon makes an ankle-deep ford of Pete's Creek and begins to climb steadily. The first avalanche slope is at mile 1.5, and this brush-choked opening allows a glimpse of the surrounding hills. After a vigorous climb the trail enters the lower end of a much larger avalanche slope. It zigzags upward through the opening for 0.5 mile, eventually reaching a zone where frequent and violent snowslides exclude all woody plants. The path then runs to the northern edge of the opening, where it meets the spur path to Colonel Bob itself. This trail is described here first, and the through hike to the Quinault Valley is discussed at the end of this trail description.

The path to Colonel Bob climbs aggressively up the west slope of Gibson Peak. The silver snags near its crest are the result of a forest fire that burned here in 1961. The track approaches the lower edge of this "silver forest," then turns east and drops through a saddle into the headwaters of Fletcher Canyon. An old trail sign half-hidden in the brush indicates a junction with the abandoned Fletcher Canyon Trail. The Colonel Bob spur turns northwest to cross Moonshine Flats, a series of level benches dotted with huge boulders and harboring a handful of shallow ponds. Local

Wooded Peak and Lake Quinault

residents once congregated in this area to "enjoy the moonshine." The flats do face east and boast spectacular moonrises; thus it is hard to say exactly what form of moonshine they were enjoying. The craggy basalt summit of Colonel Bob rises directly to the north.

After crossing the headwaters of the main stream in Fletcher Canyon, the trail skirts a meadowy basin before beginning the final pitch. The path soon becomes choked with broken rock as it ascends steeply through an open subalpine forest. Upon reaching the saddle to the south of the peak, the trail traverses across its southeast face to reach an even higher col to the east of the summit. This saddle offers fine views of Mount Olympus, and a primitive track runs down into the basin below. The main trail follows the ridgeline, climbing the last hundred yards over steps carved into

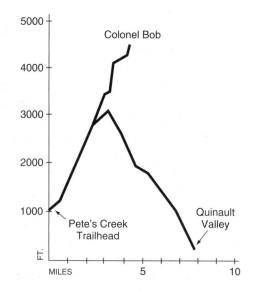

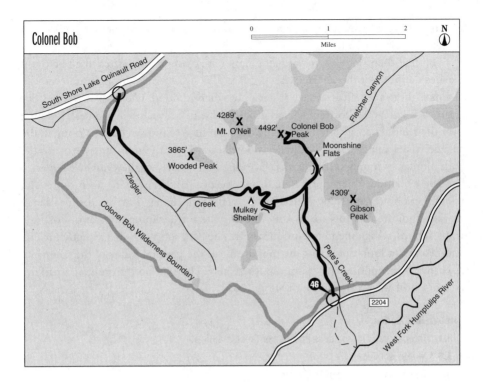

the bedrock. The old lookout site atop Colonel Bob commands a view that features Lake Quinault beyond Wooded and O'Neil Peaks, as well as the interior ranges of the Olympics.

Key Points

0.0 Pete's Creek trailhead.

0.1 Trail enters Colonel Bob Wilderness.

0.9 Trail fords Pete's Creek to reach east bank.

2.4 Junction with spur trail to summit of Colonel Bob.

3.1 Colonel Bob spur crosses pass into upper Fletcher Canyon. Junction with abandoned Fletcher Canyon Trail. Turn left.

3.2 Moonshine Flats camping area.

4.2 Summit of Colonel Bob.

Through Hike Option: The through trail runs west from its meeting with the Colonel Bob spur trail, climbing through a subalpine forest. Gaps in the trees offer views of the Humptulips Valley, surrounded by forested spires. After 370 vertical feet of climbing, the trail crests the divide over the Ziegler Creek drainage and starts down the other side. The grade is initially quite reasonable as the path drops onto a small bench that bears the Mulkey shelter. A trickle of a stream provides water, but there is no place to pitch a tent.

The trail then slogs downward at a rapid clip, crossing a dry streambed before it reaches the floor of the Ziegler Creek valley. This stream runs through subterranean channels there and offers surface water only when in flood. The track crosses its dry wash, then enters the bottom of an avalanche slope that reveals a jagged peak looming over the basin. The path then enters the trees, a refuge of mossy columns rising in the silence of the upper basin. The valley floor falls away as the trail runs west, and the path ultimately rounds a hillside that faces the broad valley of the Quinault River.

The enormous trees found here form a vertical landscape, with steep slopes and tall timber uninterrupted by undergrowth. As the trail zigzags downward, little orange markers indicate that this area is a monitoring site for declining populations of neo-tropical birds, which spend the summer here. The path soon crosses a recent clear-cut, and hikers can look out across the moonscape at the pastoral valley of the Quinault. A barnyard cacophony rises from the forest here. The trail bottoms out at a parking area just off Lake Quinault South Shore Road.

Through-Hike Option

3.1 Through trail crosses pass into Ziegler Creek drainage.

3.8 Mulkey shelter.

4.6 Trail crosses dry bed of Ziegler Creek.

7.8 Colonel Bob trailhead.

47 Lake Sundown

A 7.9-mile backpack from the Graves Creek trailhead to Lake Sundown.

Difficulty: Moderately strenuous.
Trail type: Foot.
Best season: Late June to mid-October.
Elevation gain: 3,275 feet.

Elevation loss: 70 feet.
Maximum elevation: 3,850 feet.
Topo maps: Mount Hoquiam; Custom Correct *Enchanted Valley–Skokomish.*

Finding the trailhead: From U.S. Highway 101 at mile 125.5, turn east onto Lake Quinault South Shore Road. The pavement ends after 7.8 miles, and after another 11.3 miles of bone-jarring bumps, the road ends at the Graves Creek trailhead.

The Hike

This little-used trail follows Graves Creek to a subalpine lake at the western end of the Six Ridge Trail. The lake can also be reached via Wynoochee Pass, a shorter

Lake Sundown ▶

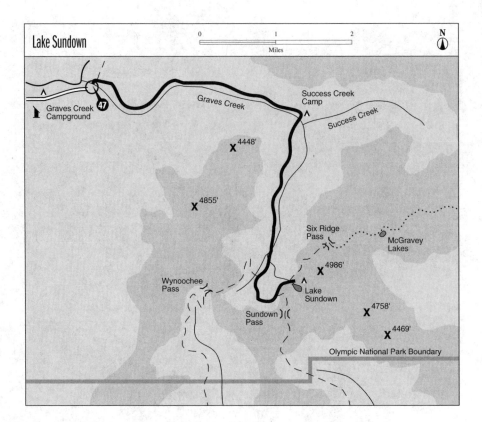

trail that requires lots of logging road driving and some route-finding skill. From the Graves Creek trailhead, cross Graves Creek on the sturdy pack bridge, then turn right onto the narrow Graves Creek Trail. This trail climbs steadily to reach a wooded bench, then runs east to track the rather steep gradient of Graves Creek. The trail dips and climbs frequently as it passes through a mixed forest of Sitka spruce, red cedar, and noble fir. At mile 2.9 the trail crosses a rocky wash that yields the first view of Graves Creek as it tumbles through a scenic waterfall.

Beyond the falls the trail continues to climb through the hillside timber. At one point the canopy is broken by a wide brushfield, where bracken fern and thimble-berry grow to shoulder height. Shortly thereafter the trail drops into a quiet creek-bottom forest, passing a primitive campsite in preparation for a ford of the stream. Although the water is shallow here, the boulders are quite slippery, and care should be taken during the crossing. On the far bank the trail gains altitude rapidly as it zigzags up a rocky path through the salmonberries.

After crossing a small brook, the trail continues up the hillside, which gives way to an unexpected pocket valley behind a creekside knob. This secluded vale offers the possibility of seeing black bear and elk, so proceed quietly. Because Graves Creek has taken a sharp southward bend, the trail once again finds itself paralleling the stream from a steep hillside. After a time the path crosses a substantial rivulet, which tumbles from pool to pool through a miniature canyon of mossy bedrock. Shortly thereafter the trail descends through old cedars and hemlocks to reach the second crossing of Graves Creek. Several campsites adorn the near bank; the ford lies 20 yards upstream from them.

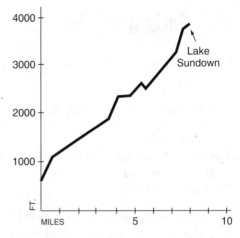

On the far bank the trail is quite brushy and may present a route-finding challenge. The brushfields soon give way to open forests, and the trail crosses three boulder-strewn washes. Just beyond the third one is the junction with the Wynoochee Pass Trail; turn left and the path becomes easy to follow once again. It climbs doggedly up the snout of a rounded spur ridge, then shoots eastward across subalpine meadows. Sword ferns mix freely with columbines, speedwell, and monkeyflowers here. Views are limited to the wooded knobs that surround the drainage.

A brief climb leads to the Sundown Pass Trail junction; Sundown Lake lies 0.3 mile to the east on a trail that rises and falls gently through a brushy subalpine forest. A few old Alaska cedars and mountain hemlocks tower in small clumps along the lakeshore, and the wooded peak at the head of the lake is adorned with a verdant avalanche slope. A snowslip lingers late into the summer here, and the evening sun burnishes it with rosy alpenglow before setting beyond the mountains. Rainbow trout abound in the placid green waters, offering the possibility of fishing to enterprising visitors. To join the Six Ridge Trail, follow the north bank of the outlet brook downstream for 20 yards to reach a marked junction.

Key Points

0.0 Graves Creek trailhead. Trail crosses Graves Creek.

0.1 Junction with Graves Creek (Lake Sundown) Trail. Turn right.

3.7 Success Creek camp. First ford of Graves Creek.

5.7 Second ford of Graves Creek.

6.3 Junction with Wynoochee Pass Trail. Turn left.

7.6 Junction with Sundown Pass Trail. Stay left.

7.9 Lake Sundown. Junction with Six Ridge Trail.

48 Enchanted Valley

An 18.1-mile backpack from the Graves Creek trailhead to Anderson Pass.

Difficulty: Moderate to Enchanted Valley; moderately strenuous beyond.
Trail type: Primary.
Best season: All year. Some higher elevation sections may not be open until mid-June.
Elevation gain: 4,328 feet.

Elevation loss: 510 feet.
Maximum elevation: 4,464 feet (Anderson Pass).
Topo maps: Mount Hoquiam, Chimney Peak, Mount Steel, Mount Olson; Custom Correct *Enchanted Valley–Skokomish.*

Finding the trailhead: From U.S. Highway 101 at mile 125.5, turn east onto Lake Quinault South Shore Road. The pavement ends after 7.8 miles, and after another 11.3 miles of bone-jarring bumps, the road ends at the Graves Creek trailhead.

The Hike

This popular route follows the Quinault River up to a spectacular open basin famous for its waterfalls. It then climbs to Anderson Pass, where it becomes the Anderson Pass Trail. Possible side trips include O'Neil Pass and the Anderson Glacier.

The trek begins from the Graves Creek trailhead and quickly crosses a pack bridge high above the waters of Graves Creek. A short distance beyond it lies a junction with the Graves Creek Trail, which runs south to Lake Sundown. Stay on the wide path that parallels the Quinault River. This old road grade climbs steadily before reaching a broad terrace high above the river. Here a grove of enormous Sitka spruce and red cedar towers skyward. The boles commonly measure more than 8 feet in diameter, and the clean trunks may rise more than 100 feet before they are interrupted by the first branch.

The roadbed ends on the rise beyond this benchland, and a picnic table marks the spot where the track narrows to a conventional path. It descends steadily to Pony Bridge, which spans the river just below a narrow gorge. Here water tinted turquoise by glacial silt rushes down through mossy palisades of rock, then swirls downstream through an intricate grouping of bedrock fingers. A few tent sites lie beside the trail here. After climbing to get around this gorge, the trail drops down to water level as it follows the north bank of the Quinault.

Riverside camping spots appear at regular intervals beyond Fire Creek, as the trail passes amid the mossy boles of the conifers. This is a true temperate rain forest, with each downed log supporting a beardlike growth of mosses and seedlings; ferns and vine maples are scattered about the understory. The bottomlands are interrupted by a sizeable hill 0.8 mile beyond Fire Creek. The trail then returns to the valley floor, keeping well inland in the silent forest. The next grade leads up to a hilltop junction

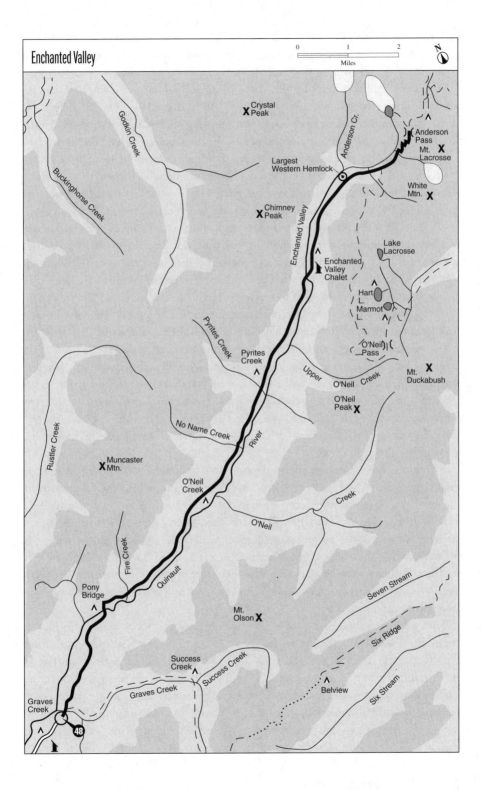

Enchanted Valley

with the spur trail to O'Neil Creek Camp. This camp is down in a brushy depression beside the river, shaded by red alders and bigleaf maples. O'Neil Creek joins the Quinault on the far bank of the river.

The main trail continues up the valley, rising and falling across forested benches before dropping down onto the floodplain. The next grade occurs just before No Name Creek as the trail makes a brief return to the conifers. It then drops back onto the river bottoms for a gentle ascent that lasts for the next 3.5 miles. This bottomland is dominated by red alder and bigleaf maple, although isolated stands of Sitka spruce, red cedar, and western hemlock rise high above the broadleaf trees. About halfway across the flats, a footlog spans the chattering waters of Pyrites Creek. An old trail once followed this streamcourse, but it has long since been abandoned.

At mile 11.8 the bottoms come to an end, and the trail climbs and dips among forested knolls. Just before reaching the Enchanted Valley, hikers are carried back to the south bank of the river on a suspension bridge. Stock parties will follow the north bank for another few hundred yards to reach a ford of the river. The path then runs across alder-dotted bottoms to reach the Enchanted Valley Chalet, located at the southern end of a grassy expanse of natural meadow. The craggy wall of Chimney Peak looms to the west, draped with dozens of ribbonlike cascades that drop from the snowy heights. The main peaks of Mount Anderson are just visible at the head of the valley, cupping between them a thick slab of glacial ice. The chalet was built of native timber in 1931 and was open until 1943 before it was taken over by the National Park Service. It recently served as a backcountry ranger station, but changes on the river course now threaten to undermine the historic structure. The camping area is spread out along the banks of the river, with a few sites scattered inland among the conifers at the head of the meadow.

From the chalet junction, hikers continuing on should bear northeast, taking an inland track along the edge of the meadows. About 0.5 mile later the open fields are replaced by a closed-canopy forest of hemlocks. This stand is soon interrupted by a wide avalanche slope filled with willow and slide alder. These brushy plants survive the frequent snowslides by virtue of their suppleness; they bend with the weight of the snow while the stiffer conifers snap like matchsticks. Soon thereafter the trail reaches a spur that runs down to the largest western hemlock on record. This behemoth was able to attain a diameter of almost 9 feet in the fertile glacial soils of the Quinault bottomland.

The main trail then begins to climb more briskly and soon crosses a footlog in the midst of the foaming cascades on White Creek. The climb steepens even more as the path ascends to its junction with the O'Neil Pass Trail. A distance marker for the Enchanted Valley Trail and several cairns mark its departure on the west bank of a rubble-filled watercourse. The forest is replaced by brushy slopes as the trail ascends, allowing views in all directions. A kink in the valley has put Chimney Peak directly behind the traveler, while the summits of Mount Anderson, White Mountain, and Mount Lacrosse are hidden above bulky pediments. Late-summer visitors will be

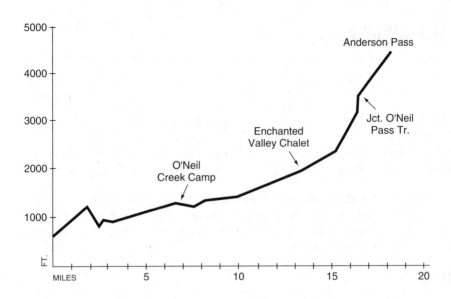

treated to an abundance of salmonberries and blueberries; be sure to yield the right-of-way to the black bears that often congregate here during berry season. After a long and grinding ascent, the trail passes into the mountain hemlocks of Anderson Pass. Just before reaching this summit, the tops of Mount Lacrosse and the West Peak of Mount Anderson become visible. Beyond the divide, trails to Anderson Glacier and down the West Fork of the Dosewallips are discussed in the Anderson Pass hike.

Key Points

0.0 Graves Creek trailhead. Trail crosses Graves Creek.

0.1 Junction with Graves Creek (Lake Sundown) Trail. Stay left.

2.5 Trail crosses Quinault River. Pony Bridge Camp.

3.5 Trail crosses Fire Creek.

6.7 Junction with spur to O'Neil Creek Camp.

8.3 Trail crosses No Name Creek.

9.8 Trail crosses Pyrites Creek. Pyrites Creek camping area.

12.7 Footbridge over Quinault River.

13.2 Enchanted Valley Chalet junction. Through hikers bear right.

15.2 Spur trail to record western hemlock.

16.0 Trail crosses White Creek.

16.4 Junction with O'Neil Pass Trail. Stay left.

18.1 Anderson Pass.

49 O'Neil Pass

An 8.6-mile extended trip from the Quinault River valley to Marmot Lake.

Difficulty: Moderate.
Trail type: Foot.
Best season: Early July to mid-October.
Elevation gain: 2,160 feet.

Elevation loss: 1,050 feet.
Maximum elevation: 5,000 feet.
Topo maps: Chimney Peak, Mount Steel; Custom Correct *Enchanted Valley–Skokomish*.

Finding the trailhead: This trail begins at a junction on the Enchanted Valley Trail (see the Enchanted Valley hike), about halfway between the chalet and Anderson Pass. There is a rushing stream at the junction that flows through a gully filled with boulders; look for a large cairn and an old, rusted trail sign to mark the spot.

The Hike

This trail offers more spectacular mountain scenery for the effort than any other on the Olympic Peninsula. It can only be reached via long treks up the Quinault, West Fork Dosewallips or Duckabush Rivers (see respective hike descriptions). The trail begins by climbing gently on a westward track to enter the drainage locally known as White Creek. It soon crosses a broad, open bowl where lush meadows rise into the steep scree slopes and rock spires of White Mountain. Look north for an excellent view of Mount Anderson with a large glacier perched high on its flanks.

The trail crosses the creek then climbs the western wall of the bowl. Upon reaching a forested rim, the trail turns south, traversing high above the Enchanted Valley. It soon reaches a steep avalanche chute, which heralds a zigzagging climb straight up. At the top of the grade, the trail turns south again and passes the remaining 6.2 miles in relatively level travel along the timberline. The mountainside traversed by the trail alternates between scattered stands of mountain hemlock and the flowery meadows of the avalanche paths. Bears and marmots are commonly seen in the meadowy openings, and the oval depressions left by bedding elk can sometimes be seen in the grass. Early on, the sandstone spires of Mount Anderson rise from the horizon like a vision from the Andes. Later the rugged east wall of Chimney Peak dominates the scenery. Look for the many tiny waterfalls that cascade across its sheer cliffs.

After traversing a particularly large and open basin, the path makes a sharp turn onto the southern slope of the ridge. The lone summit of massive stone is O'Neil Peak; a ragged and nameless

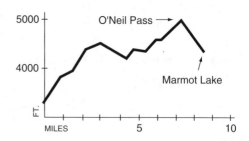

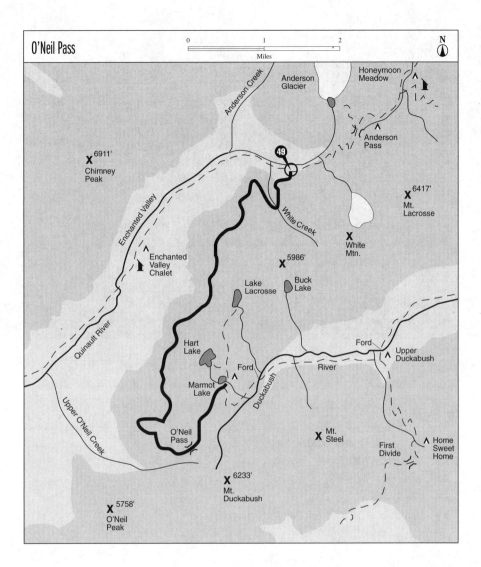

0   1   2

Miles

N

Anderson Creek

Anderson
Glacier

Honeymoon
Meadow

Anderson
Pass

49

X 6911'
Chimney
Peak

Enchanted Valley

White Creek

X 6417'
Mt.
Lacrosse

Enchanted
Valley
Chalet

X 5986'

X
White
Mtn.

Lake
Lacrosse

Buck
Lake

Quinault River

Hart
Lake

Ford

Upper
Duckabush

Ford

River

Duckabush

Marmot
Lake

Upper O'Neil Creek

O'Neil
Pass

X Mt.
Steel

First
Divide

Home
Sweet
Home

X 6233'
Mt.
Duckabush

X 5758'
O'Neil
Peak

cockscomb of rock rises beyond its eastern edge. Shortly thereafter the snow-clad summit of Mount Duckabush looms into view. The trail climbs a bit as it approaches O'Neil Pass. Shoulders of rock shield the surrounding peaks from view, but the pass does command a striking panorama of the Duckabush Valley to the north. The peaks of Mount Anderson are just visible through a depression in the ridge known locally as "Fisher's Notch," and the southern spurs of White Mountain rise above a flat shelf of meadowland. The trail then descends northward through the flower-splashed tundra as fine views of Mounts Steel and Duckabush unveil themselves to the south. The trail reaches its terminus at a junction beside Marmot Lake; for a complete description of this and other neighboring lakes, read the Duckabush River section.

Looking east from O'Neil Pass

Key Points

0.0 Junction with Enchanted Valley Trail.

0.9 Trail crosses White Creek.

2.2 Top of initial grade.

7.4 O'Neil Pass.

8.6 Marmot Lake. Junction with Duckabush River Trail.

50 The North Fork of the Quinault

A 16.4-mile backpack from the North Fork Ranger Station to Low Divide.

Difficulty: Moderate.
Trail type: Primary.
Best season: All year.
Elevation gain: 3,776 feet.
Elevation loss: 676 feet.

Maximum elevation: 3,650 feet (Low Divide).
Topo maps: Bunch Lake, Kimta Peak, Mount Christie, Mount Hoquiam; Custom Correct *Quinault-Colonel Bob*.

Finding the trailhead: From U.S. Highway 101 at mile 125.5, turn east onto Lake Quinault South Shore Road. The pavement ends after 7.8 miles, and 5 miles later is a bridge over the Quinault. Turn left to cross it, and then turn right onto North Shore Road for the remaining 3.3 miles to the trailhead and ranger station at road's end.

The Hike

This major valley-bottom route follows the North Fork of the Quinault to the Low Divide, where it meets the Elwha River Trail and a spur path to the alpine country around Martins Lakes. From the North Fork Ranger Station, the trail follows an old roadbed through a rain forest of great diversity. On drier sites enormous Sitka spruce and red cedar soar skyward. The flats of the floodplain are dominated by groves of slender red alders and pure stands of gnarled bigleaf maples draped with streamers of moss. The path runs level here, twice crossing a dry flood channel about 1.2 miles below Wolf Bar Camp. This camp is perched among tall alders and bushy clumps of sword fern beside the river.

The main trail soon works its way onto the hillside above the valley floor, and the surroundings begin to lose their rain forest aspect. Just after crossing Wild Rose Creek, the path descends onto another forested bottom, where it reaches the Halfway House camping area. This site was a rest stop for travelers on their way to the resort that once stood near the Low Divide. Although it does not appear on some maps, it is by far the most attractive campsite on the North Fork. A group site sits beneath a trailside grove of tall conifers, while others sites lie among the alders of the riverbank. At this point the river flows lazily through quiet pools between two opposing outcrops of metamorphic rock. On the far bank a waterfall splashes into its own tiny basin before joining the waters of the river.

The flats continue for a short distance beyond the camp, then give way to a series of forested finger ridges. The next campsite occupies the northern bank of Elip Creek in a ragged meadow beside the brushy stream bank. The trail passes this camp and then climbs onto the hillside beyond to reach a junction with the Elip Creek cutoff trail. The North Fork Trail continues north from this point, crossing a flat terrace covered with old-growth hemlocks. The level bench is scored with deep ravines

Mount Seattle rising beyond the larger of Martins Lakes

containing the streams that descend from the west: Three Prune, Stalding, and Kimta. A sturdy pack bridge spans each cleft, and a scattering of western red cedar lends variety to the streamside timber.

Beyond Kimta Creek lies a boggy shelf of open forest and brush that contains the Trapper shelter and camping area. After crossing this bottomland, the trail climbs onto a hillside grown thickly with young hemlock. This is the site of an old forest fire, and silvery snags still rise from the younger trees on the hillside far above the trail. The path sticks to the steep slopes high above the river on its way to Twelvemile Camp, ascending in sporadic bursts. A number of nameless tributaries drop across the hillside and are bordered by loose gravel and open brushfields that allow ever-improving views of Mount Lawson on the far side of the river. The trail then leaves the dry hillsides to return to the lush forests of the floodplain. Here Twelvemile Camp and its shelter lie among groves of alders and tall hemlocks beside the river.

After a short hump over the intervening hillside, the trail descends to ford the river. The water can be 3 to 4 feet deep in May, but decreases to a moderate knee-deep flow in midsummer. A rope is usually in place across the river to help hikers with their balance as they cross. The Sixteen Mile Camp lies among the old-growth hemlocks of the far bank. It derives its name from the time before the road was built up the North Fork and travelers hiked in from the confluence of the two rivers. From this point the trail climbs steadily for a time then levels off after attaining a height

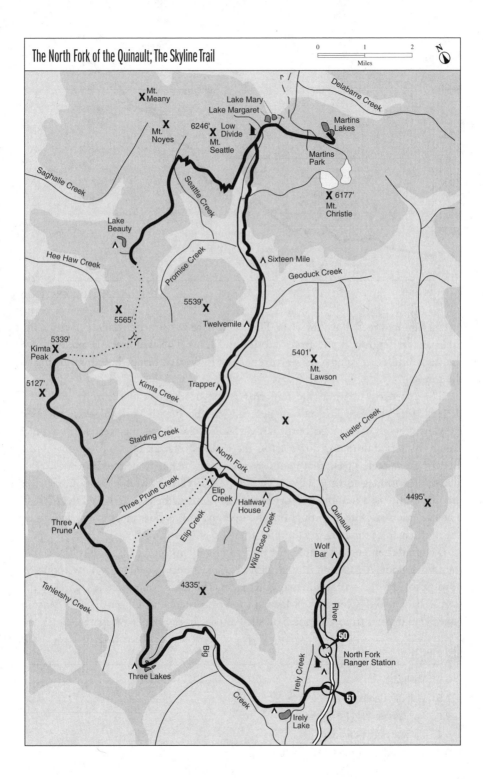

0   1   2
Miles

N

X Mt. Meany

Lake Mary
Lake Margaret

Delabarre Creek

X Mt. Noyes

6246' **X** Low Divide
Mt. Seattle

Martins Lakes

Martins Park

X 6177'
Mt. Christie

Saghalie Creek

Seattle Creek

Lake Beauty ∧

Hee Haw Creek

∧ Sixteen Mile

Promise Creek

Geoduck Creek

5539' **X**
Twelvemile ∧

X 5565'

5339'
Kimta **X**
Peak

5401' **X**
Mt. Lawson

5127' **X**

Kimta Creek

Trapper ∧

X

Stalding Creek

Rustler Creek

North Fork

Three Prune Creek

Elip Creek

Elip Creek

Halfway House ∧

Wild Rose Creek

Quinault

4495' **X**

Three Prune ∧

Wolf Bar ∧

Tshletshy Creek

4335' **X**

Big

River

50

North Fork Ranger Station

Three Lakes ∧

Creek

Irely Creek

∧

51

Irely Lake ∧

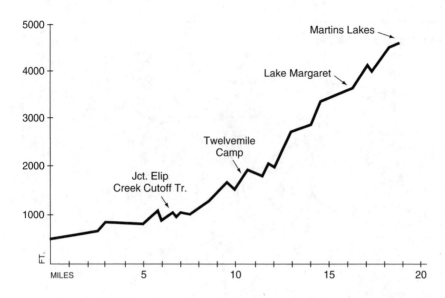

several hundred feet above the river. The forest here is distinctly montane, with a less luxuriant undergrowth and fewer mosses and ferns. The trail ascends gradually for the next 3 miles, crossing a major torrent via a lofty pack bridge before returning to the forest.

The forest opens up as the trail crosses the headwaters of the river, and soon thereafter the Skyline Ridge Trail descends to the North Fork. A series of open meadows reveals the jagged buttresses of Mount Seattle to the west, with a silver skein of waterfall dropping down across the rock. Look back for a moment for a fine view of the nameless peak that stands sentinel over the headwaters of Promise Creek. The trail continues north as willows crowd the waterway. The ranger station occupies the former site of a mountain resort in the last meadow below the Low Divide itself. The campsites are spread throughout the opening at great distances from each other; check the map at the ranger station for their exact locations.

The trail then enters the trees for the rather anticlimactic final stroll to the top of the Low Divide. A parkland dotted with heather, shooting star, and yellow monkey-flower provides the setting for two quiet lakes. The larger one, Lake Margaret, is the first to be reached, while Lake Mary lies a short distance to the north. The Martins Lakes Trail departs from a signpost on the eastern shore of Lake Margaret.

Key Points

0.0 Trailhead.

2.5 Wolf Bar Camp.

4.9 Trail crosses Wild Rose Creek.

5.1 Halfway House Camp.

6.4 Trail crosses Elip Creek. Elip Creek Camp.

6.5 Junction with Elip Creek cutoff trail. Stay right.

6.8 Trail crosses Three Prune Creek.

7.4 Trail crosses Stalding Creek.

7.7 Trail crosses Kimta Creek.

8.2 Trapper Camp.

11.5 Twelvemile Camp.

12.2 Trail fords North Fork Quinault River. Sixteen Mile Camp.

15.7 Trail crosses headwaters of North Fork Quinault River.

15.8 Junction with Skyline Ridge Trail. Bear right.

16.0 Low Divide Ranger Station and Camp.

16.3 Trail crosses Low Divide.

16.4 Lake Margaret. Junction with Elwha River and Martins Lakes Trails.

Martins Lakes Option: This primitive trail climbs into alpine country recently scoured by glaciers descending from Mount Christie. It offers a fine day trip for travelers of adventurous spirit who find themselves in the Low Divide area. It begins by running southeast through soggy country covered in a loose subalpine forest. After 0.5 mile of travel, the track comes to a dry ravine that runs between steep rock walls. The route follows the wash upward, and some scrambling is required. The path soon finds level ground again and proceeds southward. Martins Park is 1 mile into the trek, a broad expanse of wet meadow dotted with boulders brought down from Mount Christie by glaciers. The crags of this peak rise above the head of the steep rivulet that feeds the park.

The path soon finds its way into the valley of a rushing torrent that rises in the south. This stream is soon crossed, and the trail climbs steadily through the alder on its eastern bank. The upper basin of this stream lies 0.6 mile above Martins Park. Evidence of recent glaciation is everywhere: Moraines left by the retreating glacier lie across the valley floor, and patches of exposed bedrock bear deep grooves that were carved by the ice. Much of the valley floor has yet to be colonized by plants, retaining its primordial condition as bare stone and rubble. The trail soon climbs the meadowy slope opposite Mount Christie, whose spires and turrets cup the tiny vestiges of glaciers that once filled the entire basin. After a brisk ascent the trail doglegs back to the north and runs level to reach Martins Lakes. The first lake to be reached is shallow and aquamarine, while just beyond it lies the deeper tarn, a deep blue-green. The lakes occupy a lofty shelf that makes an excellent perch for viewing Mounts Seattle and Meany, which raise their rocky crests directly to the north.

51 The Skyline Trail

This is a 29.9-mile wilderness route from the Irely Lake trailhead to the North Fork Quinault Trail. (See map on page 183.)

Difficulty: Moderately strenuous to Three Prune Camp; strenuous beyond.
Trail type: Foot to Three Lakes; primitive beyond.
Best season: Late July to mid-October.

Elevation gain: 9,180 feet.
Elevation loss: 6,110 feet.
Maximum elevation: 5,330 feet.
Topo maps: Bunch Lake, Kitma Peak, Mount Christie; Custom Correct *Quinault-Colonel Bob*.

Finding the trailhead: From U.S. Highway 101 at mile 125.5, turn east onto Lake Quinault South Shore Road. The pavement ends after 7.8 miles, and 5 miles later is a bridge over the Quinault. Turn left to cross it, and then turn right onto North Shore Road for the remaining 2.6 miles to the well-marked trailhead for Irely Lake.

The Hike

This trail offers an outstanding ridge walk along the Queets–Quinault divide, with outstanding views of the wild and remote peaks of the southwestern Olympics. The path is quite difficult to follow between Kimta Peak and Lake Beauty, and some route-finding ability is required. The Skyline Ridge Trail can be combined with the North Fork of the Quinault for a loop trip of five to six days.

The trail begins in the rain forest river bottoms of the Quinault's North Fork. It runs northward among the stout trunks of old-growth red cedar and Sitka spruce, climbing in short bursts across the forested benchlands. Ferns and mosses grow from every available surface, suffusing the landscape with green. After 0.7 mile the trail crosses tiny Irely Creek and begins to follow its meandering, brush-choked channel. Salmonberries and thimbleberries grow side by side here, and are soon joined by a profusion of red huckleberries on the benches overlooking Irely Lake. This large rain forest pool is surrounded by wet meadows, forming a rare and important pocket of wetland in the midst of the conifers. Ospreys, waterfowl, and beavers are commonly seen at the lake and the surrounding marshes. There is a primitive camping area at the north end, but mosquitoes here are known to be fierce.

The main trail skirts the eastern side of the lake, then climbs aggressively as it makes its way into the valley of Big Creek. The path clings to the steep slopes several hundred feet above the stream as the forest steadily takes on a more montane character. Ferns and wood sorrel still abound in the understory, however, reminding the traveler that even the high slopes receive ample rainfall. The trail parallels Big Creek for 2.5 miles, then crosses it at an elaborate footbridge that arches gracefully above the mossy pools and rushing chutes. The trail then climbs steeply away from the stream on its way up the western wall of the valley.

Rugged crags beyond the Queets Valley

The ascent slackens a bit as the route bends westward to enter a broad, shallow basin. Along the way a signpost marks the location of the largest Alaska cedar tree ever recorded. The forest begins to open up into wet meadows and brushfields interspersed with stands of mountain hemlock and Alaska cedar. Sedges and cottongrass occupy the water-soaked swales, while a dense growth of blueberry bushes adorns the well-drained hillocks. At the head of the valley, the trail reaches the Three Lakes camping area, situated beside a large pond and surrounded by open meadows. The abandoned Tshletshy Creek Trail is discernible as it breaks away to the west, while the Skyline Ridge Trail turns north.

After crossing the headwaters of Big Creek, the path begins to descend gradually through the montane forest. It passes a tiny pond, rises through the forest obscuring nearby Reflection Lake, then crosses the almost imperceptible divide into the Elip Creek drainage. At this open and windswept spot, a broad expanse of heather allows outstanding views of the ranges to the east. The rugged crag rising from the wooded ridges due east is Mount Lawson, and Muncaster Mountain rises to a sharp point beyond the U-shaped valley of Rustler Creek.

The trail passes several gemlike pools set among the rolling meadows of the upper Elip basin, then climbs the spur ridge to the north. The first glimpse of Mount Olympus can be had atop this divide. The trail then makes a brief but rather steep descent through a loose-knit subalpine forest, then begins to follow the contours around the head of the Three Prune drainage. The Elip Creek cutoff trail soon joins the Skyline route, and 1.5 miles later the trail arrives at Three Prune Camp. This spot occupies a collection of open knolls in the northeast corner of the basin and commands views of Muncaster Mountain. Elephant's head blooms amid the cottongrass of the low spots; the drier ground is lit by the bulblike blossoms of beargrass.

The trail then begins to climb through heavy timber, passing above the headwaters of Stalding Creek. The trees thin out here, and the path follows the ridgetop northward. On two occasions the trail crosses over the ridgeline to pass west of high points; the second of these west-facing hillsides sports an open meadow that looks out over the forested drainage of Alta Creek. The next pass is covered in open fellfield, where late-blooming wildflowers brave lingering snowdrifts to bring color to the high country. The slopes beyond this pass are dotted with clumps of ancient mountain hemlocks. In this part of the range, timberline is determined not by cold or wind but by patterns of lingering snow; seedlings that take root on raised knolls where the snow melts early can be expected to grow rapidly.

The next open slope marks the ascent of Kimta Peak. The path climbs steeply through the flowery meadow, and hikers must face bushy hemlock saplings that contest the right-of-way. The trail stops climbing just below the western summit of the mountain, then begins a long descent across open slopes dissected by a number of rushing rivulets. After quite some time the trail enters a swampy forest, where the path grows faint beneath a dense growth of tall grasses. This forest soon gives way to the stark, skeletal snags of the Kimta Peak burn. This fire razed 177 acres of timber in 1987. The trail is difficult to detect as it crosses the fire-scarred landscape; look for flagging and sawed deadfalls.

On the far side of the burn, the trail embarks on one of the great killer grades in the park. This incredibly steep path ends at a high pass at the head of the Promise Creek drainage. A primordial rockscape of tilted phyllite shot through with veins of quartz stretches broadly to encompass the entire headwaters area. Follow the cairns uphill to the north as the path fades to an indistinct route across bare bedrock and scree. Mount Seattle dominates the northern skyline, while a nameless crag guards the eastern approaches to Promise Creek. After nearing the ridgetop, travelers should follow cairns on a long downhill arc. The descent ends where the rock is covered with trees and meadows; here the trail climbs and drops dramatically as it picks its way among the vertically tilted strata that block its path. Excellent views of Mount Christie open up before the trail climbs into a pass above the head of Hee Haw Creek.

The steady descent continues across the western side of the ridge, where open slopes allow outstanding views of Mount Olympus and the crags that trail away to the west of it. These peaks are nameless, but mountaineers call them "The Valhallas." The next saddle in the ridgetop is riven so deeply by erosion that the uplifted sheets of bedrock rise from the soil like bared bones. The junction with the Lake Beauty Trail lies at the northern edge of this pass. This path descends steeply for 0.3 mile to reach a campsite beside the lake. The water is tinted such that the deeper parts appear

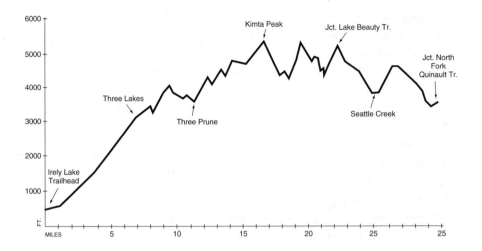

dark blue, while the shallows are a shade of turquoise. The meadowy hummocks surrounding the lake offer fine views of the Olympus massif across the deep Queets Valley, which is often filled with low clouds.

The main trail jogs east from the rocky saddle, maintaining its altitude with a series of gentle rises and descents. As the trail rounds a bend in the hillside, the sparsely forested slopes give way to meadowy benches that hold a scattering of ponds and rivulets. These meadows provide the picturesque foreground for the towering rock mass of Mount Seattle, which rises above the head of Seattle Creek along with its companion peak, Mount Noyes. After departing the high benchlands, the trail begins a gradual descent into the valley, then switchbacks downward through the trees at a more workmanlike pace. Near the bottom of the grade, the path traverses northeast once more, paralleling the meadowy course of Seattle Creek. The creek bottoms possess a subalpine character due to the snows that linger here into the summer, creating a sort of reverse timberline.

After a boulder hop across the rushing waters, the trail begins to climb the forested east wall of the valley. It switchbacks high onto the shoulders of Mount Seattle, where rolling country is covered with heather and blueberry bushes. After rounding the corner into the North Fork Quinault valley, the trail maintains its altitude to pass through rocky forest openings. The rocky spires of Mount Christie rise sheer above the deep trench carved over the course of millennia by glaciers. The trail soon zigzags down through the timber, then turns northeast to parallel the course of the North Fork. After 0.5 mile it reaches a junction with the North Fork Quinault Trail in a meadow just below the Low Divide Ranger Station.

Key Points

0.0 Irely Lake trailhead.
0.7 Trail crosses Irely Creek.

1.1	Spur path to Irely Lake.
4.0	Trail crosses Big Creek.
6.0	Trail passes record Alaska cedar.
7.0	Three Lakes Camp. Junction with abandoned Tshletshy Creek Trail. Turn right.
8.9	Trail crosses divide into Elip Creek drainage.
9.6	Trail enters Three Prune drainage.
9.9	Junction with Elip Creek cutoff trail. Stay left.
11.4	Three Prune Camp.
12.6	Trail crosses divide into Stalding Creek drainage.
17.0	Trail passes Kimta Peak.
19.3	Trail enters Promise Creek basin.
22.5	Junction with spur to Lake Beauty. Through hikers bear right.
25.5	Trail fords Seattle Creek.
29.9	Junction with North Fork Quinault Trail.

52 The Queets River

A 16.1-mile backpack from Queets River Road to the Pelton Creek shelter.

Difficulty: Moderate.
Trail type: Secondary to Bob Creek; primitive beyond.
Best season: Early July to mid-October.
Elevation gain: 540 feet.

Elevation loss: 70 feet.
Maximum elevation: 810 feet.
Topo maps: Salmon River, Kloochman Rock; Custom Correct *Queets Valley.*

Finding the trailhead: From the village of Queets, drive southeast 7 miles on U.S. Highway 101, then turn north onto Queets River Road at mile 144.6. Follow this narrow gravel road (unsuited to trailers and RVs) 13.8 miles to reach the trailhead at road's end. Queets River Road was washed out at Matheny Creek at press time (but the trail remains open); check at a ranger station for current conditions.

The Hike

This trail follows the Queets River into some of the most remote and primitive country in Olympic National Park. The Queets derives its name from a tribal legend in which the Great Spirit waded across the cold river, then rubbed his legs to warm himself. He threw the rolls of mud and skin into the river, and out came the first man and woman of the Quaitso tribe. Thus, Queets is laterally translated, "out of the dirt of the skin."

The trek begins with a waist-deep ford of the swift-flowing river. Approach the crossing in early morning, before the daily pulse of glacial meltwater raises the river

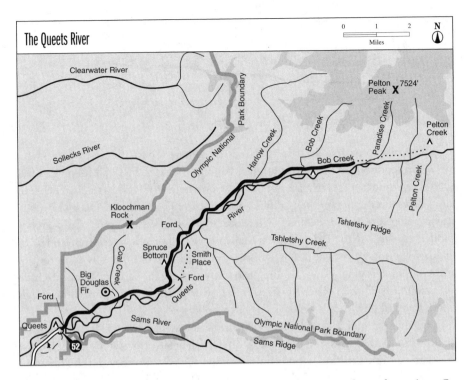

level. It is best to look for braided channels and cross them one channel at a time. On the far bank the trail runs northeast through a sparse stand of tall alders, with grass carpeting the forest floor. After a short time the trail arrives at the Andrews homestead, where a decaying barn lies in ruin amid tall grasses and thistles of the meadows. Kloochman Rock is visible to the north, perched atop a wooded ridge.

The trail then delves back into the rain forest, where streamers of moss hang from the vine maples and clumps of sword fern grow to the size of bushes. The foundation of an old one-room schoolhouse occupies the edge of a smaller opening near the junction with the old Kloochman Rock Trail. Here, on the banks of Coal Creek, a spur path runs 0.2 mile to reach a Douglas fir that was once the largest of its species. Storms have taken the top of this venerable giant, but it retains an impressive girth of 17 feet.

The main trail crosses Coal Creek and continues to follow the river. At mile 4.2 a signpost marks the lower crossing of the Queets on a trail that once ascended Tshletshy Creek. Bear left and continue through the forest as the trail climbs and drops in crossing small ridges. The Spruce Bottom camping area lies on the riverbank amid the huge trunks of rain forest conifers, and just beyond it lies an unmarked trail junction. The more heavily worn path turns southeast to cross the river on its way to the Smith Place, a popular campsite on the south bank of the river. The main trail bears left, becoming a bit faint as it crosses grassy savannas dotted with the gnarled forms of bigleaf maples.

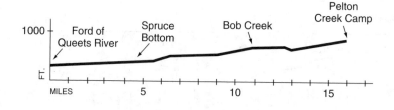

The trail approaches the riverside at its confluence with Tshletshy Creek, and oddly formed foothills rise beyond the far bank of the river. The trail follows a series of level riverside benches that are important winter range for Roosevelt elk. These rain forest herbivores maintain the parklike appearance of the river bottoms by browsing out invading shrubs and seedlings. There are several impressive stands of old-growth conifers on the way to Harlow Creek. Many of these enormous trees seem to rise on stilts, with a hollow core at the base of the trunk. Such trees originally took root on nurse logs or decaying stumps, sending roots down along the dead wood to reach the forest soil below. When the dead wood rotted away, these roots supported the weight of the tree and grew stout with age around a hollow center.

The massive bulk of Tshletshy Ridge rises across the river as the trail crosses Harlow and Bob Creeks in rapid succession. The shelter at Bob Creek burned down long ago, but one can find good campsites along the river just beyond it. The trail is maintained infrequently beyond this point, so travelers should expect blowdowns and route-finding problems for the remaining distance to the Pelton Creek shelter. The trail soon climbs over a steep hillside, where a square outcrop of bedrock looms out of the steep slope. The path then returns to the bottomland, crossing Paradise Creek and one other stream on its way to the Pelton Creek shelter. The shelter itself is located in a rather brushy and unattractive spot; good campsites along the river bar offer views of Pelton Peak.

Key Points

0.0   Trailhead and ford of Queets River.

1.7   Andrews Field.

2.3   Spur path to former record Douglas fir.

2.4   Trail crosses Coal Creek.

4.2   Junction with lower ford trail. Bear left.

5.1   Spruce Bottom Camp.

5.8   Junction with upper ford trail. Turn left.

9.5   Trail crosses Harlow Creek.

11.2   Trail crosses Bob Creek.

13.6   Trail crosses Paradise Creek.

16.1   Pelton Creek shelter.

53 The South Fork of the Hoh River

This is a remote 4-mile day hike or short backpack to the east end of Big Flat.

Difficulty: Moderate.
Trail type: Foot.
Best season: All year.
Elevation gain: 110 feet.

Elevation loss: 140 feet.
Maximum elevation: 850 feet.
Topo maps: Mount Tom; Custom Correct *Mount Olympus Climber's Map.*

Finding the trailhead: From mile 176 on U.S. Highway 101 (just south of the Hoh Oxbow Campground), turn southeast onto paved Clearwater Road. Drive 8 miles and turn left at signs for the South Fork Campground. Follow markers for Road 1000 for 10 miles, past the South Fork Campground, to the trailhead at road's end.

The Hike

This remote trail offers a quiet stroll through the rain forest and big timber along the South Fork of the Hoh River. From the trailhead the path descends through a strand

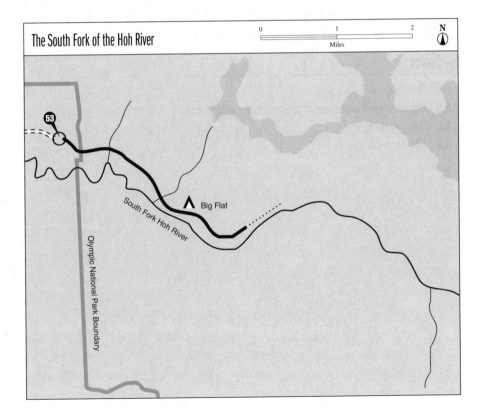

of young spruce, passing a hairpin turn on a closed logging road before veering away to the east. The forest
is less dense beyond the park boundary, with a complex overstory featuring a variety of canopy heights.
Huge Sitka spruce and western hemlock tower above
all, while their younger relatives vie for openings in the

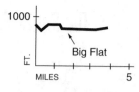

canopy. Vine maple is a common understory shrub, and a variety of forbs and ferns
decorate the forest floor.

The descent continues past a fair-size stream before dropping the traveler onto
Big Flat, a broad swath of bottomland on the north bank of the South Fork. Potential campsites abound as the trail continues eastward just out of sight of the river.
Ancient spruce trees are spaced hundreds of feet apart, with an understory sometimes
crowded with red alder and vine maple and at other times almost entirely absent. The
path swings next to an overlook of the river, then crosses through a dense growth of
salmonberry on its way inland again. Higher, well-drained benches support stands of
Sitka spruce that commonly exceed 10 feet in diameter.

As the track nears the river once again, grassy savannas separate the conifers and
render the trail difficult to detect. It can be followed, however, beyond the next river
overlook that features views of Hoh Peak. After crossing a considerable amount of
deadfall, the trail peters out on the eastern end of the flats. A hillside descends steeply
to meet the river here, blocking further progress to the east.

Key Points

0.0 Trailhead.

0.5 Olympic National Park boundary and registration station.

1.5 Trail enters Big Flat.

4.0 End of trail.

54 The Hoh River

A 17.5-mile backpack from the Hoh Rainforest Visitor Center to Glacier Meadows, with an extra 0.6-mile hike to reach the Blue Glacier overlook.

Difficulty: Easy to Olympus Meadows; moderately strenuous beyond.
Trail type: Primary to Martin Creek; foot beyond.
Best season: All year.
Elevation gain: 4,200 feet.

Elevation loss: 100 feet.
Maximum elevation: 4,700 feet (Blue Glacier overlook).
Topo maps: Mount Tom, Mount Olympus; Custom Correct *Seven Lakes Basin–Hoh*.

Finding the trailhead: From Forks, drive south on U.S. Highway 101 to mile 178.5. Turn east onto paved Hoh River Road. Drive 18 miles to the trailhead and visitor center at road's end.

The Hike

This trail offers an outstanding sample of the diverse habitats of Olympic National Park, from primeval rain forests to windswept icefields. Its easy access makes it one of the most popular treks in the park, and travelers may want to schedule their visit here off-season to avoid the crowds. Permits are obtained at the Hoh Rainforest Visitor Center, although reservations are not currently required. *Hoh* is an adaptation of the Salish *ohalet,* meaning "white water."

The journey starts on the paved walkway that is shared with the Spruce Nature Trail. The Hoh River Trail soon splits off to the northeast, a wide, smooth path that runs across the forest duff. The lower portion of the Hoh valley is robed in a magnificent rain forest, where the enormous boles of the Sitka spruce rise like pillars from the verdant forest floor. Mosses, ferns, and conifer seedlings carpet every level spot, including fallen logs and standing stumps. The trail wanders close to the river at times, affording campsites for short-range travelers. It soon crosses a substantial stream, and soon afterward a smaller cousin. At this point Mount Tom can be glimpsed to the southeast through a curtain of foliage.

Soon afterward, a spur path leads to Tom Creek Meadows, a camping area situated in a grassy grove of red alder on the riverbank. The Hoh River meanders across a broad bed of outwash gravel, shifting its course after every major storm. Beyond this point a handful of western red cedars are conspicuously present in the overstory; some attain magnificent proportions. At mile 4.5 the trail crosses a well-drained terrace. Here ancient spruces rise rank on rank with little intervening vegetation to mask the magnificent vertical landscape.

The route then drops to the river bottoms, crossing dry sloughs and tarrying among tall alders and squat, moss-draped vine maples. There are unmarked campsites among the bottomland at mile 5. At mile 5.8 the Happy Four shelter looms into

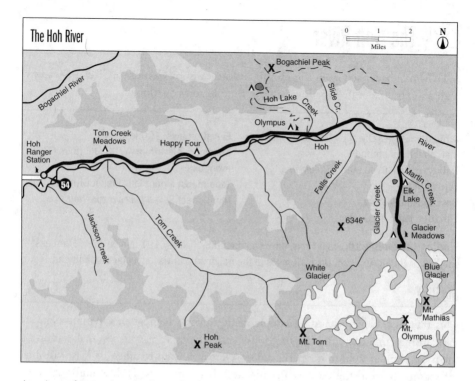

The Hoh River

0   1   2
Miles

N

Bogachiel Peak

Bogachiel River

Hoh Lake

Slide Cr.

Creek

Olympus

Tom Creek
Meadows

Happy Four

Hoh

Hoh
Ranger
Station

54

Jackson Creek

Tom Creek

Falls Creek

River

Martin Creek

Elk
Lake

X 6346'

Glacier Creek

Glacier
Meadows

White
Glacier

Blue
Glacier

X
Mt.
Mathias

X
Mt.
Olympus

Hoh
X Peak

X
Mt. Tom

view in a gloomy stand of conifers. The campsites are on an alder-covered river bottom to the south. Beyond this point broadleaf trees become increasingly prevalent in the forest canopy, with only a scattering of conifers overtopping them. The spruces and cedars fall away entirely for a long stretch as the trail wanders through a green gallery of overhanging vine maples. A few old, wolfy bigleaf maples rise above their low-growing cousins, and these gnarled giants are twisted into odd shapes and hung with streamers of moss.

The trail then swings back toward the river, heralding the return of the conifers. From the floodplain, visitors can glimpse the destruction wrought by the Hoh Lake Fire of 1978 on the ridges to the north. The trail soon climbs across a hillside consumed by the blaze. The forest heals itself quickly in these moist environs, and the burn site is host to a profusion of alder, bracken fern, and salmonberry. A few Douglas fir seedlings have also made a start here and will provide the next generation of climax forest. The snowy tops of the Bailey Range are partly visible from the burned hillside.

The path soon returns to the valley floor, crossing a slough and running out onto the meadowy bottoms that shelter Olympus Guard Station. A few old cottonwoods grow to enormous sizes on this fertile bottomland. Tents can be pitched at designated sites among the alders of the riverside, and black-tailed deer commonly visit the meadows in front of the patrol cabin. In the interest of keeping these animals in a wild state, take extra precautions to make sure that they do not get food from unnatural sources. Half a mile beyond the ranger station, the Hoh Lake Trail (see the Hoh Lake hike) takes off to the left. The main trail continues up the valley through a forest in transition between lowland and montane communities: Sitka spruce is steadily replaced by Douglas fir and western hemlock, although red cedar maintains a minor presence. After crossing the dry bed of Hoh Lake Creek, the trail wanders past Lewis Meadow. This opening, frequently visited by deer and elk, offers a last glimpse of the Bailey Range.

Beyond this meadow the valley walls close in around the surging waters of the Hoh, and the trail leads uphill at an increasingly steady pace. There are several fine riverside campsites set among the sun-dappled conifers of the riverbank. After a brief climb the trail drops down to a bridge that spans a deep chasm carved by the rushing torrent. The upper basin of the river was once a hanging valley carved by glacial erosion, but the river has worn its way through the headwall of the lower valley and now links the two basins without the interruption of a waterfall.

Once on the far bank, the path begins a vigorous ascent through a forest lit in early June by the tiny white blossoms of twinflower. It emerges at a crossing of Martins Creek, where a horse camp offers the last chance for campfires before the trail enters the subalpine zone. After a brief wander through the forest, the trail arrives at the shore of Elk Lake. Waterlilies crowd its still waters, which reflect the craggy spurs of the Olympus massif. There is a shelter and numerous campsites in the grove of old hemlocks above the lake, and a healthy population of brook trout cruises its waters and provides fair fishing.

Beyond this point the trail climbs swiftly into the avalanche fields overlooking the lake. These openings offer fine views of the snowy ridgecrest to the west. The trail passes through a forest of silver fir and Alaska cedar for a time, then emerges as it rounds a series of steep, washed-out spurs. Numerous landslides provide outstanding views of one of the buttresses of Mount Olympus, which hides the summit of the peak behind its massive bulk. The path then descends into a vale forested in young subalpine firs to reach the Glacier Meadows campground.

From this point a rough track runs to the east, passing the ranger tent as it runs toward the terminal moraine of Blue Glacier. This massive wall of rocky debris was bulldozed into place by the relentless grinding of the glacier over the course of many millennia. The path makes its way up the western slope of the moraine, which is being colonized by the subalpine forest. It soon reaches a marked junction, where travelers have two choices. The path straight ahead climbs onto the lateral moraine of the Blue Glacier and allows climbers to access the ice. The lateral moraine offers sweeping views of the Blue Glacier icefall, and the summits of Mount Olympus rise beyond the ice.

The path to the right runs southward among the loose boulders and pioneering vegetation. The trail reaches its terminus in a notch between two monolithic outcrops, with a panorama of rock and ice so powerful and primordial that viewers may experience a temporary loss of speech. The enormous ice mass of the Blue Glacier

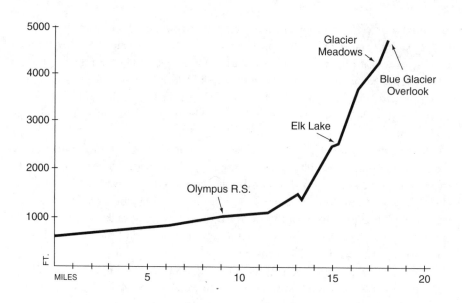

flows down from the summit of Olympus, carving a channel through the stark precipices that surround it. The main summits of Olympus are hidden behind the mass of the Snow Dome, but the sawtooth spires of Mount Mathias loom above the ice in plain view. Deep crevasses in the glacier glow with an ethereal blue light; these chasms are a deadly peril to climbers who venture out onto the ice. Before leaving, examine the bedrock underfoot for striations that indicate the passage of the ice over this lip during colder times.

Key Points

55 Hoh Lake

A 6.5-mile trip from the Hoh River to the High Divide Trail.

Difficulty: Strenuous south to north; moderately strenuous north to south.
Trail type: Secondary.
Best season: Early July to mid-October.

Elevation gain: 4,300 feet.
Maximum elevation: 5,300 feet.
Topo maps: Bogachiel Peak; Custom Correct *Seven Lakes Basin–Hoh*.

Finding the trailhead: This trail begins at mile 9.8 on the Hoh River Trail (see the Hoh River hike), just east of Olympus Guard Station.

The Hike

This trail climbs steadily up the north wall of the Hoh valley, passing the alpine basin of Hoh Lake on its way to meet the High Divide Trail. Most of the climb is

Mount Olympus from the Hoh Lake Trail

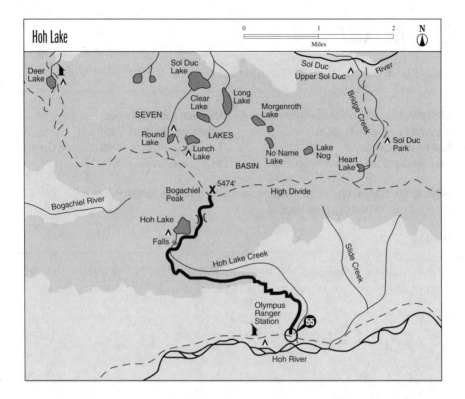

across open slopes burned in 1978, and this area is baked by the sun from midday on. Campsites at Hoh Lake and CB Flats require reservations, which can be obtained at neighboring ranger stations.

The trail departs from the Hoh River Trail just east of Olympus Guard Station and runs northward across the valley floor. The chuckling sound of Hoh Lake Creek can soon be heard to the east of the trail. As the trail scales the valley wall, the trees soon give way to the brushy slopes of the Hoh Lake burn. This blaze started with a lightning strike on the lower slopes, and winds fanned the flames uphill toward Hoh Lake. The entire ridge was burned, making this one of the largest fires ever recorded in Olympic National Park. The next 2.5 miles of climbing alternate between strips of surviving trees and the brushlands of the burn, where the transpiration of the plants hits the traveler in humid waves on sunny days.

The trail completes the initial ascent atop a razor-edge ridge, which it follows across dips and rises toward the west. The open country of the burn reveals a vista of the Hoh's braided channels meandering across its gravel bed, with the snow-dappled peaks of the Olympus massif rising above it. After entering the forest, the path makes a shallow descent into the vale of Hoh Lake Creek before resuming the climb. A marked campsite offers the last opportunity for campfires as the trail moves into alpine country, crossing seeps and streamlets that run across flowery glades.

The forest opens up when the hiker reaches CB Flats; this grassy opening offers the first glimpses of the summit of Mount Olympus. The path runs straight across the meadow, then passes beneath the first of three delightful cascades that are draped across the headwall below the foot of the lake; permits for this area must be obtained at a ranger station. The climb picks up a bit as the trail makes one long switchback to the east before depositing the traveler on the shore of Hoh Lake. This aquamarine gem sits in a compact basin with steep walls covered in alpine meadows. Marmots frolic amid the flowers and issue piercing alarm whistles upon the approach of hawks and eagles. There are several fine campsites on the far side of the outlet stream below the foot of the lake.

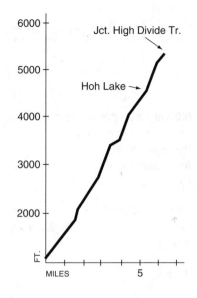

The main trail turns east, climbing the spur ridge above the lake. It occasionally wanders through openings that offer superb aerial views of the clear waters of the lake. The trail soon pops through a saddle in the ridgeline, and spectacular vistas open up on all sides. The glacier-clad crests of Mount Olympus preside over the scene, with Mount Mathias and Mount Tom flanking them on either side. Cat Peak rises to the east at the tail end of the Bailey Range. The path then works its way north across grassy slopes to the base of Bogachiel Peak, where it meets the High Divide Trail.

Key Points

0.0 Junction with Hoh River Trail.
3.1 Top of ridge.
4.5 CB Flats.
5.3 Hoh Lake. Turn right for the High Divide.
6.5 Trail meets High Divide Trail.

56 The Bogachiel River

A 23.2-mile backpack from Forest Road 2932 to the Mink Lake–Little Divide Trail.

Difficulty: Moderate to Fifteen Mile Camp; moderately strenuous beyond.
Trail type: Secondary.
Best season: All year.
Elevation gain: 4,685 feet.

Elevation loss: 1,005 feet.
Maximum elevation: 4,304 feet.
Topo maps: Slide Peak, Hunger Mountain, Indian Pass, Reade Hills; Custom Correct *Bogachiel Valley.*

Finding the trailhead: From Forks, drive south on U.S. Highway 101 to Bogachiel State Park. Turn left (east) onto Undie Road, which becomes FR 2932. Drive about 5 miles to the trailhead at road's end.

The Hike

This trail runs through a stunning rain forest as it ascends the wild and remote Bogachiel valley. *Bogachiel* (pronounced BO-guh-sheel) is a Quileute word that can be roughly translated as "waters that become muddy from rainstorms." The waters of the river are crystal clear throughout most of the summer, however, and support winter and summer runs of steelhead. At its terminus, the trail links up with the Mink Lake–Little Divide Trail. Because the area has a relatively low maintenance priority, travelers should expect to clamber over a few deadfalls and make occasional creek fords. Horse parties should ask about trail conditions before beginning a trip.

The trek begins as the path drops into a stand of red alder to cross Morgenroth Creek. On the far bank a spur path runs a short distance to a wetlands interpretive site, while the main trail runs east up the river valley. It crosses swales and bottoms robed in alder and second-growth spruce. The scenery changes little beyond the park boundary: This entire area was extensively logged before being added to the park in the 1940s. The forest community found here is a regrowth that sprang up in the wake of clear-cutting.

The trail soon climbs over a hillside where the Bogachiel River meanders close to the edge of the bottomlands. The path then crosses Mosquito Creek, where there is a riverside campsite. The country flattens out again, and after 1.3 miles the trail crosses Indian Creek. From this point onward the landscape takes on the aspect of an ancient rain forest, with tall cedar, hemlock, and Sitka spruce scattered amid a lush undergrowth of ferns and shrubs. Just beyond a junction with the Rugged Ridge Trail, the Bogachiel camping area occupies a riverbank graced with the stately columns of age-old conifers. Many of the tent sites have been washed away by the river, but camping sites are available on riverside gravel bars. The river meanders widely across a broad peneplain of gravel, changing its course frequently during winter floods.

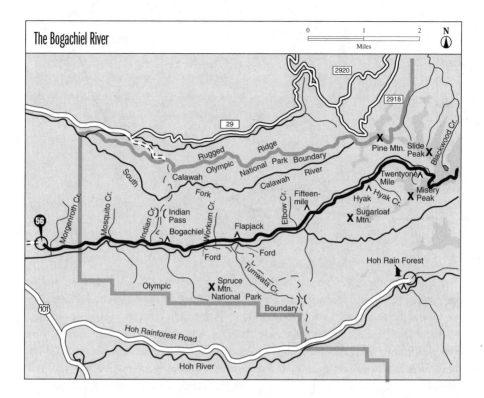

The Bogachiel River

0   1   2   N

Miles

Another 1.9 miles of easy bottomland hiking brings the traveler to the lower ford junction, where the Hoh–Bogachiel Trail crosses the river and runs south over a lofty ridge. The main trail climbs and falls vigorously for the next several miles, avoiding the riverbanks in favor of the forested hillsides to the north. Warkum Creek is a scenic landmark to mark one's progress through the trackless forest. It tumbles through a narrow channel carved into the mossy bedrock with several attractive cascades inter-rupting its flow. Just before the upper ford junction is a smaller but equally interesting stream that pours in a thin sheet across a rounded face of stone. The erosive power of this rivulet is not quite sufficient to wear a channel into the bedrock. The upper ford trail runs to Flapjack Camp on the gravel bar of the river, then on across the waters to link up with the Hoh–Bogachiel Trail.

The main trail crosses another long stretch of flat bottomland, with tall spruces underlain by moss and sword fern. The path meanders back to the riverside to meet a pair of campsites, then crosses tiny Spawner Creek. Above this point the valley constricts around the river, whose emerald waters swirl through placid pools amid the bedrock. Thick brakes of salmonberry grow beside the numerous streams that meander down from the north, providing a trailside treat for hikers and black bears in midsummer. The spruce and Douglas fir benchlands found here support a lush understory of vine maple and sword fern.

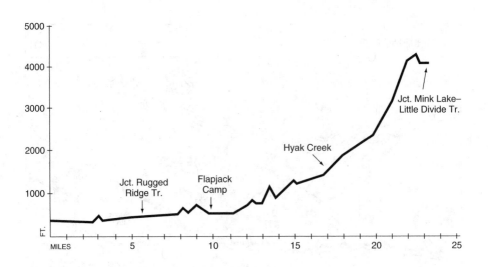

At mile 13 the main branch of the river splits away to the south unseen, and the trail begins to climb vigorously above the North Fork of the Bogachiel. High above the waters the trail reaches the Fifteenmile shelter, which is set in a grove of old western hemlocks (there are no good tent spots here). A pack bridge soon spans the North Fork, leading to a hearty climb above its south bank. The rain forest is replaced by a more montane plant community, and the forest becomes more ragged. The trail soon drops into a small, overgrown meadow with the Hyak shelter at its lower edge.

The path then arcs uphill again, crossing Hyak Creek and several lesser streams along the way. Near the head of the valley, the Twentyone Mile shelter is perched beside a stream amid a ragged grove of hemlocks. Beyond this point the trail climbs steadily for a long stretch to a flattened terrace on the ridgetop. The ascent continues along the crest of the ridge, bearing west. Before long, open meadows spangled with blossoms of all descriptions open up vistas of the surrounding country. All around, unblemished ridges clothed in virgin forest stretch away to the horizon, while the snowbound masses of Mount Olympus and Mount Tom rise above the verdant hills to the southeast. The trail continues to climb in fits and starts, ultimately reaching its end at a junction with the Mink Lake–Little Divide Trail (see that hike description).

Key Points

0.0 Trailhead.

0.2 Trail crosses Morgenroth Creek. Spur path to wetlands interpretive site.

1.6 Olympic National Park boundary and registration station.

3.2 Trail crosses Mosquito Creek.

4.5 Trail crosses Indian Creek.

5.6 Junction with Rugged Ridge Trail. Stay right.

5.7	Bogachiel Camp.
7.6	Junction with lower ford to Hoh-Bogachiel Trail. Stay left.
9.8	Junction with trail to Flapjack Camp and ford to reach Hoh-Bogachiel Trail. Stay left.
11.4	Trail crosses Spawner Creek.
12.1	Trail crosses Lotloh Creek.
13.7	Fifteenmile Camp.
13.9	Trail crosses North Fork Bogachiel River.
16.5	Hyak Camp.
16.9	Trail crosses Hyak Creek.
19.4	Twentyone Mile Camp.
23.2	Junction with Mink Lake-Little Divide Trail.

57 Rugged Ridge

A 6.6-mile day hike or backpack from the Rugged River trailhead to the Bogachiel River.

Difficulty: Moderate north to south; moderately strenuous south to north.
Trail type: Foot.
Best season: All year.
Elevation gain: 880 feet.

Elevation loss: 1,190 feet.
Maximum elevation: 1,640 feet.
Topo maps: Spruce Mountain; Custom Correct *Seven Lakes Basin-Hoh.*

Finding the trailhead: From Forks, drive north on U.S. Highway 101 to mile 193.2. Turn east onto Forest Road 29 and drive 11.5 miles. At the junction with Forest Road 29-070, turn right at the sign for the Rugged Ridge Trail. Follow this narrow gravel road 2.3 miles to the trailhead at road's end. The trail begins a short distance downhill from the parking area.

The Hike

This trail offers an alternate and perhaps more interesting route into the lower valley of the Bogachiel River. It begins by snaking up to the top of Rugged Ridge through a mature forest that blocks out the sun. Atop the ridge, a registration station at the park boundary provides the backcountry permits that all backpackers must carry. The path then plots a sinuous course among finger ridges so numerous that it is difficult to determine when Rugged Ridge has actually been crossed. The forest here is dominated by Douglas fir and western hemlock and retains a lowland character despite its position on the crest of a ridge. Deer fern and woods sorrel are common on the dimly lit forest floor, and clumps of sword fern occupy the occasional damp swale.

After 1.8 miles the trail begins its descent into the South Fork Calawah valley. It passes through an old-growth forest that has remained undisturbed. The route runs

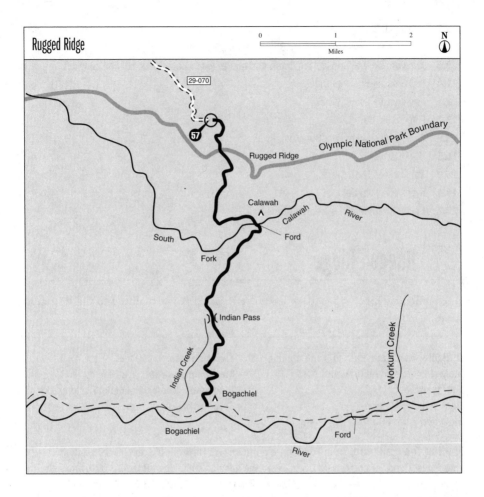

westward as it drops, and holes in the canopy allow brush to grow in the sunny gaps. Soon after reaching the valley floor, the traveler must make a shallow ford of the South Fork of the Calawah River. The primitive campsite once found here was washed out by flooding in 2003, and it is now difficult to find a spot to pitch a tent here. Dark rain forest awaits on the far shore.

The trail then bends southwest as it climbs through the damp forest to reach Indian Pass. This low saddle in an otherwise unbroken ridge is a bit of a geological mystery. It is loosely forested with giant conifers, whose massive boles rise through a multistoried canopy of younger trees. The tallest of these trees are Douglas fir and Sitka spruce, while western hemlocks rise to lesser heights. The trail then winds gradually downward across a series of level terraces to enter the spectacular rain forest bottomland of the Bogachiel River. It joins the Bogachiel River Trail (see previous hike) in an ancient stand of spruces just west of Bogachiel Camp.

Key Points

0.0 Trailhead.

0.4 Olympic National Park boundary and registration station.

3.2 Site of Calawah Camp. Trail fords South Fork Calawah River.

4.7 Indian Pass.

6.6 Junction with Bogachiel River Trail.

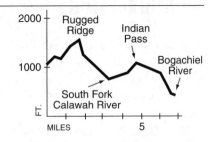

Additional Trails

The **South Fork Skokomish Trail** is a well-maintained route through old-growth bottomlands as far as the park border, where it turns into a faint track that runs over Sundown Pass to join the Lake Sundown route.

The **Wynoochee Pass Trail** is an overgrown, hard-to-follow shortcut to Lake Sundown.

The **West Fork Humptulips Trail** is being rehabilitated all along the river to provide a horseback route. It visits a number of river-bottom meadows.

The **Quinault Loop** complex is a series of interconnected trails that begins at the Lake Quinault Lodge. It visits waterfalls and impressive groves of ancient timber. A spur links it to the Rainforest Village area.

The **Fletcher Canyon Trail** once linked up with the Colonel Bob route, but now it is maintained only as far as a waterfall at the 2-mile mark.

The **Maple Groves Nature Trail** makes a short, self-guided loop behind the Quinault (NPS) Ranger Station.

The **Cascading Terraces Nature Trail** offers a self-guiding walk from the Graves Creek Campground through a bottomland rain forest of great diversity.

The **Sams River Loop** is a 2.8-mile trek through the bottomland rain forest that surrounds the Queets campground.

The **Tshletshy Creek, Kloochman Rock, Pyrites Creek, Rustler Creek, Mount Tom Creek,** and **Geodetic Hill Trails** have long been abandoned and swallowed by the forest; they are no longer worth looking for.

The **Spruce Nature Trail** and **Hall of Mosses Trail** provide two outstanding nature walks in the Hoh rain forest. Illustrated placards interpret the ecological principals at work here.

The **Hoh–Bogachiel Trail** provides a rather strenuous and viewless trek over the high ridge that separates these two major rivers. The hiker then has a choice of two fords of the Bogachiel before meeting the Bogachiel Trail.

The Olympic Coastline

The wild and rugged Olympic coast is the site of ceaseless change. Wave action weathers arches and sea stacks from resistant blocks of sandstone, then slowly abrades them down to nothing. The fractured rock of the coves is constantly slumping onto the beach, then is carried away by the tides. Flood-gorged rivers discharge great plumes of silt and debris into the ocean, forming long spits at their mouths. Enormous logs are washed out to sea by these rivers, and these are stripped and polished by the surf and then cast up on the beach. The incessant pounding of the waves, as well as the periodic tempests of wintertime, are constantly at work tearing down the coastline and building it anew.

This environment of endless upheaval is also the site of one of the most diverse biological communities in the Pacific Northwest. Tidepools harbor an almost infinite array of invertebrate life amid a lush growth of aquatic plants. Gulls, mergansers, ospreys, and bald eagles wheel on the ocean breezes, while oystercatchers and sandpipers patrol the beaches and rocks. The offshore islands teem with marine mammals, featuring sea otters, gray whales, orcas, harbor seals, and the endangered Steller's sea lion. Such a bounty of marine life forms the economic backbone of the coastal Indian villages that have stood here from time immemorial.

Most of the coastline can be hiked, although Quateata and Teahwhit Head are completely impassable, and the Queets, Hoh, and Quillayute Rivers are always too deep to ford. A tide table is a must because heavy surf renders most of the headlands impassable at high tide. Tide tables are posted at most trailheads, and free copies are usually offered as well. Avoid hiking on an incoming tide, and use common sense at all times. Changing weather patterns can result in higher tides than expected, especially when a storm is brewing. In addition the surf often tosses huge (and deadly) logs around like matchsticks, and in many cases these surf logs are waterlogged and invisible beneath the waves. Do not swim in the surf of unprotected beaches; venture into the water only in protected areas that have little wave action. NOTE: The water is extremely cold, even in summer.

Developed areas near the coast can be found at Ozette Lake, Mora, and Kalaloch. Kalaloch has its own lodge, and campgrounds and ranger stations can be found at all

Sea anemones in an Olympic coastline tidepool

of these locations. Ozette Lake is a popular destination, and its campground is often full. Call ahead to ask if space is available because there are few alternatives for camping elsewhere in the area. Clallam Bay, Forks, and, to a lesser extent, Kalaloch offer groceries and other supplies.

58 Elephant Rock

A day hike along the beach to a series of arches and sea stacks, 3.6 miles one way.

Difficulty: Moderately strenuous.
Trail type: Coast route.
Best season: Spring, summer, fall.
Elevation gain: None.

Elevation loss: 90 feet.
Maximum elevation: Sea level.
Topo maps: Tunnel Island, Queets.
Jurisdiction: Quinault Indian Reservation.

Finding the trailhead: Take U.S. Highway 101 southeast from the town of Queets to mile 150.4. Here an improved gravel road runs westward past several small work centers. After 0.5 mile the road splits; continue straight ahead on the right for an additional 0.3 mile and park at the old gravel pit on the bluffs above the beach. A Quinault Reservation beach pass is required to visit these tribal lands; it must be obtained at the town of Taholah, which lies at the end of Highway 109, accessible from Hoquiam via Ocean Beach Road or from the Moclips Highway, a gravel road that departs US 101 a few miles south of Lake Quinault.

The Hike

This day hike visits a cluster of arches and sea stacks at the mouth of the Raft River, including fanciful Elephant Rock. This hike is on the Quinault Indian Reservation; visitors must get a beach pass from the tribal government for a nominal fee. Overnight camping is not allowed on the reservation; visitors must approach the trek as an out-and-back affair in one day. Although the hike is almost level, the very tricky descent to the beach and the soft nature of the beach sands and gravels make for a physically demanding trek. Time your hike to round the headland beside Tunnel Island and ford the Raft River at low tide. Coastal access to Elephant Rock from the south is blocked by Pratt Point, an impassable headland, so this trek approaches the formations from the north.

The hike begins with a very steep and tricky descent along a footpath that departs from the south side of the parking area. Watch your footing as the track drops precipitously down an eroded hillside. Near the bottom an almost sheer ravine with a fixed-rope rappel plummets the last 15 feet or so to the beach. Take a bearing on the landmarks here, to be sure you can locate the exit route on the return leg of your trip.

On the beach turn south along the sandy strand that runs along the base of eroded cliffs of conglomerate. Far ahead the tree-covered mass of Tunnel Island protrudes into the surf, marking the hike's destination. About halfway there the two forks of Whale Creek form a small lagoon, and the shell of an old summer cabin is sagging into ruin nearby. Watch for signs of landslides and slumping to the south of Whale Creek, as the twin forces of wave action and seeping groundwater combine to undermine the stability of the bluffs and cause mudslides.

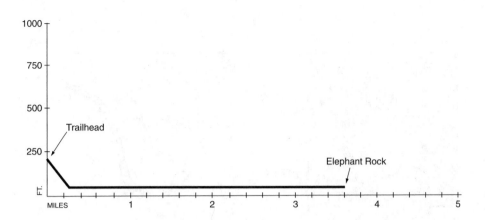

There is one rocky headland to negotiate just north of Tunnel Island, and you may have to do some rock-hopping to keep your feet dry if the tide isn't at its low ebb. After rounding the headland you will reach the mouth of the Raft River as you draw abreast of Tunnel Island. At low tide the ford is knee-deep to ankle-deep, with a significant current. Expect problems getting across at high tide. A wrack of giant logs and roots guard the estuary of the Raft River, where bald eagles are sometimes sighted.

On the far bank the origins of Tunnel Island's name soon become apparent, as the grotto at its south end has been drilled all the way through the bedrock of the island. The south side of the island is replete with multiple arches, including the fancifully shaped Elephant Rock, with its multiple arches and pillars resembling an ossified pachyderm. Off in the distance the Hogsback rises at the edge of the surf, and sea stacks including Willoughby Rock and Split Rock are scattered across the face of the sea. Several of the stacks that flank Tunnel Island serve as rookeries for seabirds such as pelicans and cormorants, making this a great spot for bird-watching. Elephant Rock marks the end of the hike; after enjoying the area, turn around and retrace your steps to the parking area.

Key Points

0.0 Trail leaves parking area near East Entrance.
0.1 Path reaches the beach. Turn left (south).
1.7 Whale Creek.
3.3 Headland beside Tunnel Island. CAUTION: Passable at low tide.
3.5 Ford of Raft River—ankle to waist deep at low tide.
3.6 Route draws even with Elephant Rock.

◀ *Elephant Rock rises at the mouth of the Raft River.*

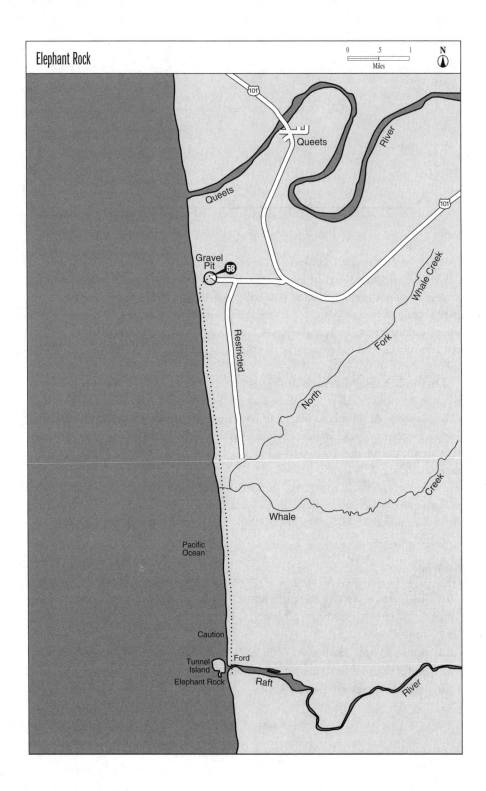

Elephant Rock

0 .5 1
Miles

N

101

Queets

River

Queets

Gravel
Pit

58

Whale Creek

Restricted

Fork

North

Creek

Whale

Pacific
Ocean

Caution

Tunnel
Island

Ford

Elephant Rock

Raft

River

59 The Kalaloch Beaches

A series of day trips of varying lengths along coastal routes in the Kalaloch area.

Difficulty: Easy.
Trail type: Coast routes.
Best season: All year.

Topo maps: Destruction Island, Queets; Custom Correct *South Olympic Coast.*

Finding the trailheads: All beaches are accessed from pullouts or parking areas along U.S. Highway 101 between the Hoh River and the town of Queets: Ruby Beach at mile 164.7; Beach 6, mile 162.7; Beach 5, mile 162.1; Beach 4, mile 160.5; Beach 3, mile 159.9; Beach 2, mile 156.2; Beach 1, mile 155.3.

The Hikes

These beaches stretch along the southern coast of the Olympic Peninsula, surrounding the resort village of Kalaloch (pronounced "kuh-LAY-lock"). US 101 runs along the coast here, and a number of short trails descend from the bluffs to reach the broad and almost unbroken strand that stretches between the Hoh and Queets Rivers. Day trips of any length can be undertaken, but camping on these beaches is not allowed. Pets, however, are permitted on these beaches. The beaches will be discussed in detail with reference to their access points; in general, extremely short wooden causeways lead from bluff-top parking areas to the shore.

Ruby Beach: This beach is known for its pinkish sands, which derive their color from the presence of tiny grains of garnet. Ruby is set apart from the other beaches by the presence of sea stacks at its northern end; Abbey Island is the largest of these. Cedar Creek forms a wide lagoon near the stacks, and piles of drift logs litter its edges. Destruction Island can be seen far to the southwest. This mighty rock has lived up to its name over the years, being the site of at least five major shipwrecks.

Beach 6: The trail to this beach passes through a grove of mature Sitka spruce, many of which have been infected with parasitic organisms. In response, the trees have produced a bulbous growth of wood known as a burl around the infected trunk or limb. Note the dwarfed growth form of the spruces nearest the beach. Lashed by winter gales, these hardy trees have adopted aerodynamic shapes that deflect the wind. The beach itself is mostly cobble, and there is a scattering of large drift logs near the high-tide mark.

Beach 5: This track starts from an unmarked pullout just south of the Big Cedar exhibit. The beach is almost indistinguishable from Beach Six.

Beach 4: The trail follows a grassy ravine down to the ocean. This beach features exposed strata of shale and sandstone that were tilted and folded as the Juan de Fuca

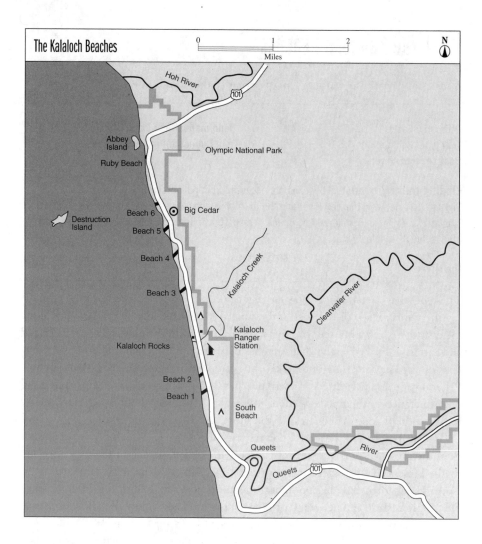

The Kalaloch Beaches

0   1   2
Miles

N

Hoh River

101

Abbey Island

Olympic National Park

Ruby Beach

Beach 6   Big Cedar

Destruction Island

Beach 5

Beach 4

Kalaloch Creek

Beach 3

Clearwater River

Kalaloch Ranger Station

Kalaloch Rocks

Beach 2

Beach 1

South Beach

Queets

River

Queets   101

Plate submerged itself beneath the Continental Plate. Outcroppings of bedrock near the north end of the beach offer opportunities for tidepool exploration. Remember that these tiny worlds are fragile; avoid disturbing their inhabitants.

Beach 3: This short stretch of fine sand derives its dark shade from an abundance of black magnetite. It is tucked between tawny headlands capped by Sitka spruce and alder. These trees have been pruned by windblown sand and salt into twisted forms that bring to mind the art of a Japanese bonsai gardener.

Beach 2: This beach has extremely limited parking. The path begins from the north side of the Beach 2 highway sign and makes a very brief and easy descent to the seashore. This beach is part of a broad, sandy strand that stretches north beyond Kalaloch Campground. Drift logs have been weathered into fascinating shapes, as have the spruces that cling to the seaside bluffs.

Stacks in the fog at Ruby Beach

Beach 1: This beach is almost a twin of Beach 2, but with safer and more spacious parking facilities. It also offers a spur trail through groves of Sitka spruce that sport impressive burl. Gray whales are commonly seen in March and April.

60 The South Wilderness Coast

A 17-mile backpack from the Third Beach trailhead to Oil City Road.

Difficulty: Moderate.
Trail type: Coast route.
Best season: Spring, summer, fall.

Topo maps: Quillayute Prairie, Toleak Point, Hoh Head. Custom Correct's *South Olympic Coast* is most recommended.

Finding the trailhead: From Forks, drive north about 1 mile on U.S. Highway 101 to La Push Road. Turn left (west) and drive 11.3 miles, following road signs for La Push, to the well-marked Third Beach trailhead on the left. The south end of the route is accessed at the end of the 11-mile Oil City Road, which departs US 101 just north of the Hoh River bridge. WARNING: Do not leave valuables in your car at the Second or Third Beach trailheads. Both are sites of frequent break-ins.

Hiking past the Giant's Graveyard

The Hike

This extended beach hike runs from the La Push Road to the old Oil City site on the north bank of the Hoh River. The coastline is typified by sandy beaches interrupted by impassable headlands that require the use of trails that have been built over the bluffs and wood-and-cable ladders to help hikers up steep slopes. From the Third Beach trailhead, a wide path runs southeast through a young coastal forest of Sitka spruce and western hemlock. Gravel steps lead down to Third Beach, which is the former site of the first oil drilling efforts in the state of Washington. A tangled growth of vegetation has covered over all traces of oil exploration. The wide sweep of Strawberry Bay is bounded to the north by the sheer cliffs of Teahwhit Head, and a sandy strand stretches away to the south.

Taylor Point soon looms out into the surf, and travelers must take an overland trail to navigate around it. After a sojourn through the forest, the trail returns to the beach at a narrow cove flanked by towering cliffs. Due south, the stacks of the Giant's Graveyard rise from the sea like so many scattered bones. This diverse assortment of defiant sandstone is the feature attraction for the next several miles. Keep an eye out for bald eagles, which hunt the coastline in search of fish or beach carrion. Pods of killer whales are also spotted in this area on rare occasions. After about a mile of beach travel, a brief climb around Scotts Bluff is advisable under all but the lowest tide

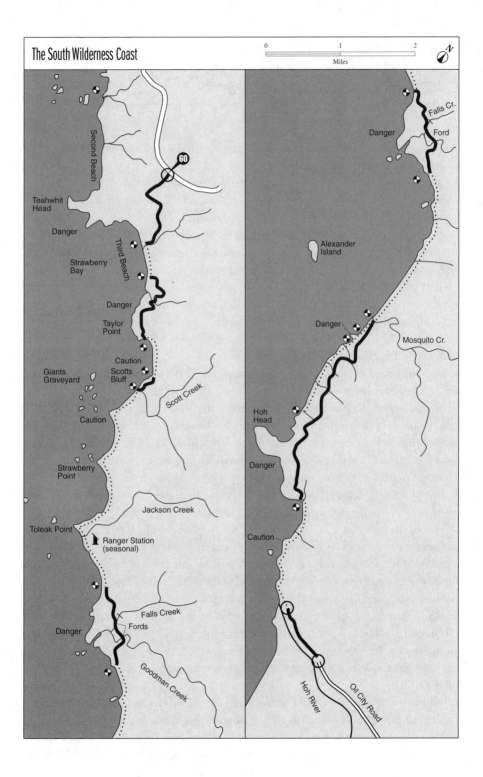

The South Wilderness Coast

0   1   2
Miles

N

Second Beach

60

Teahwhit Head

Danger

Third Beach

Strawberry Bay

Danger

Taylor Point

Caution
Scotts Bluff

Giants Graveyard

Scott Creek

Caution

Strawberry Point

Jackson Creek

Toleak Point

Ranger Station (seasonal)

Falls Creek

Fords

Danger

Goodman Creek

Falls Cr.

Danger

Ford

Alexander Island

Danger

Mosquito Cr.

Hoh Head

Danger

Caution

Hoh River

Oil City Road

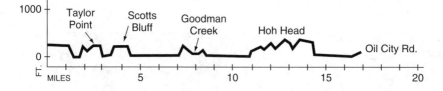

conditions. The headland trail ends at a beachside emergency shelter, and a stretch of mostly sandy beach lies ahead.

The second headland after Scotts Bluff is Strawberry Point, which extends to a large stack that can be reached on foot at low tide. Well-stratified sandstone and siltstone is visible here. Another mile of crescent-shaped beach leads to Toleak Point. There is a summer ranger tent here and an emergency shelter above Jackson Creek, a dependable supply of fresh water. This point was a traditional summer camp for the local coastal tribes. When the tide is out, numerous pockets of water remain among the rocks. These tidepools are a microcosm of the shoreline ecosystem, allowing close inspection of its diverse inhabitants. Starfish, sea anemones, turban snails, shore crabs, and sculpins thrive here amid a veritable jungle of varicolored algae and sea grasses. Look in on the lives of these delicate creatures, but avoid disturbing them as they go about their daily rounds.

A mile beyond Toleak Point is the long trail that circumnavigates the rugged, impassable headland bearing Goodman Creek. This trail climbs steeply into the forest, then descends to pass an elegant 50-foot waterfall on Falls Creek. The path soon fords this stream and then the much larger Goodman Creek; these fords can be quite deep at high tide or after rains. The coastal forest is sprinkled with nurse logs, those decaying deadfalls that serve as aerial seedbeds for the next generation of trees. The trail soon returns to the ocean's edge, where it encounters a lonely reach of coastline with sea stacks scattered sparsely near the headlands. The flattened mass of Alexander Island is a dominating presence here, rising from the brine a mile out to sea.

A long and curving beach trek ends at a ford of Mosquito Creek. At this popular camping spot, the traveler faces a choice. At extremely low tides the shoreline route is passable for an additional 2 miles, interrupted by one brief but strenuous headland crossing. For complete safety take the Hoh Head Trail inland from the south bank of Mosquito Creek. This trail climbs into a coastal forest of Sitka spruce and western hemlock, frequently straying close to the edge of the bluff in the early going. After 2.2 miles it is joined by a steep spur trail from the shoreline route and then proceeds south around the promontory of Hoh Head, which is impassable from the beach. The trail then makes a steep and often slippery descent, returning to the beach at Jefferson Cove.

Shortly thereafter the next headland poses a treacherous crossing of jumbled boulders of conglomerate, covered in algae below the high-tide mark. Offshore is a final cluster of rocky spires, featuring Diamond Rock near shore and North and Middle Rocks farther out to sea. The route follows the coastline around the sand spit at the mouth of the Hoh River, which is too deep to ford at any time. Upstream is the site of "Oil City," a scheme perpetrated by speculators to sell plots of land in an area of oil seeps in anticipation of drilling efforts that never amounted to anything. Look for the target that marks a trail following the river inland through a forest of red alder and Sitka spruce to reach the end of the Oil City Road.

Key Points

0.0 Third Beach trailhead.

1.4 Trail reaches Third Beach. Turn south.

1.8 Taylor Point. DANGER: Use headland trail.

3.0 Taylor Point overland trail returns to beach. CAUTION: 4.5-foot tide.

3.6 Scotts Bluff. CAUTION: 1-foot tide. Overland trail begins.

3.9 Scotts Bluff overland trail returns to beach.

4.4 Nameless point of land. CAUTION: 4-foot tide.

5.1 Strawberry Point.

6.2 Toleak Point.

7.1 Goodman overland trail. DANGER: impassable coastline.

7.9 Trail fords Falls Creek.

8.1 Trail fords Goodman Creek.

8.6 Goodman overland trail returns to beach.

10.9 Ford of Mosquito Creek. Hoh Head Trail begins.

13.1 Junction with spur trail from extreme-low-tide coast route.

14.4 Hoh Head overland trail returns to beach.

15.0 Headland near Diamond Rock. CAUTION: 4-foot tide.

16.4 Target marks beginning of Oil City Trail.

17.0 Oil City trailhead.

61 The Quillayute Needles (Second Beach)

A 2.4-mile day hike from the Second Beach trailhead to the base of Teahwhit Head.

Difficulty: Easy.
Trail type: Coast route.
Best season: All year.

Topo maps: La Push, Quillayute Prairie; Custom Correct *South Olympic Coast.*

Finding the trailhead: From Forks, drive north about 1 mile on U.S. Highway 101 to La Push Road. Turn left (west) and drive 12.7 miles (following signs for La Push) to the well-marked Second Beach trailhead.

The Hike

This trail begins on the Quileute Indian Reservation, and disputes over territorial sovereignty have sometimes led to the closure of this route. The route follows the Second Beach Trail down to a sandy stretch of coastline, offering a short day hike or

Quateata guards the northern approach to Second Beach.

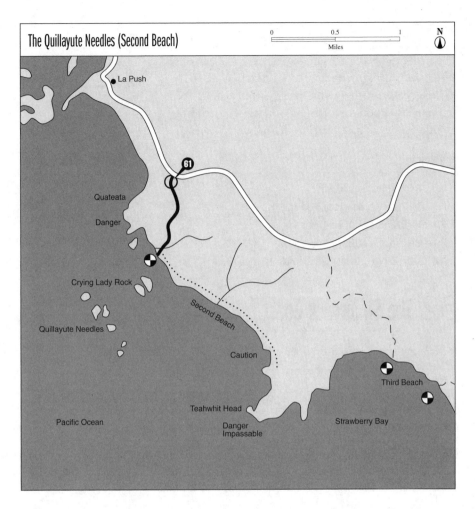

0   0.5   1
Miles

N

La Push

61

Quateata

Danger

Crying Lady Rock

Quillayute Needles

Second Beach

Caution

Third Beach

Teahwhit Head

Pacific Ocean

Danger
Impassable

Strawberry Bay

a good family overnight. The trail begins by winding through a forest of Sitka spruce and western hemlock that sprang up in the aftermath of logging that occurred early in this century. After wandering the wooded blufftop for a time, a wooden boardwalk and steps drop down to the north end of Second Beach. An enormous block of contorted stone named Quateata blocks the northern approaches to the beach, and it is pierced by a natural arch. The Quillayute Needles are scattered across the sparkling waters of the Pacific. This formation is an old wave-cut terrace that has been elevated and weathered into sandstone pillars. Some are massive and stout while others form slender spires.

Turn south and follow the coast as it bends away toward Teahwhit Head. The beach spreads out into a wide stretch of fine sand, raked ceaselessly by turbulent combers. Near its south end sheer cliffs march down to the water's edge, and tortured stacks stand among the breakers. Tidepools among the rocks showcase delicate sea anemones and colorful starfish. A passage can be made around the first headland, which guards an isolated beach. From this point a natural arch can be seen among the jagged spires of Teahwhit Head. The next headland is trickier to negotiate and can only be crossed during extremely low tides. Beyond it is a secluded cove much like the previous inlet, and a rugged jumble of boulders stretches southwest toward the forbidding and impassable cliffs of Teahwhit Head.

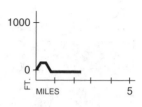

Key Points

0.0 Second Beach trailhead.

0.7 Trail reaches beach. Turn south.

2.1 Headland. CAUTION: 4-foot tide.

2.2 Headland. CAUTION: 1-foot tide.

2.4 Teahwhit Head. DANGER: impassable headland.

62 The Shipwreck Coast

A 20.1-mile backpack from Rialto Beach to the Ozette Ranger Station.

Difficulty: Moderately strenuous.
Trail type: Coast route.
Best season: Spring, summer, fall.

Topo maps: La Push, Allens Bay, Ozette; Custom Correct's *North Olympic Coast* is most recommended.

Finding the trailhead: From Forks, drive about 1 mile north on U.S. Highway 101 to La Push Road. Turn left (west) and drive 7.6 miles to the fire station. Turn right here on the road to Mora, and continue 4.8 miles to the Rialto Beach trailhead at road's end.

The Hike

This wild and beautiful expanse of coastline stretches from Rialto Beach in the south to Sand Point in the north. It is commonly approached as a three-day trip, but it can also be combined with the Ozette Loop and Point of the Arches route for a much longer trip. The coastline is typified by boulder-strewn coves and rocky headlands, which makes for more difficult traveling than the sandy beaches found farther south. There are few trails navigating around the headlands because most are passable during low tide. By the same token, hikers can be easily isolated at high tide, so it is imperative to pay close attention to tide levels while exploring this area. A quota system is in effect from the Yellow Banks northward to the campsites north of the Ozette River. Advance reservations are required for this zone. Call the park's Wilderness Information Center at (360) 452-0300.

A view of Jagged Island from the old coastwatcher's shack

The trek begins at Rialto Beach; the registration station is located along a barrier-free path to an overlook. The cobble-strewn beach extends north for 3 miles. Enormous drift logs have been brought down the river during winter floods, battered and polished by wave action, then heaved high onto the beach by storms. These same winter gales have sculpted the Sitka spruce that crowd the beach in low-growing forms that resemble the krummholz of timberline. A long spit extends south from the mouth of the Quillayute River toward the James Island archipelago. This cluster of islands sports stout, wave-carved cliffs of sandstone topped with spruce and alder. The Quileute tribe once used this cluster of islands as a natural fortress when fierce bands of Makah swept down the coast during the course of intertribal warfare.

As the route runs northward, Cake Rock is the major stack that rises far out to sea, while the more ragged crest of Dahdayla Island rises from the surf closer to the beach. The traveling is easy all the way to Hole-in-the-Wall Rock. True to its name, this minor promontory is pierced by a rounded aperture worn through the stone by centuries of wave action. A short trail climbs around the head, which can be passed on the ocean side only at low tides. Upon rounding the first major headland (use caution), the trail encounters a broad ledge of bedrock guarded by a constellation of igneous rock spires. This shelf drains free of water at low tide, allowing excellent opportunities for tidepool exploration.

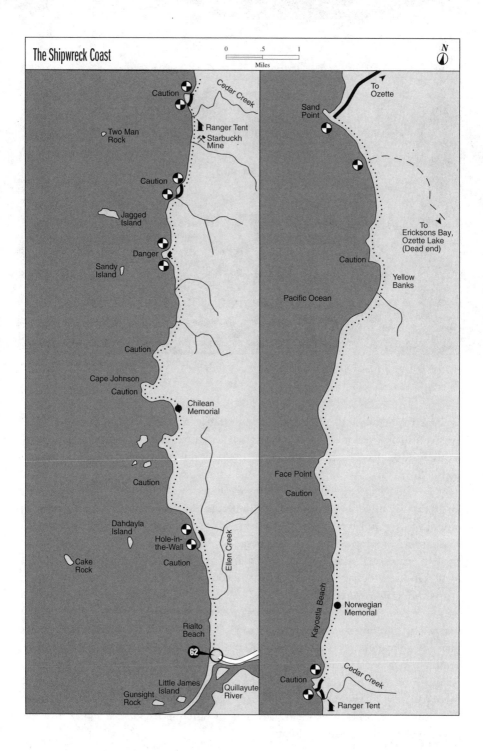

The Shipwreck Coast

After rounding a sharp, forested point of land, the route enters a rather rocky cove. Here a plaque commemorates the wreck of the schooner *W. J. Pirrie*, a cargo vessel of Chilean registry. This ship went down in a fierce winter storm in 1920, with the loss of all hands. The next headland is Cape Johnson, and it marks the beginning of 1.2 miles of tricky boulder-hopping across the algae-covered rocks of the intertidal zone. Deep tidepools reveal the denizens of the marine environment in pursuit of their daily activities. Hermit crabs and purple shore crabs scuttle about in search of scraps, sea anemones strain the water for plankton with their stinging tentacles, and starfish crawl about with glacial slowness in pursuit of their immobile bivalve prey. Harbor seals commonly haul up onto the outer banks to sun themselves, and the occasional bald eagle may be seen patrolling the coastline.

After rounding the next head (once again impassable at high tide), Carroll and Jagged Islands can be seen to the north. Carroll Island is a major rookery for Steller's sea lions and also has nesting colonies of auklets, puffins, and storm petrels. The route then returns to a beach of coarse sand for easy traveling as far as "Saddle Rock." A short traverse provides access around this small head, then returns the traveler to beach level. Here wide stretches of sand beckon, and outgoing tides trap shallow lagoons of salt water on the flats. Look for rafts of seabirds in the shallows; cormorants and black brant are sometimes seen amid the ever-present gulls.

A steep cliff known locally as "Coastie Head" lies 0.8 mile north of Saddle Rock. The trail that navigates over it is well worth the effort even at low tide: It offers a fine viewing platform of the neighboring sea stacks and passes a historic coastwatcher's shack. This observation post was manned periodically during World War II, when the threat of invasion by the Japanese was an ever-present concern. The strand of coastline to the north is bordered to the landward side by a dike of cobbles and storm-tossed driftwood. Several small streams form brackish lagoons behind this natural dam. The summer ranger tent and old Starbuch Mine site lie near the center of the bay. This was the site of a placer mining operation that produced small quantities of gold between 1910 and 1920. The Cedar Creek emergency shelter is nestled among the spruces near the north end of the bay.

After rounding the next headland, the route reaches Kayostla Beach. There is a small stream here, and plenty of good campsites are located among the trees. At the north end of the beach, the Norwegian Memorial gives silent testimony to the wreck of the bark *Prince Arthur* in 1903. The granite obelisk is set back in a forest glade, but a trail sign visible from the beach marks its location. Beyond this spot a series of rocky headlands slow northward progress to a crawl. At first the heads are of naked bedrock, with arches and grottoes carved out by the waves. This soon gives way to a barren peneplain of sandstone, pocked with tidepools that harbor darting sculpins and scuttling crabs. Climb up the bluffs to glass for sea otters, which are commonly seen in this vicinity.

Beyond "Face Point" is a rocky cove preferred by seals for hauling out. Wooded bluffs crowd the waters of this small bay, and more barren stone, paired later with

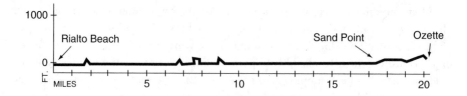

beaches of deep gravel, make traveling a toilsome affair. The sandy strands return below the Yellow Banks, a series of steep, eroded bluffs of glacial loess. This sediment was carried by the wind from glacial outwash plains to be deposited far out on the flats during the Pleistocene and earlier ice ages. At the north edge of the cove lies a tricky point, through which a tunnel has been dug for easier access.

Hikers must then clamber over pillars of bedrock, but this rough stretch passes quickly. A long expanse of sandy beach stretches away to Sand Point, where most travelers turn inland toward Ozette Lake. The first target to be reached marks the Ericksons Bay Trail, which is a dead-end spur to Ozette Lake. The Sand Point Trail lies 0.7 mile to the north, in a grove of young Sitka spruce. It can be followed for the remaining 3 miles to the Ozette Ranger Station, or the longer route along the coast to Cape Alava can be used to reach the same terminus. This latter route and the Sand Point Trail are discussed in detail under The Ozette Loop hike.

Key Points

0.0   Rialto Beach parking area. Turn north at the shoreline.

1.6   Hole-in-the-Wall Rock. CAUTION: 5-foot tide. Optional overland trail.

2.3   Headland. CAUTION: 5-foot tide.

3.8   Chilean Memorial.

4.5   Cape Johnson. CAUTION: 4-foot tide.

5.2   Headland. CAUTION: 5.5-foot tide.

6.7   "Saddle Rock." DANGER: Use overland trail.

7.5   "Coastie Head." CAUTION: 4-foot tide. Optional overland trail.

7.7   Coastie Head overland trail returns to beach.

8.7   Cedar Creek.

8.8   Headland. CAUTION: 5.5-foot tide. Optional overland trail.

10.0   Norwegian Memorial.

11.9   "Face Point." CAUTION: 6-foot tide.

14.5   Yellow Banks.

15.0   Rocky point. CAUTION: 5-foot tide. Optional tunnel.

16.4   Target marks Ericksons Bay spur trail. Keep going north.

17.1   Sand Point target. Turn east for Ozette Lake.

20.1   Ozette Ranger Station.

63 The Ozette Loop

A long day hike or short backpack, 9.3 miles round-trip.

Difficulty: Moderate.
Trail type: Coast route.
Best season: All year.

Topo maps: Ozette; Custom Correct *Ozette Beach Loop.*

Finding the trailhead: From Sappho on U.S. Highway 101, drive north on Highway 112 to Clallam Bay and the village of Sekiu. At 2.3 miles west of Sekiu, turn left (south) onto Ozette Road, which is paved for most of its 20-mile length. The trailhead is located beside the ranger station at road's end.

The Hike

This trail offers a short-range day hike or backpack along a part of the coast that is inaccessible by car. It receives heavy use due to its ease of access, and a permit reservation system is in place for overnight camping between the Yellow Banks and the Ozette River. Reservations should be sought by phone, mail, or in person at least two days before the planned trip; weekends are particularly busy, and getting reservations a week in advance for these days is advisable. Backpackers should bear in mind that the only reliable fresh water along the coastal part of the route is at Cape Alava and Sand Point. The hike is described here going counterclockwise around the loop, but it could be done either way.

The trail leaves the Ozette Ranger Station heading west, and a broad bridge soon arches above the sluggish waters of the Ozette River. Soon after entering the forest, the trail branches into two paths. The right fork heads toward Cape Alava and the left fork to Sand Point (the return leg of this loop). Bear right on the Cape Alava Trail, which wanders west through young spruce and hemlock underlain by deer fern. The gigantic leaves of skunk cabbage appear in clumps in the boggy pockets of the forest.

The trail soon becomes a boardwalk causeway that may be quite slippery during rains. At mile 2.3 the trail passes a large rest area that is actually the site of Lars Ahlstrom's barn, long since burned down. The broad stretch of coastal prairie to the west of it is named Ahlstrom's Prairie in honor of this man, who built the original causeway and was for a time the westernmost homesteader in the United States. A few fruit trees remain to the south of the trail, while the deteriorating buildings of the homestead lie out of sight to the north. This coastal prairie is really a wet bog, filled with sedges, crowberry, and sundews. The sundew is carnivorous: Hairs on the leaves produce droplets of a sticky, sweet-smelling substance that traps ants and flies. After crossing an opening the trail enters a superb coastal rain forest dominated by Sitka spruce and sword fern. It then descends from the bluff to reach the shoreline at Cape Alava.

Upon reaching Cape Alava, visitors are immediately impressed by the collection of large, spruce-encrusted islands that loom offshore. To the north is Tskawayah Island, so close to shore that it can be reached on foot at low tide. This island is part of the Ozette Indian Reservation, and climbing onto it is not permitted. Far to the west the Bodelteh Islands appear to be a single mass from this vantage point. The long, lean ridge of Ozette Island rises across a rocky tidal flat to the southeast. Cape Alava is reputed to be one of the best places on the coast to see marine mammals, including the majestic gray whale. This whale is unusual in that it lives on a diet of amphipods that it filters from seafloor sediments. There are campsites among the trees and a tiny creek for fresh water; campers should be aware that raccoons are particularly persistent pests in this area. The Makah Ranger Station lies a short distance to the north. A Makah village stood here for untold centuries, and a succession of mudslides buried the site from time to time. The result was one of the most important archaeological digs in North America. The dig site is currently inactive but should not be disturbed. A binder at the site contains a laminated magazine article that offers additional information on this historic village site. The last permanent residents of this village had departed by 1917, but the Makah still return to a small reservation just to the north on a seasonal basis.

Turn south, following a narrow strip of gravel that is deep and soft. A rocky shelf borders the beach, and at low tide the numerous tidepools provide windows into the world of sea creatures. The first headland to be reached is the site of the Wedding Rocks, where a collection of 300-year-old petroglyphs grace the soft graywacke boulders. The petroglyphs are on boulders above the high-tide mark, clustered in two groups: One group is centered 50 yards to the north of the headland, while the other group is 25 yards southeast of it. There are more than fifty petroglyphs in all, featuring marine mammals, a two-masted sailing bark, and human figures. The most famous petroglyph is the "wedding scene," from which the rocks derive their name. It consists of a male and female figure surrounded by bisected circles, which are a sort of sexual symbol. Carving or defacing of the petroglyph site is a federal crime; please report any violations immediately.

The traveling continues to be rather laborious as the trail rounds the next headland to the south of the Wedding Rocks. Here isolated spires rise in a surreal landscape like forgotten chessmen on an enormous playing board. Far out to sea the stately walls of White Rock rise sheer from the open ocean. Cormorants, common murres, and glaucous-winged gulls nest on this isolated stack, and their droppings give the island its white color. After rounding a rocky head, the trail crosses the shallow bay that leads to Sand Point. True to its name, sandy beaches surround this long spit that juts into the Pacific. There are campsites and a shelter among the trees to the south of the point, and the acidic waters of a tiny creek provide the only supply of water.

◄ *Stacks and tidepools south of the Wedding Rocks*

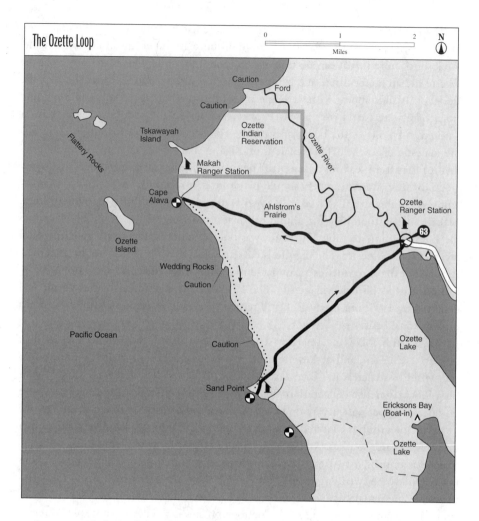

The Ozette Loop

0   1   2   **N**

Miles

Caution

Ford

Caution

Tskawayah
Island

Ozette
Indian
Reservation

Ozette River

Flattery Rocks

Makah
Ranger Station

Cape
Alava

Ahlstrom's
Prairie

Ozette
Ranger Station

63

Ozette
Island

Wedding Rocks

Caution

Pacific Ocean

Caution

Ozette
Lake

Sand Point

Ericksons Bay
(Boat-in)

Ozette
Lake

Just around the point a target marks the trail returning to the Ozette Ranger
Station. This path is almost entirely boardwalk and has lots of stairs on it. After beginning in a Sitka spruce forest, the causeway breaks out into an old burn that is now a
jungle of salal and other shrubs. A few old cedars survived the fire and rise high above
the brushy understory. Shortly after returning to the forest, the trail rejoins the Cape
Alava Trail for the final 0.2 mile to the Ozette Ranger Station.

Key Points

0.0   Ozette Ranger Station. Trail crosses Ozette River.

0.2   Trail splits into Sand Point and Cape Alava Trails. Bear right.

3.3   Cape Alava. Turn south along the coast.

4.3   Wedding Rocks. CAUTION: 5-foot tide.

4.8   Headland. CAUTION: 5.5-foot tide.

6.2 Sand Point.

6.3 Sand Point target. Follow trail east for Ozette Lake.

9.1 Trail rejoins Cape Alava Trail.

9.3 Trail crosses Ozette River to return to Ozette Ranger Station.

64 Point of the Arches

A 13.4-mile backpack from Ozette Lake to the north end of Shi Shi Beach.

Difficulty: Moderately strenuous.
Trail type: Coast route.
Best season: All year.

Topo maps: Ozette, Makah Bay; Custom Correct *North Olympic Coast.*

Finding the trailhead: From Sappho on U.S. Highway 101, drive north on Highway 112 to Clallam Bay and the village of Sekiu. At 2.3 miles west of Sekiu, turn left (south) onto Ozette Road, which is paved for most of its 20-mile length. The trailhead is located beside the ranger station at road's end.

The Hike

This route covers a wild and beautiful stretch of coastline north of Ozette Lake. There are some steep climbs aided by fixed ropes near Will Point. The former northern access to Shi Shi Beach is no longer open to the public, so travelers to Point of the Arches must count on returning by the same route that they came. A new northern access route has been blazed to Shi Shi Beach, which means that this historically remote backcountry area becomes crowded at times with day hikers. Detailed descriptions of the trail to Cape Alava as well as the Cape area itself can be found under The Ozette Loop hike.

From Cape Alava turn north and cross the spit that goes to Tskawayah Island, staying on the mainland. The first headland to be encountered is attended by a number of small, picturesque sea stacks. Beyond a small and shallow cove is a second head, this one an imposing promontory of rock. Wave action has carved deep grottoes into the bedrock, and these can be explored when the tide is out. Just beyond this point is a ford of the Ozette River. It is really no more than a medium-size creek and is less than knee-deep at low tide.

Beyond the river lies a long arc of beach, guarded to the north by the Father and Son formation standing far out to sea. Traveling is initially quite easy across firmly packed sands. The bluffs above the beach are composed of a fractured form of bedrock known as melange and are continually slumping down onto the beach in the face of incessant erosion. Alders cover these unstable slopes, pioneering a forest stand

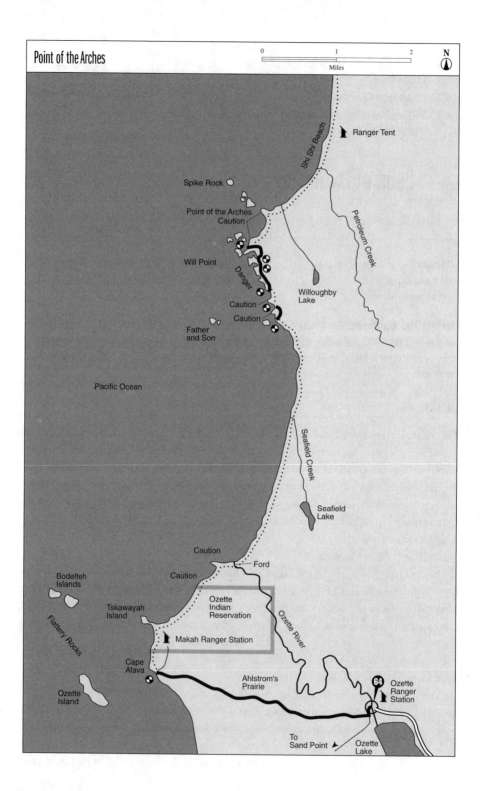

Point of the Arches

0   1   2

Miles

N

Ranger Tent

Shi Shi Beach

Petroleum Creek

Spike Rock

Point of the Arches
Caution

Will Point

Danger

Willoughby
Lake

Caution

Caution

Father
and Son

Pacific Ocean

Seafield Creek

Seafield
Lake

Caution

Ford

Bodelteh
Islands

Caution

Flattery Rocks

Tskawayah
Island

Ozette
Indian
Reservation

Ozette River

Makah Ranger Station

Cape
Alava

Ahlstrom's
Prairie

64

Ozette
Ranger
Station

Ozette
Island

To
Sand Point

Ozette
Lake

and growing rapidly on the exposed soils, only to be cast down by the next mudslide. About halfway across the shallow bay, the sand gives way to deep gravel, and traveling becomes more taxing.

The sand returns on the far side of Seafield Creek, and numerous boulders pock the intertidal zone with sand tidepools. Turban snails thrive here, and mussels and barnacles coat the rocks. As the tides recede this area presents a remarkable exhibition of the Olympic coast's diverse assortment of starfishes. These spiny-skinned animals are a relative to the sea urchin and the sand dollar, and more species of starfish occur in Olympic coastal waters than anywhere else in the world. Do not disturb these fragile creatures; they are easily killed by handling.

The headland that marks the northern boundary of the bay is a real challenge to traverse: Its jumbled piles of large boulders require time-consuming and strenuous acrobatics. After this point has been successfully crossed, an optional headland trail leads over the top of the next point. Atop the saddle are a few ancient Sitka spruces that demonstrate a radically different growth form than their lofty rain forest cousins. One more headland must then be negotiated before the Will Point Trail is reached. Here the impassable cliffs are guarded by sharp teeth of stone that send up plumes of spray as the surf beats against them. Will Point is an isolated pluton of metamorphic rock, with eroded stacks stretching far out to sea.

The Will Point Trail runs for 0.3 mile along the bluff tops, then drops into a narrow cove hemmed in by sheer walls. After crossing the cove the path returns steeply to the bluffs. It cruises through a dark forest of young spruce as it rounds a small bay, then makes its way out onto a neck behind Will Point. This high saddle boasts an excellent view of the Father and Son, and the booming surf surges through a tunnel of bedrock at the foot of the cliffs. The jagged stacks of Point of the Arches rise from the breakers to the north.

The path then makes an extremely steep descent to return to sea level, dropping the traveler into a wonderland of rock towers and tunnels. The route passes through an arch in the bedrock, making a fitting approach to Point of the Arches. A string of stacks and islands runs into the sea from this point, and the waves have carved an assortment of stout tunnels, deep grottoes, and delicate arches into the stone. Some of these are best viewed from Shi Shi Beach, a broad expanse of sandy coastline that stretches away to the north. Pronounced "shy-shy," this sandy strand is 2.3 miles long. Petroleum Creek and several smaller streams provide fresh water, and a backcountry ranger is usually stationed here. Its northern end signals the park boundary and is itself guarded by a small collection of spires and arches.

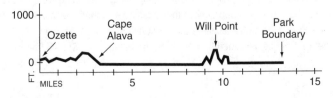

Key Points

0.0   Ozette Ranger Station. Trail crosses Ozette River.

0.2   Trail splits into Sand Point and Cape Alava Trails. Bear right.

3.3   Cape Alava. Turn north along the coast.

3.8   Makah Ranger Station.

4.0   Tskawayah Island.

4.8   Headland. CAUTION: 5-foot tide.

5.2   Headland. CAUTION: 4-foot tide.

5.5   Ford of Ozette River.

6.0   Headland. CAUTION: 6-foot tide.

7.6   Seafield Creek.

8.9   Headland. CAUTION: 5.5-foot tide.

9.0   Headland. CAUTION: 4-foot tide. Optional overland trail.

9.3   Headland. CAUTION: 4-foot tide.

9.4   Beginning of Will Point overland trail. DANGER: impassable coastline.

10.0   Trail drops briefly into narrow cove.

10.4   Will Point overland trail returns to beach.

10.7   Headland crossing. CAUTION: 6-foot tide.

11.1   Point of the Arches. CAUTION: 4.5-foot tide. South end of Shi Shi Beach.

12.0   Petroleum Creek.

13.4   National Park Boundary, north end of Shi Shi Beach.

65 Shi Shi Beach

An out-and-back day hike or short backpack from the Makah Reservation to the northernmost beach in Olympic National Park, 2.2 miles one way.

Difficulty: Moderate.
Trail type: Foot.
Best season: All year.
Elevation gain: 195 feet.
Elevation loss: 235 feet.

Maximum elevation: 180 feet.
Topo maps: Makah Bay; Ozette (for Point of the Arches); Custom Correct *North Olympic Coast.*
Jurisdiction: Makah Indian Reservation and Olympic National Park.

Finding the trailhead: From the west end of the town of Neah Bay, take Cape Flattery Road. After 2.5 miles, turn left onto the Hobuck Road, staying left and following signs for the Makah National Fish Hatchery. The road approaches the coastline at Hobuck Beach, swings inland to cross the Sooes River, then swings close to the coast again at Tsoo Yess Beach. At the far end of the beach, the road climbs a wooded bluff to reach the well-marked Shi Shi Trailhead at mile 4.5.

The cantilever bridge leads through a grove of old-growth spruce and hemlock.

The Hike

This new trail was recently rebuilt to offer access for day hikers to Shi Shi Beach, one of the more striking areas on the Olympic coastline. The good news is that access to this beach is now fast and easy; the bad news is that Shi Shi Beach, once a secluded destination for backcountry beach hikers, has turned into a somewhat busy day-hike destination, spoiling the remoteness once found here. All visitors on this trail will need a visitor's pass from the Makah Tribe to cross the tribal lands along the way, and overnight campers will also need a backcountry permit from Olympic National Park (the nearest ranger stations are far away at Ozette and Forks). Visitors should leave their pets at the car, as they are not allowed past the Olympic National Park boundary or along Shi Shi Beach itself. For a long day hike, travelers can walk the beach southward for an additional 3 miles to reach Point of the Arches.

The trek begins on a mix of boardwalk and footpath that winds through several logged-over areas, by turns a dense growth of young hemlocks and a clearing crowded with a riot of underbrush. After crossing a well-worn track (the former Shi Shi Trail, which crosses private property), the path tunnels through heavy vegetation to reach a cantilever bridge that spans a boggy rivulet choked with skunk cabbage. Here the path visits a wonderful grove of ancient spruce, hemlock, and cedar. Watch for the

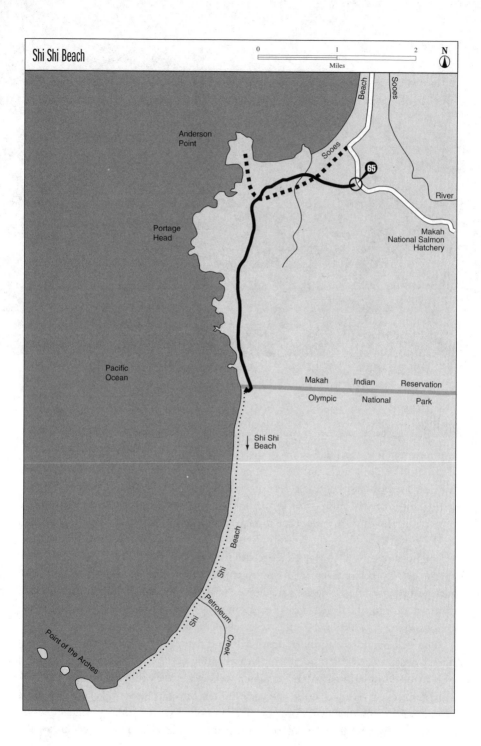

Shi Shi Beach

0   1   2
Miles

N

Anderson
Point

Soees   Beach   Sooes

65

Portage
Head

River

Makah
National Salmon
Hatchery

Pacific
Ocean

Makah   Indian   Reservation

Olympic   National   Park

↓ Shi Shi
Beach

Shi Shi Beach

Shi Shi Petroleum Creek

Point of the Arches

telltale buttress roots at the base of the big trees, indicating that they got their start atop elevated stumps or nurse logs as young seedlings.

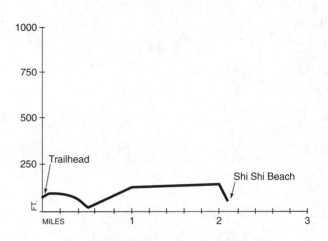

The path now climbs several small hills as it rises through the forest to intersect the original trail, arrowing through the forest. The hike adopts this original trail for a gradual climb through a stand of red alders. A narrow defile between two steep hillsides marks the high point of the hike. As the trail drops gradually through the trees, a series of muddy spots must be negotiated. Soon the path is wandering through groves of stately hemlocks, punctuated here and there by scruffy Alaska yellow cedars and massive specimens of Sitka spruce. The pounding of the surf is now audible below, but it is not until the trail reaches the top of the grade down to Shi Shi Beach that you will get an unobstructed view of the water.

At the boundary of Olympic National Park, a veritable staircase of tree roots plummets down the forested face of the bluffs to deposit the traveler at the north end of Shi Shi Beach. A small cluster of arches and pinnacles graces the surf near at hand, while the jagged teeth of Point of the Arches rise to the south, a 3-mile beach walk away.

Key Points

0.0 Trailhead on Hatchery Road.

0.6 Cantilever bridge.

0.9 Trail crosses through narrow saddle.

2.1 Olympic National Park Boundary. Trail begins a steep descent.

2.2 Shi Shi Beach.

66 Cape Flattery

A short day hike across the Makah Indian Reservation to a craggy headland that marks the northwesternmost point in the lower 48 states, 0.6 mile one way.

A wind-torn hemlock guards the tip of Cape Flattery.

Difficulty: Moderate.
Trail type: Foot.
Best season: All year.
Elevation gain: None.
Elevation loss: 200 feet.

Maximum elevation: 320 feet.
Topo maps: Cape Flattery; Custom Correct *North Olympic Coast*.
Jurisdiction: Makah Indian Reservation (tribal visitor's permit required).

Finding the trailhead: From the west end of the town of Neah Bay, take Cape Flattery Road. After 2.5 miles, stay right at the intersection and follow the signs for Cape Flattery as the road turns from pavement to gravel and ends at the trailhead.

The Hike

This hike makes a short traverse through the Makah tribal wilderness to reach the crest of Cape Flattery, where stark cliffs rise above sea stacks and grottoes carved out by the thundering surf. This spot is one of the most dramatic "land's ends" on Earth, marking the northwesternmost point in the coterminous United States. Cape Flattery was named by Captain James Cook, the European discoverer of the Hawaiian Islands, who named this important nautical landmark that "flattered" him with the hopes of finding a safe harbor (there was none). Of course, the Makah people and other Native Americans had been using this area for many thousands of years to hunt, fish, and gather seagull eggs.

The hike begins on a wide path that descends steadily through heavy forest. Most of the big trees are red cedar and western hemlock, with red alder present in

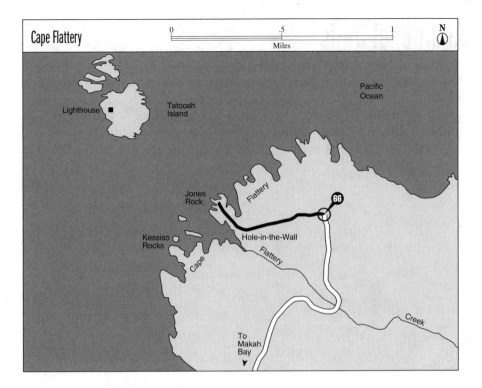

abundance as well. The path soon levels off to become a boardwalk crossing a small swamp on an elevated bench, then becomes a steady (and sometimes slippery) drop through the hemlocks. Watch for giant specimens of Sitka spruce as the path makes its way onto a narrow, wooded promontory high above the surf. Soon the first observation platform can be seen to the south, offering views of sea stacks and the Hole in the Wall, a deep, fjordlike cove guarded by sheer cliffs. There are two more observation decks on the north side of the promontory en route to land's end, and these high perches overlook deep caves and grottoes whittled into the sandstone of the Cape by the booming surf.

The path ends at a platform atop the farthest-reaching pillar of stone on Cape Flattery. From here panoramic views take in the striking architecture of coves and pillars both north and south, as well as the turtle-shell back of Tatoosh Island with its squat lighthouse. This islet, named for the fierce leader Tatooche of the Makah people, provides a rookery for sea lions and sea birds, which are often spotted hunting in the surrounding waters.

Key Points

0.0 Trailhead.

0.3 First observation platform above the Hole in the Wall.

0.6 Trail ends at the tip of Cape Flattery.

Additional Trails

The **Slough Trail** runs a mile from the Mora Ranger Station to the Quillayute River.

The **Ericksons Bay Trail** links the beach with a western arm of Lake Ozette. It is made up of rickety boardwalk that is quite slippery when wet.

The **Allens Bay Trail** has been abandoned and the planking removed. It is no longer a viable route.

Appendix A
Extended Trips

Most of the trails penetrating the Olympic Mountains interconnect, offering infinite possibilities for extended treks of varying lengths. Here are just a few possible routes for the traveler who seeks a long journey.

The Press Expedition Route (45 miles)

This trek is one of the easier trips that penetrates into the Olympic Range. It follows the Elwha River into the heart of the mountains, then crosses the Low Divide and descends down the North Fork of the Quinault. Possible side trips include the alpine Martins Lakes as well as Hayden Pass. This trip, which took the Press Expedition six months and a full case of whiskey to complete, can now be covered easily in a week.

The Northern Traverse (31 miles)

This journey offers a sampling of the most outstanding features of Olympic National Park: hot springs, vistas of glacier-clad peaks, and mysterious rain forest. It begins by following the Appleton Pass Trail past Olympic Hot Springs and into the high country. It then drops into the Sol Duc Valley, following this basin upward to the High Divide. It follows this striking ridge westward to Bogachiel Peak, where it descends past Hoh Lake into the valley of the Hoh River. It then follows this mighty torrent down through the magnificent Hoh rain forest to end at the visitor center. Possible side trips include the Seven Lakes Basin and the Blue Glacier at the end of the Hoh River Trail.

The Quinault Loop (56 miles)

This route is strenuous and remote, and follows some little-used trails that require some route-finding skill. It begins by ascending Graves Creek to Lake Sundown, where it meets the Six Ridge Trail. It follows this demanding alpine route to reach the North Fork of the Skokomish, where it turns north. After crossing First Divide, the trek drops into the headwaters of the Duckabush. Turn west to follow the Duckabush Trail up to the alpine lakes at its head. The O'Neil Pass Trail then winds through the high country to the head of the Quinault Valley. Turn left onto the Enchanted Valley Trail to complete the loop, as the trail passes the waterfall-decked cliffs that loom above the chalet and then disappears into a deep rain forest for the remainder of the loop.

The Mount Lacrosse Circuit (41 miles)

This trail makes a shorter loop into the high country from the eastern side of the range. It begins by following the Anderson Pass Trail to a junction just above Honeymoon Meadows. Turn south here, following the Lacrosse Pass Trail over a lofty divide and down the long grade into the valley of the Duckabush. The route then turns west, climbing to Marmot Lake, where it meets the O'Neil Pass route. This trail takes travelers high above the Enchanted Valley, then deposits them at the head of the Quinault drainage. Turn east here, crossing Anderson Pass to complete the loop. Travelers must then retrace their steps down the West Fork of the Dosewallips to return to the trailhead. Short side trips include the Anderson Glacier and the Enchanted Valley.

The Tour of the Buckhorn (27 miles)

This route takes the traveler through the fantastic crags that guard the eastern approaches to the Olympics. It begins by climbing over Mount Townsend, then hooking up with the Dirtyface Ridge Trail to descend to Silver Creek. It crosses a logging road to hook up with the Tubal Cain Trail, which it follows past a historic mine and up to the lofty crest of the Buckhorn Wilderness. The route then descends past Marmot Pass to reach the Boulder shelter, where it turns south toward Home Lake. It passes beneath the massive edifice of Mount Constance, then climbs through Constance Pass and onto a high ridge for fantastic views of the Olympic Range. It then drops past Sunnybrook Meadows and down into the valley of the Dosewallips, which it follows downstream to the Dosewallips Ranger Station.

The Grand Valley Loop (27 miles)

This trek makes a loop around the Grand Creek basin. It can be approached from Deer Park, but the lack of a suitable campsite near Obstruction Point makes this latter trailhead a better starting point. The trek follows the Grand Valley route along Lillian Ridge and then down into the Grand Valley. It passes Grand, Moose, and Gladys Lakes on its way to a crossing of the often-snowbound Grand Pass. A steep grade then leads down into the Cameron Creek drainage. The trail follows the Cameron Pass Trail downstream to Three Forks, where the Three Forks cutoff trail makes a steady ascent to Deer Park. Once here the traveler can turn west along the ridgeline, climbing across Maiden Peak and Elk Mountain on the way back to Obstruction Point.

Appendix B
Backcountry Camping Areas in Olympic National Park

Ratings

5 – Camping area is a scenic attraction in itself.
4 – Camping area is in an area of high scenic value.
3 – Camping area is in an area of moderate scenic value.
2 – Camping area is in an area with low scenic value.

Comments

a – Can be reached only by boat.
b – Shelter only; no tent sites.
c – Horses and llamas allowed.
d – Llamas allowed.
e – Campground washed out as of this writing.
G – Group camp; groups of 7 to 12 allowed.
S – Small.
M – Medium.
L – Large.
Q – Quotas in effect; reservations required.
Y – Yes.
N – No.

Camping Area	Rating	Size	Fires	Privy	Bear Wire	Comments
Anderson Pass	4	L	N	Y	Y	
Appleton Pass	5	M	N	N	N	
Bear Camp	4	M	N	Y	Y	
Belview	4	S	N	N	N	
Big Flat	3	M	Y	N	N	
Big Log	3	M	Y	Y	Y	
Big Timber	3	L	Y	Y	Y	c
Bogachiel	3	M	Y	N	N	
Boulder Creek	2	L	Y	Y	N	
Boulder Lake	4	M	N	N	Y	
Calawah	2	S	Y	N	N	e
Cameron Basin	5	S	N	N	N	
Camp Ellis	2	S	Y	N	N	
Camp Pleasant	3	L	Y	Y	Y	
Camp Wilder	3	M	Y	Y	Y	
Canyon Camp	3	M	Y	N	Y	

Camping Area	Rating	Size	Fires	Privy	Bear Wire	Comments
CB Flats	3	S	N	N	Y	Q, G
Chicago Camp	3	M	Y	N	N	
Deception Creek	3	M	Y	N	Y	c
Deer Lake	3	L	N	Y	Y	d, Q, G
Diamond Meadows	3	M	Y	Y	Y	c
Dodger Point	5	S	N	N	N	
Dose Forks	3	M	Y	Y	Y	
Dose Meadows	4	M	N	N	Y	
Elip Creek	2	S	Y	Y	Y	
Elkhorn	2	M	Y	Y	N	Y
Elk Lake	4	M	N	Y	Y	
Elwha Basin	4	S	Y	N	N	
Enchanted Valley	5	L	Y	Y	Y	
Erickson Bay	3	L	Y	Y	Y	a
Falls	3	M	Y	N	N	
Fifteenmile	3	S	Y	N	N	b
Five Mile Island	3	M	Y	Y	N	c, G
Flapjack Camp	3	S	Y	N	N	
Flapjack Lakes	4	L	N	Y	Y	Q
Glacier Meadows	3	M	N	Y	Y	
Grand Lake	4	M	N	Y	N	Q
Gray Wolf	3	M	Y	N	N	
Halfway House	4	M	Y	N	N	
Happy Four	2	M	Y	N	N	
Happy Hollow	3	S	Y	Y	N	
Happy Lake	3	S	N	N	N	
Hart Lake	5	S	N	N	N	
Hayes River	2	M	Y	Y	N	
Heart Lake	3	M	N	Y	N	Q
Heather Park	4	S	N	N	N	
Hoh Lake	4	S	N	Y	Y	Q
Home Lake	5	S	N	N	N	
Home Sweet Home	5	S	N	Y	Y	c
Honeymoon Meadows	4	L	N	Y	Y	
Humes Ranch	3	L	Y	N	Y	
Hyak	2	S	Y	N	N	
Irely Lake	3	S	Y	N	N	
Lake Angeles	4	M	N	N	N	
Lake Beauty	5	S	N	N	N	
Lake Constance	5	M	N	Y	Y	Q
Lake Mills	3	S	Y	N	N	

Camping Area	Rating	Size	Fires	Privy	Bear Wire	Comments
Lake Sundown	4	S	N	N	N	
Lewis Meadow	4	S	Y	N	N	c
Lillian Camp	4	M	Y	N	Y	Y
Low Divide	3	L	Y	Y	Y	
Lower Cameron	2	S	Y	N	N	b
Lunch Lake	5	L	N	Y	Y	Q
Marmot Lake	4	M	N	Y	Y	
Martins Creek	3	S	Y	N	N	c
Mary's Falls	2	M	Y	Y	N	Y
Mink Lake	3	M	Y	N	N	
Moose Lake	5	L	N	N	N	Q
Mt. Tom Meadow	3	M	Y	N	Y	
Nine Stream	2	S	Y	Y	Y	c
North Fork Sol Duc	2	S	Y	N	N	
Olympus Guard Station	3	L	Y	Y	Y	
O'Neil Creek	2	M	Y	Y	Y	
Pelton Creek	2	S	Y	N	N	
Pony Bridge	2	S	Y	N	N	
Pyrites Creek	2	S	Y	N	Y	
Round Lake	4	S	N	Y	Y	Q
Seven Mile	3	M	Y	N	Y	c
Sixteenmile	3	M	Y	Y	N	
Smith Place	3	M	Y	N	N	
Sol Duc Park	3	M	N	Y	Y	Q, G
Sourdough	3	S	N	N	N	
Sprice Bottom	3	S	Y	N	N	
Stony Point	3	M	Y	Y	N	Y
Success Creek	3	S	Y	N	N	
Sunnybrook Meadows	5	S	N	N	N	
Tenmile	3	M	Y	N	N	c
Three Forks	2	S	Y	Y	Y	
Three Lakes	4	S	N	N	N	
Three Prune	4	S	N	N	N	
Trapper	2	M	Y	N	Y	
Twelvemile	3	M	Y	Y	N	
Twentyone Mile	3	S	Y	N	N	
Two Bear	2	S	N	N	Y	
Upper Duckabush	3	M	Y	Y	Y	
Upper Lena Lake	5	L	N	Y	Y	
Wolf Bar	3	M	Y	N	N	

Appendix C
Backcountry Camping Areas in Olympic National Forest

Campground	Rating	Size	Fires	Privy	Bear Wire	Comment
Boulder	4	M	N	N	N	
Camp Handy	3	S	Y	N	N	
Camp Mystery	4	M	N	N	N	
Fivemile	3	M	Y	N	N	
Mulkey	2	S	Y	N	N	b
Tunnel Creek	2	S	Y	N	N	

Appendix D
Backcountry Camping Areas on the Olympic Coastline

Site Types
I – Inland sites, off the beach and within the forest
B – Beach sites, dispersed camping on sandy benches above the high tide mark.

Attractions
SS – Sea stacks
TP – Tidepools
All coastal camping areas have fresh water available.

Campground	Rating	Site Types	Privy	Bear Wire	Attractions
Cape Alava	4	I	Y	Y	SS
Cedar Creek	3	I, B	Y	Y	SS
Kayostla Beach	3	I, B	Y	Y	SS
Mosquito Creek	2	I	Y		
North Ozette River	3	I, B	N	N	
Sand Point	3	I	Y	Y	
Scott Creek	4	I, B	Y	Y	SS
Second Beach	4	B	Y	Y	SS, TP
Shi Shi Beach	5	I, B	Y	Y	SS
South Ozette River	2	I	Y	N	
South Sand Point	3	I, B	Y	Y	
Third Beach	3	I, B	Y	Y	
Toleak Point	4	I, B	Y	Y	TP
Yellow Banks	3	I, B	N		

Appendix E
Useful Addresses

Custom Correct Maps, c/o Little River Enterprises, 3492 Little River Road, Port Angeles, WA 98363; (360) 457-5667; www.customcorrectmaps.com.

Eagle Ranger Station (Sol Duc Hot Springs), (360) 327-3534.

Elwha Ranger Station (NPS), 480 Upper Elwha Road, Port Angeles, WA 98363; (360) 452-9191.

Forks Information Office (NPS/USFS), 551 South Forks Avenue, Forks, WA 98331.

Hoh Ranger Station (NPS), HC 80, Box 650, Forks, WA 98331; (360) 374-6925.

Kalaloch Ranger Station (NPS), HC 80, Box 2200, Forks, WA 98331; (360) 962-2283.

Mora Ranger Station (NPS), 3283 Mora Road, Forks, WA 98331; (360) 374-5460.

Olympic National Park Headquarters, 600 East Park Avenue, Port Angeles, WA 98362; (360) 565-3000; www.nps.gov/olym.

Ozette Ranger Station (NPS), Box 39A, Clallam Bay, WA 98326; (360) 963-2725. Ozette Reservations, (360) 452-0300.

Pioneer Visitor Center (NPS), 3002 Mount Angeles Road, Port Angeles, WA 98362; (360) 565-3000.

Quilcene Ranger Station (USFS), P.O. Box 280, Quilcene, WA 98376; (360) 765-3368.

Quinault Ranger Station (USFS), Route 1, Box 9, Quinault, WA 98575; (360) 288-2525.

Storm King Ranger Station (NPS), 343 Barnes Point Road, Port Angeles, WA 98363; (360) 928-3380.

U.S. Geological Survey, Denver, CO 80225; (703) 648-4090.

Index

About the Author

Erik Molvar has hiked more than 10,000 miles of trails, from the Arctic Ocean to the Mexican border. Erik has a master's degree in wildlife management from the University of Alaska Fairbanks, where he performed groundbreaking research on moose in Denali National Park. He currently is director of the Biodiversity Conservation Alliance, one of the West's most effective conservation organizations (www.voiceforthewild.org).

Also by the author:
Best Easy Day Hikes Olympic National Park
Hiking Arizona's Cactus Country
Hiking Colorado's Maroon Bells-Snowmass Wilderness
Hiking Glacier and Waterton Lakes National Parks
Best Easy Day Hikes Glacier and Waterton Lakes National Parks
Hiking the North Cascades
Best Easy Day Hikes North Cascades
Hiking Wyoming's Cloud Peak Wilderness
Hiking Zion and Bryce Canyon National Parks
Alaska on Foot: Wilderness Techniques for the Far North
Scenic Driving Alaska and the Yukon
Hiking Montana's Bob Marshall Wilderness
Wild Wyoming

The author at work in his office.